Ferenczi's Language
of Tenderness

Ferenczi's Language of Tenderness

Working with Disturbances from the Earliest Years

Robert W. Rentoul

JASON ARONSON
Lanham • Boulder • New York • Toronto • Plymouth, UK

Published by Jason Aronson
An imprint of Rowman & Littlefield Publishers, Inc.
A wholly owned subsidiary of The Rowman & Littlefield Publishing Group, Inc.
4501 Forbes Boulevard, Suite 200, Lanham, Maryland 20706
http://www.rowmanlittlefield.com

Estover Road, Plymouth PL6 7PY, United Kingdom

British Library Cataloguing in Publication Information Available

Library of Congress Cataloging in Publication Data

The hardback edition of this book was previously cataloged by the Library of Congress
as follows:

Rentoul, Robert W., 1930
  Ferencziís language of tenderness : working with disturbances from the earliest years /
Robert W. Rentoul.
    p. cm.
  Includes bibliographical references and index.
 1. Ferenczi, S ndor, 1873 1933. 2. Psychoanalysis. 3. Psychotherapy. I. Title.
  RC438.6.F47R46 2010
  616.89í17   dc22   2009037047

ISBN: 978 0 7657 0757 4 (cloth : alk. paper)
ISBN: 978 0 7657 0758 1 (pbk. : alk. paper)
ISBN: 978 0 7657 0759 8 (electronic)

Printed in the United States of America

For Annie and James

Contents

Acknowledgments

This book is dedicated to all who were willing to share their life with me in therapy, especially those who have consented to their stories being mentioned individually. I am indebted too to the lively, appreciative and interactive trainees in lectures and seminars; to Dr John Ryder, who encouraged me to write this particular book; and to Paul Stibbe, who helped to give the book its final shape. I would also like to thank Julie Kirsch, my editor at Jason Aronson, for her perception and wise counsel, as well as my production editor, Jayme Bartles Reed, for making working with her a pleasure as well.

Above all, I owe much more than the book to my wife, my daughters and my sons, without whom neither the book nor I would have come to fruition.

READER'S NOTE

Ferenczi's major publications are on occasion indicated by the following abbreviations:

CD   *The Clinical Diary of Sandor Ferenczi.* Ed. Judith Dupont. Harvard University Press, 1995.

FC   *Final Contributions to the Problems and Methods of Psychoanalysis.* Brunner/Mazel, 1980. Originally published by Hogarth Press, 1955.

FrC   *Further Contributions to the Theory and Technique of Psychoanalysis.* Karnac, 1994. Originally published by Hogarth Press, 1926.

I wish to thank Jason Aronson Publishers, Inc., publisher of Dr. Lawrence Hedges's *Interpreting the Countertransference* (1992, 212 213) for allowing me to use the original material incorporated in the table on page 100.

Introduction

LOOKING FOR A LANGUAGE

The evocatively named language of tenderness is the language of childhood, of innocence and sensuality. It contrasts with the language of passion, which belongs to the adult, to awareness and genitality. The distinction between the two was first made within psychoanalysis by Sandor Ferenczi (1873 1933). He observed that there was always a child in every analysis (or therapy), even if the person presenting should appear to be an adult. The language used should therefore be that suitable for a child. His insight provided the germ of a new ethos for psychoanalysis alternative to that of Freud. It laid the basis of a psychoanalytic psychotherapy which could work effectively with distur bances dating from the very earliest years of infancy.

This book is the account of a practice that found its home in the writings and work of Ferenczi. In the course of this practice it became clear that there is a significant group of people who miss out on a vital aspect of life in their infancy. That something is touch, and the fundamental care which a loving touch represents. This group of people appears largely to have been over looked by conventional psychoanalysis, and certainly by its classical Freud ian form. Following a Ferenczian emphasis makes it possible to do something to meet their need, but also raises questions as to the possibility and extent of its universal application.

The people concerned in the therapeutic encounter may be of either sex, and I try to use they and its cognates so as to preserve some anonymity for the particular individuals to whom I may refer. It may on occasion seem awkward, but it avoids constant repetition of he or she and other forms of those words. I trust that the context makes it clear when I am referring to an individual.

My own path through therapy was triggered by a dream. That started the process which led to a personal therapy extending over many years, and eventually into the practice of psychoanalytic psychotherapy over several decades. The personal therapy brought both agony and change: some of the agony was completely unnecessary, and was a by product of the first train ing analysis which I underwent. That experience provided the dynamic for seeking a more human and respectful way of practicing psychoanalysis and any therapy derived from it. Other parts of the agony were associated with the process of change, brought about by the second training analysis to which I moved. My practice in turn entailed much questioning and struggle, until I found the answer to most of my questions in the work of Ferenczi and of those influenced by him. This also opened my eyes to aspects of human suf fering and deprivation untreatable by classical psychoanalysis.

TWO ANALYSES

I was a minister of the church, and had been working in India. I had known for years that there was something wrong. I sought career guidance at the Tavistock Clinic in London, and was told that I needed psychotherapy. I was also thinking of making a new career for myself within counseling or psycho therapy, for which I would need a training analysis. I, accordingly, after much travail, entered my first training analysis.

This was conducted by a Contemporary Freudian analyst of the British Psychoanalytic Society. It was a disaster. I traveled three or four times per week from Wolverhampton, where I lived and worked, to London, and, against my protests, lay dutifully on the analyst's couch, to enjoy some mi nor releasing moments, but on the whole to be subjected to a form of torture. I felt that the analyst was treating me as a stroppy and rebellious nuisance. He eventually succeeded in reproducing the very scenario of my childhood and early life from which I was seeking to be freed. After two years it was unbearable: even though it meant being rejected by my training body (which was then the British Association of Psychotherapists), if I moved to someone who was not on their list of approved analysts, it became a matter of life or death to leave such a destructive encounter.

I chose life: I went one day from my training analysis to the concurrent weekly supervision of my work. The supervision was with someone who had a quite different attitude to the work of psychoanalysis from that of my analyst. I burst into tears of distress and frustration, and begged this man to take me into therapy with him. I had been told all my life what was wrong with me, and did not need more of it in my analysis, day after day, three times a week. Surely there must be some good in me too and I asked him if he would help me to find it. He agreed, and a new life began. I moved to a very different form of analysis, in which I felt loved and valued rather than disliked and criticized. It was the difference between this and the previous analysis which made it possible for things to change.

Later, when my psychoanalytic reading had extended to books by Ameri can psychoanalysts, I came across a page in one of them which suddenly made crystal clear to me just what had been wrong about this first training analysis: the number of the page, 190, at the conclusion of the book, is forever stamped in my brain. The book was Stolorow and Lachmannís *Psychoanaly sis of Developmental Arrests* (1980): the page provided an explanation of therapeutic failures (developmental arrest refers to people who appear to be stuck at some earlier level of development than that appropriate to their age). The methods of classical psychoanalysis, the writers of that book said, were being applied to someone who was not at that level, for whom such an approach was unsuitable, indeed positively contra indicated, and whose real needs had never been recognized. That is, they were being applied to people who were suffering from much earlier disturbances, with very negative and counter therapeutic consequences.

It was a tremendously liberating message to come across. Reading it gave me a great fillip in mind and body. It was a pivotal point, to find that people who identified themselves as psychoanalysts had recognized, and managed to put into words, exactly what had lain behind the devastating experience of my first analysis.

LIBERATION

It is difficult to write about my second analysis in any way that can do suf ficient justice to it. It was a profoundly transforming experience: fundamental enough to shift me out of my adamantine cage into a freer and a fuller life: a task which some others evidently considered impossible.

This analysis was with Ben Churchill, who had been my supervisor for the preceding two or three years. I had learned a lot from him in that role: about working with deeply damaged and puzzlingly disturbed people; about adopt ing an open and understanding approach towards those who came for therapy, and about having a skeptical and questioning approach towards the world of assessment, diagnosis and closed thinking. It was he who introduced me to the saving words of Bion (1990): In every consulting room, there ought to be two rather frightened people (13). I loved him, and I knew that he loved me not in the same way, but it was enough.

Laing!

Ben Churchill had worked with Ronald Laing in the Philadelphia Associa
tion, had been a co founder of the Guild of Psychotherapists, and was now
himself on its training committee, and at one time was the Guildís chairman.
This brought an occasionally unwelcome dimension into my work with him
in that I could not be rid of the feeling that to some extent he was sitting in
judgment of me, as I had now moved from my previous training body to
training with the Guild. It has been important to me ever since that a training
therapist should keep separate from the qualification process.

It was with him that I learned the immeasurable value of silence. My most
important session with him was one in which nothing was said apart from
 hello at the beginning and thank you at the end: except that at a point
when I felt I might have been expected to start talking but instead wanted
to continue the silence, I said, Donít go away. He said, I wonít ; and the
silence remained. He allowed me to remain quiet until the end.

It was full of meaning, without parallel for me, that I was able to sit in a
room with another person and not feel obliged to say or do anything: just to
 be, and to know that he would still be there with me. It normally only hap
pens with mothers and babies, or with lovers, or perhaps in nursing, though
the last is more focused. With Ben Churchill there was none of the usual
sort of psychoanalytic interpretation of the silences. In my experience of the
classical tradition silence is almost always interpreted in a hostile or suspi
cious manner, as hiding feelings of anger or sexuality. It did indeed in this
case conceal (or rather, as it always does, it revealed) deep emotion; but the
emotions were of love, of peace, of safety, of gratitude. I have learned from
that experience always to value and to honor silence; to permit it as long as
it lasts if it feels comfortable, and to ask, if it should feel tense or doubtful. It
is a powerful form of communication.

 This did not mean that my therapist indulged me: he frequently reproved
me and goaded me out of my set patterns. If he felt that I could, which ap
peared to be most of the time, he left me to work out problems for myself,
whether they were intellectual, emotional or practical. We talked often about
my own work of psychotherapy, and he encouraged me also to solve the prob
lems of that. He recognized that I was pioneering in a place far from others
similarly engaged; in a part of the country where, apart from the visits of one
London analyst to restricted locations, analytic psychotherapy was new and
not yet understood including by me.

Ben Churchill lent me books, among them the one referred to earlier: I ap
preciated his openness and his freedom from pointless rules in this respect,
and I continued this practice with my own therapees and trainees. My initial
introduction to the writings of Ralph Greenson (1967), George Klein (1976),
Roy Schafer (1976), Michael Balint (1968), Heinz Kohut (1971, 1977) and

others was all thanks to books which he lent me. My training therapy was an apprenticeship, as he felt it should be, with me learning from him, and him teaching me and sharing with me; yet it did not cease also to be curative. He told me much later that apprenticeship was the model which he and one of the other founders of the Guild of Psychotherapists had envisaged for psycho therapy training. It is a good one: the Hungarian model of training (Ferenczi's tradition) was nearer that than the model which eventually came to prevail.

THE TURNING POINT

I settled into this new analysis. Before long a pivotal event occurred. On it turned the whole subsequent course of my therapy and of my life. It was, as tonishingly, brought about by an accident which turned out to be little short of a miracle. It must have been waiting to occur: if it had not been that particular happening which restored me to life, I imagine that the emotional power of this therapy would nevertheless have brought the awakening at some other time and by some other means. It could not have been avoided if movement were to occur.

My therapist's wife telephoned one day to cancel my meetings with him for the subsequent week. I was plunged immediately into an enormous sense of loss and sadness, out of all apparent proportion to the event. I don't know how I survived, except by sheer determination fortified by the promise that at the end of that week I would see him once more. When we met again I told him how devastating the experience had been for me (I wasn't very con cerned about how it had been for him). From my previous analysis I might have expected to be told that I was angry with him, that I didn't mean what I said, that I was being inconsiderate, that it was reaction formation to cover up my anger. It would have resulted in a fruitless argument whose self fulfilling result would certainly have been the anger alleged. But it was not so in this analysis: my therapist accepted what I said, and listened to my account. He didn't make any of the usual conventional dismissive   but supposedly sooth ing   remark cither: he accepted the reality and power of my experience.

This enabled me to say that in the week of losing him an event from child hood had come back to me which I had apparently forgotten for decades. The intensity of my feeling at his being unable to see me had brought with it a feeling of similar but forgotten intensity. It was a profound feeling of loss, dating from my infancy, when, without warning or explanation, I had lost someone to whom I was devotedly attached. When I was two or three years old she suddenly disappeared from my life. I woke up one morning, and she wasn't there. I ceased to feel. I lost all emotion. I became a good baby.

I never wept again (I cried when hurt, but didn't weep), until at the age of forty six I recovered this memory with all its attendant feelings, and wept. The dam had burst. *oh yes*

This was the turning point which set me free. The knowledge of that rup tured attachment made sense of so many puzzles in my life. My subsequent understanding is that I had formed that very strong bond in the context of a failure of attachment to my mother. This was as a result of my mother hav ing had a serious breakdown at my birth, and rejecting me. The feeling of rejection was the one which had remained with me, though without my con sciously knowing its cause. It was evidently easier to cope with it than with the feeling of loss.

I never saw my nurse again: but the recovery of my feeling for her restored my emotions and re started the life which had been choked so long before. There had fortunately been a fault line in the hard shell that had come to encase me, although fault line gives the wrong sense: it was a lifeline, an Ariadne's thread to help me out of the maze. I had at one time known some thing different.

There were other, though lesser, turning points along the way of this analy sis. Change required letting go the straitjacket that had grown to be part of me: each turning point played an incremental part in this process. It required risking the amorphous and volatile feelings that succeeded the straitjacket, and letting a new structure for my life come into existence, one which could result in a new identity and mode of being. *existential - bodily*

METAMORPHOSIS

I find it hard to describe quite what life was like during those years   from the desperate frustration of my first analysis through to the liberation of my second   but one event in nature strikes me as a very close analogy, express ing well the state of vulnerability, confusion and emptiness through which it was necessary to pass. It is the miracle of metamorphosis as it occurs in the life cycle of a butterfly. In this miracle the caterpillar is literally liquefied and re assembled. (The quotation is taken, with gratitude, from the website of the Victoria Butterfly Gardens, British Columbia.) It is still not understood how this process occurs, any more than exactly how the changes effected in psychotherapy take place.

An additional vivid parallel with the process of metamorphosis is given by a further statement, to the effect that the first evidence that a butterfly is about to emerge is usually a transparency of the chrysalis, revealing colours beneath. If one reads emotions for colours, it is an excellent parallel:

the first sign of change in psychotherapy is the one that reveals emotions beneath. (For a brilliant description of human metamorphosis through psy chotherapy, see Bernard Brandchaftís chapter 5, To Free the Spirit from Its Cell, in Stolorow, Atwood and Brandchaft [1994]. He brings out the terror engendered by the prospect of change).

FUTURE PRINCIPLES

The way was now slowly forward: hard going, but sometimes with an end in sight. I had experienced the importance of the therapeutic relationship, and I had learned the ultimate importance of a personís childhood to their subsequent life. My experience of therapy having been both good and bad meant that there were certain practices and expressions which I would for the future take great care to avoid, and others which I would try to promote. Things to avoid included unnecessary withholding, judgmental remarks, ag gressive confrontation, rigid attachment to theory, intellectualization, exces sively wordy comments, and neglect of the relationship. Things to promote and express were such things as sensitive listening, flexibility, tentativeness, openness, bonding, humor, paradox and respect.

I can say with certainty that only Freudian based psychoanalytic therapy could have rescued me from the state in which I had been originally and brought me to the healthier state in which I now was. It embraces, if it is al lowed to do so, a wide range of approaches, some helpful, and some, damag ing. One of my experiences of it was definitely damaging, and one was both human and liberating. Only that last had been deep and powerful enough to crack the carapace in which I had been encased. It was this psychoanalytic psychotherapy, rooted in Freud, that enabled me to reach new life. Notwith standing that it was rooted in Freud, it did not take the classical form but was mediated through my therapist in his own individual way, which he himself had learned under the influence of the Independent tradition within the British Psychoanalytic Society. Peter Lomas had been his analyst, and Peter Lomasís analyst had been Charles Rycroft.

STARTING TO PRACTICE

Throughout my training analyses I had also been starting to practice. This caused me as much questioning as the analyses. I became more and more unsure of what I was supposed to be doing and what psychotherapy was about. I was full of questions. I was also becoming increasingly aware that the people I was working with did not match Freudian literature nor the approach and theory that some of my supervisors spoke about. The theory did not match the facts. Many of the books I read were not of much help either; the people they talked about did not seem to be the same as those with whom I worked.

One supervisor, in response to my asking what it was that psychotherapy was doing, said that its purpose was to resolve neurotic conflicts; but this failed to carry any conviction with me. A neurotic conflict in Freudian us age refers to conflict arising from a clash between two incompatible uncon scious impulses or drives, which happens at a time after the resolution of the Oedipus complex at ages three to five (or the failure to resolve it). This is subsequent to the development of language. Most people who came to me appeared to be troubled by things long before that which were far more amorphous: I was quite unable to identify any neurotic conflicts in them. What is more, neurotic conflicts respond to verbal interpretation: the earlier phenomena do not, having occurred before language. They need something else first before they can take on board verbal interpretation (Lomas 1987).

It soon became clear that those who sought therapy in an unsophisticated area such as that in which I was working were very different from those who might end up in a London analyst's room. In the latter, selection and exclusion operated: people were selected who were considered suitable for psychotherapy and they were excluded if they were deemed not to be. This was bound to produce a highly specialized group of patients matching pre conceived criteria. Those with whom I worked covered a much wider range of life and of problems than those whom some of my supervisors talked about. The latter had presumably been weeded out according to criteria of analyzability until only those with neurotic conflicts remained, with the result that those particular supervisors found what they were looking for and knew little of people outside that range.

My own hunch, from my background in academic psychology, was that psychotherapy was concerned with increasing the flow of information in the brain across the corpus callosum. This was, in fact, what Freud indicated in other words with his statement that the aim of psychoanalysis was to make the unconscious conscious. Nowadays modern neuroscience is opening up this exchange between the two hemispheres of the brain to scientific inquiry (Schore 1994, 2003; Levin 2003: Solms and Turnbull 2002). However, that knowledge was not available in Freud's time, and was not common knowl edge at the time I was starting to practice, though it did seem to be common sense. It highlighted the way in which psychoanalysis kept itself apart from academic and experimental psychology.

In consequence of not being given a clear answer as to what psychotherapy was about, I floundered, although with some help, prominent amongst which were my own therapy and my discussions with my therapist. The next most prominent was my moving to a more experienced and understanding supervisor, in the person of Dr. Harold Stewart.

THE CHILD WITHIN

I learned an immense amount from Harold Stewart. Most was learned from his supervision of my work with one particular person sent to me by a perceptive psychiatrist. This person had run the whole gamut of psychiatric treatments over many years   chemistry, electricity, hospitalization; drugs, ECT, pentothal abreaction, LSD   all to little avail. The problems were emotional, not medical, and outside the range of conventional psychoanalytic criteria. The work with that person took me into the work of regression, but it was by no means plain sailing. I had to learn to deal with silence, with aggression, with physical expression, and with long stretches of apparently nothing. Work with this particular person was absolutely central to my development as a therapist.

They soon developed a full blown   transference psychosis.   In more natural parlance they were soon   re-living their childhood : I think that it was Bion who described psychotic bits as unresolved bits of childhood. In this I became the hated, feared but clung to, mother, together with all the mother's successors in the multitude of teachers and psychiatrists along the way. For years I was subjected to constant attacks, which on two occasions became physical. This was followed up by angry letters between our meetings, intermixed with agonizingly puzzled ones. The person's need, perseverance and a sensed underlying attachment were incentive for us both to keep going. I am forever grateful to them. The regard was evidently mutual: on one occasion when they were asked by their psychiatrist how the psychotherapy was going, they replied   Fine, thank you: it reaches the parts other therapies can't reach   (this was an adaptation of a well known advertisement for Heineken lager at the time).

The person's verbal attacks often contained a good deal of trenchant wit. On one occasion they said that it was about time that I stopped practicing, and did psychotherapy properly. On another, they suspended momentarily an angry verbal assault and looked carefully at the books in the bookcase beside their chair. I wondered what was coming.   Are all those books about psychotherapy?   the person asked. I said,   Yes.   They said,   Don't you think it would be a good idea if you read them? You might learn how to do it. Some sessions ended with me feeling totally useless, drained, no good for anything (which was assuredly how the person felt also about themselves).

Sometimes many times, and for long periods nothing seemed to be happening at all; at other times all hell broke loose. Everything I did took on some hidden meaning, usually indicating a deliberate covert and cunning attack on them by me. For that person everything included things seen out side my house or inside it on entering, with which I may well in reality have had nothing whatever to do. My accuser was incontrovertibly convinced that I already knew what it was all about.

The person was similarly plagued with bodily sensations, each of which carried an underlying meaning. I came to understand them as the eruptions of repressed and forbidden emotions which had been extraordinarily power ful and which had been sunk without other trace early in childhood, so as to reappear later as somatic symptoms all over the surface of the body, like an underground nuclear explosion being reflected in disturbances of the earthís surface. The emotions were still there, but were denied any appropriate expression. It became our task painstakingly to decipher the often multiple meanings of these signs and sensations.

Much time was spent just waiting patiently, and hoping. In so many ses sions nothing appeared to take place. Fortunately for both parties to the therapy, Dr. Stewart understood perfectly what was happening and through his supervision encouraged perseverance.

It may have become clear to the reader that what was happening in this therapy was that the person was reverting (regressing) to childhood, and though in an adult body and at times reacting to me as an adult, was predomi nantly reacting as a child, locked in their childhood world, with their experi ences from that period active though unrecognized within them, such that I actually became the figures from that time, and nothing could persuade them otherwise. They needed to be responded to as the child of that time.

I was taught this by Harold Stewart on an occasion when my therapee had taken physical action towards me. Other supervisors and mentors told me that I should stop seeing the person immediately. Dr. Stewart pointed out the crassness of such a procedure (as, to my great surprise, did Freud, in relation to the erotic transference [see chapter 6], though I didnít know that then). I had been trying through many years of psychotherapy, he said, to help the person to get at their anger: now that they had, it was out of the question to punish them for it by abandoning them: that was precisely what had happened earlier in their life. Dr. Stewart added that the curative way was to accept that they were acting as a child, and to treat them as such. If they had caused dam age, they should pay for it, and gradually be taught that there are alternative and more constructive ways of expressing themselves. This is one of the tasks that childhood should accomplish.

Dr. Stewart taught me too about unconscious communication   how a person's apparently superficial remarks may have an underlying meaning which requires discerning, deciphering and feeding back to them. This particular therapee thus told me one day a story about going for a bath on the previous evening and fearing that the water might be too hot for them to get in. Harold Stewart said that undoubtedly the person had been talking about their fear of going any further with me in therapy as it might get them into hot water. I thought that such an interpretation was pretty fanciful but took the risk of feeding it back to the person concerned   to find to my great surprise that they accepted it with some relief. It had been exactly what they had meant.

The bodily sensations and symptoms too served to communicate meaning unconsciously: one method of communication is verbal, symbolic; the other, and earlier, is non verbal, physical, directly effected through the body. The person's bodily sensations thus gave a sure indication both of the earliness of the original damage and of the difficulty in communicating it. It needed someone outside the person to recognize what the symptoms and sensations might mean (as a sensitive mother might), and to feed their understanding back. Ultimately it requires the person themselves to become able to recognize the meaning for themselves, as this person duly came to do.

AN UNEXPECTED NEED

interesting, – bodily (sb's) as communication

Someone else with whom I worked in those early days revealed an unexpected and disconcerting need. They were very deeply damaged, but were able, with immense difficulty, to keep the disturbance within the agreed framework for the therapy, though every parting was hell. It was with this person that I first became aware that some people lacked the most basic experience of human warmth, touch and skin contact that is so necessary to assure us of our worth and root us in the ground. The very fact of skin contact can bring about attachment. This is so for all animals, including humans. To be deprived of it means being deprived both of individual grounding and of that warm bond with a fellow human being, which together form the foundations of life.

Such deprivation can result in a permanent erosion of firmness, confidence and value, or, of the ability to stand on one's own two feet. This particular person, though physically adult and holding a responsible position in life, had never matured into emotional adulthood but remained a child within. The physical contact sought was a warm and comforting sensuality, not something genital. I came to wonder if there were the possibility of any answer to such a person's piercing need, yearning and pain. I discovered through later experience in my practice that there are many such people, both men and women, who suffer from this aching void while carrying on apparently adult and successful lives. Because of the universal reaction to any appearance of weakness and to any expression of clamant need, it is kept well hidden by those who suffer from it; but it is there.

It was while working with this person that I first noticed something which was confirmed for me many times subsequently. That is, that someone who has suffered early damage frequently appears to be years younger than their chronological age. When I was sufficiently sure of this I mentioned it to one or two colleagues, who said on reflection that it did seem to be confirmed in several of those with whom they themselves worked. This suggests that the original experiences affect our hormonal development. Benign experiences have certainly been shown to do so (Schore 1994 et seq.; Gerhardt 2004); it is reasonable to expect that adverse experiences should have the opposite effect. The old term of arrested development would seem to be highly appropriate, except that that may suggest a static state, which is not necessarily so.

It was my work with the two people mentioned in these last two sections, which proceeded alongside working with many others with more conventional problems, which helped me in the end to discover a strong foundation for my practice. To what I had already learned from my own therapy it added the phenomena of unconscious communication, and it alerted me to the trauma of deprivation of bodily comfort and warmth. It took me into long term, intensive, regression work; and it taught me to see and respond to the child who lives within the adult. This child can allow itself, if the atmosphere is suitably responsive, to be most evident and vulnerable in therapy, where there is then hope that growth can be resumed.

Your order of January 12, 2012 (Order ID 102-1380241-7213004)

Qty.	Item	Item Price	Tota
1	**Ferenczi's Language of Tenderness: Working with Disturbances from the Earliest Years** Paperback (** P-3-B124B112 **) 0765707586	$29.95	$29.95

Subtotal	$29.95
Order Total	$29.95
Paid via credit/debit	$29.95
Balance due	$0.00

This shipment completes your order.

||||| |||||| ||| ||||| ||| ||| |||||| ||||| |||

4/DDMfIM7yR/-1 of 1-//1F/second/5852598/0113-14:00/0113-10:57/therescl

V3

Part One

FUNDAMENTALS

Chapter One

Finding Ferenczi

A CONFUSED FIELD

I was reading widely. I was confused at this early stage by the plethora of books on psychoanalysis and psychotherapy which were available but which seemed to say quite different things. They used unnecessary jargon; they gave different meanings to the same word, and they used different words to express much the same meaning; yet all of them claimed to be Freudian. It was only later that I began to notice that while many of the books started off with an acknowledgment of Freud as the ultimate authority, frequently accompanied by a suitable quotation from his works, several of them then proceeded to say something markedly at variance with what Freud actually said. The difficulty for innovative thinkers to break free from the Freudian grip on psychoanalysis seems to have been too great to permit them to do it fully.

Admittedly, Freud was an intellectual giant: but he was only human, and in some respects he might have been wrong. For one thing, he was a child of his age. Originally a neurologist, he did not have available to him the advances in neuroscience, neuropsychology and neuropsychoanalysis which have occurred since his day. As a scientist, he was locked into a Helmholtzian physical universe where energy was understood to be part of a closed system, and he used hydraulic and drive models to describe it. He did not have the advantage of modern studies of motivation and of emotion which suggest that our dynamics are instead to be found there, in an open system. Thus a book review in *The International Journal of Psychoanalysis* (*IJPA*) (1995, **76**, 6, 1281a) said, Over the last twenty years affect [emotion] . . . has gradually replaced Freudís drive discharge theory as a major factor motivating human behaviour. Intersubjective writers agree that most important . . . has been

3

the shift from drive to affect as the central motivational construct for psycho
analysis (Stolorow, Atwood, and Brandchaft 1994).

Since Freud three paradigm shifts have occurred, each affecting both
theory and practice. First, emotion has replaced drive as the primary moti
vating factor, with the consequence that the emotions and their recovery are
now the main focus of psychotherapy; secondly, psychoanalysis has shifted
to a relational rather than an instinctual basis, which highlights the relation
with the therapist / analyst as the chief arena of psychodynamic work. This is
in contrast with the study of the isolated inner workings of someoneís mind
which had been the previous dominant model. Thirdly, workers since Freud
have pushed back the boundaries of investigation, to find earlier origins for
the development of disturbances. This has brought with it an emphasis on
supplying a deficit in peopleís lives as being an alternative focus for the work
of psychoanalysis to the previous emphasis on solving conflicts.

MARKERS ON THE WAY

I soon began to read the works of American psychoanalytic authors. These
were almost without exception illuminating, liberating, fresh and encourag
ing; yet they are not much referred to within British psychoanalysis. A recent
book review by an American analyst deplored the apparent lack of awareness
on the part of British psychoanalysts of American authors and their work: he
held that in America there is a considerably greater awareness of British writ
ers and their outlook (Bass 2004, **85**, 249). The bridging of the gulf would, I
am sure, make British psychoanalysis much richer, gentler, wider, more open
and almost by definition more human and effective. Certainly these Ameri
can authors helped greatly to bring some order into my work and thinking,
to widen my horizons, to deepen my awareness of the range and nature of
early developmental disturbances and to suggest effective ways of working
with people suffering from them. I was becoming more aware of this wider
range of psychoanalytic work and theory and of the differences between that
and the old.

I have already mentioned the first book which I read which came from
American psychoanalysis. This was Stolorow and Lachmannís *Psychoanal
ysis of Developmental Arrests* (1980), which made clear what was wrong
with the classical Freudian analysis that I had experienced as so destructive.
Things became even clearer when a little later I came across Balintís book
The Basic Fault (1968), which was initially lent to me by my therapist. In
that book I found a story that made sense of my puzzles and questionings:
an account of how, long before neurotic conflicts develop, there can be a

stage in infant life where nurturing in primary love is all important. The lack of primary love causes a basic fault which leaves a life long scar, and leads to a deep inner distress which affects all of oneís subsequent life (the word fault is used in a geological sense). I recognized immediately that this was the fault, or damage, both in me and in most of those with whom I worked. The confusion about psychotherapy cleared, and I realized that my task as a psychotherapist was to work with this fault. I was now able in a more focused way to set myself to learn more about it, how it occurred, and how it might be helped.

A contemporaneous happening that made sense of my experience in the practice of psychotherapy was, as previously mentioned, my move into super vision with Dr. Harold Stewart. He had been an officer of the British Psycho analytic Society, and (though at that time this was unknown to me) had had Michael Balint as one of his own supervisors. He, like Balint, worked with regression. He understood immediately the people with whom I was working and the work that I was trying to do with them. He understood, too, my dis satisfaction with my training: as he put it, my unease at feeling that they were trying to force me into a mold.

THE BRITISH INDEPENDENTS

Balint and Stewart were both members of the Independent Group within the British Psychoanalytic Society. This is not quite co terminous with the Object Relations School, although the two terms are often used interchangeably. The latter is slightly wider and earlier, and included Melanie Klein. She nominally adhered to Freudís drive theory, though hers was a purposeful rather than an impersonal drive, and she was more interested in fantasy and a personís internal world than others of the Object Relations School. Her followers therefore became, and remain, a group separate from both the Freudians and the Independents.

Overall, the British Independents pushed back the boundaries within which Freud had worked, and the ranges of age and of disorder which he had consid ered it possible to work with. He had held that only the experience of children after the age of five was suitable for psychoanalysis: and that the Oedipus complex, involving the triad of the child and its parents, was the focal event of the work. The Independents, on the other hand, went back to include the earlier years and the dyadic interaction of mother and child. Thus Balint (of GP Balint Groups) studied and worked with these early interactions using regression, in which he allowed people to go back to the formative years of childhood and to use their therapy as a transference of their entire childhood situation. So also did Winnicott, though with a slightly different emphasis (1965, 127).

Balint had been an analyst, colleague and deputy of Ferenczi in Hungary, and came to Britain before the Second World War. Here he both promoted Ferencziís work and continued it in his own; though because of the schism between Ferenczi and Freud, and the continuing suppression of Ferencziís work within psychoanalysis, he had to do this somewhat covertly. He brought with him to Britain not only Ferencziís influence, but also his papers; and when the time was ripe he released these for publication. Unlike Ernest Jones, who had been a dominant figure in the formative years of British Psychoanalysis, and was also an analysand of Ferencziís, Balint remained loyal to his former analyst and enabled us to rediscover in time the insights of the man who earlier had been hailed, with Freud, as one of the founders of psychoanalysis.

There were many others in the British group both then and subsequently, all of whom helped to open up for investigation and healing the early years of childhood with their associated disturbances. Besides Balint, Winnicottís work with mother and child has been fundamental. Others, among the more familiar of the British Independents, were Charles Rycroft; John Bowlby, of Attachment Theory fame (1969 et seq.), who like Winnicott was originally supervised by Melanie Klein; and, nearer the present time, Peter Lomas. All of these three were to leave the British Psychoanalytic Society as their work developed. The Independents have amongst their number in addition the equally notable figures of Eric Rayner, Harold Stewart, Christopher Bollas and Patrick Casement, the last two perhaps representing in Britain a third psychoanalytic generation. Their contribution has done much to change the face of British psychoanalysis. The debt they all owe to the work of Ferenczi is fundamental.

Balint and Regression

Balint is of particular importance in that he developed work with regression, and was the first to delineate a particular stage in therapy which heralded its onset (see chapter 4). Regression above all needs sensitivity: what Ferenczi called tact. This tact or sensitivity is instinctively elicited by Ferencziís insight that there is a child, and a wounded child at that, at the heart of every analysis. To accommodate this, we need a different way of understanding and working in psychoanalytic psychotherapy from that of Freudian theory and classical psychoanalysis.

Besides Balintís work, two other advances helped towards consolidating this sort of approach to therapy. One is Kohutís work on narcissistic wounds, which helps to inform our understanding of and response to outbursts of long ing, need, and rage; helping us to respond in a more human and patient way, as to a child (see further, chapter 8). The other is the developing awareness of counter transference, which encourages us to take note of, to trust, to un derstand and to use our own reactions to the therapy and therapee. It helps us to identify something of the problem or time warp in which the other person is caught up.

DEVELOPMENTS IN AMERICA

I continued to read American writers too. The US, as compared with the UK, had different patterns of immigration from Europe, which resulted in a different range of psychoanalytic influence. There were very few Kleinians, and very many Freudians, the latter of whom formed the dominant school of Ego Psychology. Out of this school there developed, among several, the important offshoot of Self Psychology originally associated with Kohut. In many ways the growth of this school parallels the development of the British Independents, who are not themselves otherwise represented in American psychoanalysis; as if similar insights were bound to break out of the old tem plate regardless of the particular culture.

Kohut and the Self

I was introduced to the work of Heinz Kohut by the loan of a book once again by my therapist (*The Analysis of the Self*, 1971). It was written in dense psy choanalytic language, and was very closely reasoned. I thought it was miles above my head, though when I reported this to my therapist he mocked my difficulty. He saw no reason why I should be unable to understand it, and he thought that I could in fact do so very well. I was probably reacting against the psychoanalytic language, for when I re applied myself to the book I found that I did indeed understand it and was fired up by it and by Kohutís other works which I then went on to read. His language seemed to get easier as his years of writing advanced (and possibly too with his increasing distance from his roots in classical psychoanalysis); however, the clearest introduction to his work, for me, is Allan Siegelís *Heinz Kohut and the Psychology of the Self* (1996), possibly because it is not written in such esoteric language.

Kohut, originally a neurologist like Freud, founded the school of Self Psy chology. His work in the US has many similarities to that of Balint and of Winnicott in the UK, though Kohutís emphasis was more on the structures needed by the developing self, while Balintís and Winnicottís were more

on the effects on the child of its interaction with the mother. These different
foci are of course closely related, but led to different levels or perspectives
in their therapy (Hedges 1983). Kohut was originally a training analyst and
supervisor of the Chicago School of Psychoanalysis, teaching and practic
ing classical drive theory, with its individualistic understanding. In a radical
development from that he became interested in the development of the self
and in the disorders resulting from mishaps in that development. These had
not been a concern of classical psychoanalysis, and are clearly aspects of the
relationships with which the self is involved. Although he was anxious at the
start to present his theory as merely a modification of Freudís, Kohut moved
over the years from being an exponent of classical drive theory to being a
fully relational theorist, for whom interaction was the essential theme.

Like Balint with his identification of the need for primary love in infancy,
Kohut, too, focused on the child carer interaction and stressed how vital it
is for our development that that interaction should supply certain essential
needs of the self. These he called our narcissistic needs. Deprivation of them
leads to various types of disturbance, notably those which nowadays are
themselves termed narcissistic. Kohut saw the central element in the sup
plying of these needs and the building of a cohesive sense of self to be the
formation of certain essential structures between the self and its surroundings.
The self internalizes these structures until they become part of it. He called
these structures selfobjects, spelled without any hyphen in order to stress that
they constitute structures independent of both the self and the other. These
structures can be supplied in later life under suitable conditions, such as can
exist within therapy, or indeed within friendships and partnerships.

The needs find expression in therapy through the development of transfer
ences which take specific forms: these he termed mirror, idealizing, and
 twinship (or alter ego) transferences. The mirror transference reflects the
need of an infant to receive a mirroring admiration of his or her self from their
carer: the consequence of not doing so is an oversensitivity to rejection or
criticism. The idealizing transference represents the need of the infant also to
have someone whom they in turn can admire or idealize: the absence of this is
held to lead to the loss of a goal and purpose in life. The third type of transfer
ence, twinship or alter ego, while it is exciting to find anyone identifying
and writing about it, seems to me to be an amalgam of these first two, though
Kohut himself sees it as something separate. It seems better understood as
being earlier in origin than the development of the self, and is something to
do with lack of early tactility and bonding (see chapter 9).

Kohutís account of the contrasting styles of analysis or therapy resulting
from adherence to drive theory or to self theory was contained in his moving
paper The Two Analyses of Mr. Z (1979), in which he conducted a second

analysis according to the model of Self Psychology of someone whom he had already analyzed some years previously according to the drive model. My reading of that paper made me identify strongly with Mr. Z: the differences between my two training analyses are profoundly similar to what Kohut de scribed. The contrast is put well by Basch (*Practising Psychotherapy* 1992, 92): I well remember how it felt when many of my analytic patients and I tried, literally year after year, to move forward only to spin our wheels, as my attempts to fit them into the oedipal scheme of understanding pathology failed time and time again, until Kohutís understanding of narcissistic pa thology became known to me. With this new organizing framework again, literally the patient in question progressed in days further than they ever had in years.

Coming across the work of Kohut thus linked up for me with what I had already come to know of the work of Balint and the British Independents, and what I was later to come to know of the work of Ferenczi. Together they moved the work of psychoanalytic therapy into the realms of infancy, the maternal dyad, and the earliest years of life. Basically it calls for a re writing of the whole theory of psychoanalysis. It made sense for me of my own life experience and of that of so many of the people who came to me, and it made sense of analysis as I had experienced it to date. My first analysis had been geared to the old focus, to later years, to neurotic conflict, using exclusively verbal material: the second had been focused on the earlier years, on narcis sistic and borderline deficits, and on non verbal, pre genital, pre oedipal ma terial. Experience, theory and practice were beginning to come together.

Greenberg and Mitchell

The 1980s were exciting times. In the middle of that decade I came across a further, revolutionary, book. It was exactly what the psychoanalytic world needed, an ordering of all the varied theories, volumes and writers into a coherent frame. The book was Greenberg and Mitchellís *Object Relations in Psychoanalytic Theory* (1983). In it the two authors, themselves belonging to the Relational School in the US, introduced the idea that the various theories of psychoanalysis were fairly clearly divided into two groups, drive and relational. They pointed out how since the beginning all contemporary theorists are concerned with a common problem: how to account for the pre eminent importance in all clinical work of relations with other people. . . . Freudís original drive theory takes the discharge of psychic energy as its fun damental . . . building block, assigning to relations with others a status which is neither central nor immediately apparent. Every major psychoanalytic theorist has had to address himself to this problem (379). They have done so in many and often bewildering ways: bewildering, that is, until Greenberg and Mitchell discerned the basic division into drive and relational theories. What is more, and more important for clinical work, the two different sets of theory have completely different effects on practice. (The word *clinical* is used in this book to mean the face to face encounter that takes place between two or more people within the context of healing.)

The drive group of theories includes all those which follow the classical Freudian model, holding that undirected instincts or drives are the moving force in human behavior, and seeing people to be at the whim of those imper sonal forces which then have to be tamed and harnessed. The relational group covers those theories for which our primary motivation is directed towards other people, and which hold that it is the people to whom such motivation is directed who ultimately determine our behavior.

The latter group thus embraces British Object Relations theories, Attach ment Theory, Self Psychology and its offshoots, and Relational theories. The drive theories include those of Freud, of Contemporary Freudians in the UK (including his daughter Anna), and the theories of Ego Psychologists in the US. Melanie Klein claimed allegiance to Freud but occupies a sort of compro mise position, as her drives, while still the basic units of motivation, were actually already directed towards some sort of object.

From then on the reading of books became much easier, and things began to fall into place. I could recognize that I myself was a psychoanalytic psycho therapist working on the relational model, and working chiefly with people who had been damaged very early in life, mostly through their interaction or lack of it with their mother or other primary carer. All had suffered trauma in those first years which had affected their self confidence, their emotional growth, their attachments, and their trust in other people. It was the task of psychotherapy to try to restore some of these things. Further, because the trauma had happened so early in childhood it was going to take many years of intensive psychotherapy to counter its effects. Only an intensive relational psychodynamic therapy could hope to touch it; one in which emotions would be deeply engaged.

This is one of the things which make classical drive theory psychoanalysis contra indicated for this sort of work. Not only that, it eschews relationship from the beginning, but perhaps inevitably with an approach which requires abstention or withholding on the part of the analyst, it seems to tend towards intellectual interpretation rather than emotional engagement. I experienced this myself in practice, and the publications of classical writers reflect the same. This is in spite of the fact that one of the criteria for a mutative inter pretation is held out to be emotional impact, at least on the part of the patient (Strachey 1934); it does not, however, emphasize any emotional exchange, or mutual engagement.

The nature of early damage involving traumatic experiences, over whelming at the time and consequently buried, also means that any therapy dealing with this is faced with the need to permit, and indeed encourage, regression to childhood. In this, the person can be allowed, in a safe en vironment, to go back to their earliest experiences within the relationship offered, to re live those experiences and to find new ways of coping with them and of correcting their results. It means, in other words, allowing the person to become a child again. As Cozolino (2004) states, The things most people need to learn in psychotherapy are related to attachment, abandonment, love, and fear. We are trying to access basic emotional processes that are organized in primitive and early developing parts of the brain. The language of these emotions is also very basic; it is the language of childhood (25).

In the light of this, there seems to be a further radical division between different types of theory and practice: that is, a division between those consid ered suitable for an adult and those more suited to work with a child (the child in the adult). I sense this, especially in clinical work, as a deeper division than that between drive and relational theories. For one thing, to work with a child essentially requires a relationship, by definition: that is how a child grows. Further, as I hope has become fairly clear by now, for a variety of reasons I personally do not think that practice based on drive theory is appropriate for an adult either.

Intersubjectivity and Interaction

The 1980s and 1990s were also times of great development, especially in America. Alongside the publication of Greenberg and Mitchellís book from within the Relational stream, the school of Self Psychology (Kohut) gave birth to offshoots which have been as seminal as their parent in advancing psychoanalytic understanding of people and of practice. These developments from Self Psychology arose, and prosper, on the West Coast of America (San Francisco and Los Angeles). They are the two schools of Intersubjectivity and of Listening Perspectives. Arising as it did out of Freudian Ego Psychol ogy, whose focus was primarily on the individual, the dominant focus of Self Psychology was originally on the development of the individual self. Inter subjectivity extended this to the encounter between two individual selves, and reflects the general move in psychoanalysis towards a systems approach. The Intersubjective movement is primarily associated with the names of Robert Stolorow and associates (1994 et seq.). Intersubjectivity itself is a philosophical term, and refers to the meeting of two inner worlds (Benjamin, in Skolnick and Warshaw 1992, 45). As did Buber (1937), it emphasizes the difference between being a subject and being an object, and the movement tries to make explicit what it is that makes a subject a subject rather than an object. As an interpretation of psychodynamics intersubjectivity stresses that what occurs in therapy is the meeting of two persons as subjects and explores what happens within that meeting.

We have moved a long way from 19th century classical theory and its early scientific background: from Freudís original spotlight on the id, through to the study of the ego with its various sub divisions; to the emphasis on the self and its development; and now to the analysis of the interaction between the two people involved. As Levine (1994) said more than a decade ago:

> In recent years classical psychoanalytic theory has been undergoing a slow, but discernible, evolutionary change. Our interests have extended beyond a focus on the mind of the patient to include the psychology and experience of the analyst, and beyond that . . . to the interactive dimension inherent in the relation between analyst and analysand. Traditional classical views of the psychoanalytic process have depended upon an unquestioned assumption of a clearly demarcated split between analyst and analysand, between the observer and the observed. By contrast, more contemporary formulations . . . have shifted their emphasis from a predominantly patient centered focus to a field theory, in which analysis is viewed as a two person process that evolves in a mutually determined fashion from the engagement between analyst and analysand. (**75**, 4, 665, 667)

A NOTE ON COUNTER-TRANSFERENCE

We come now to a tremendously important phenomenon in the practice of psychoanalysis and psychotherapy which is central to the interaction between the two participants: the phenomenon of counter transference. At first con sidered by Freud to be an obstacle and requiring fresh analysis of the analyst experiencing it, it later came to be seen as an important component of analy sis. Important is an understatement: it is crucial. To detect it and respond to it we require to be finely tuned instruments: tuned by life experience, therapy and supervision to its recognition and to a sensitive emotional response. Counter transference refers, in brief, to the reactions of the therapist to the therapee, in particular those brought about by the therapeutic interaction. Chediak (1979) gives a good overall analysis of the various possible types of counter transference; Maroda (1991) gives a brilliant account of its use.

One of the most important types of counter transference which Chediak identifies is the puzzling way in which therapists are asked to act as contain ers for the therapeeís forbidden feelings. That is, they experience feelings which actually belong to the other person: what might be called   direct communication of feeling. Ferenczi (1995) referred to it as the dialogue of unconsciousnesses (84). This phenomenon seems to be what the Kleinian concept of projective identification is referring to when it is used in this context. I hope that I am not being presumptuous in understanding that Nev ille Symington (2007) shares this view (61 62).

Counter transference in the form of the direct communication of feeling is an immensely valuable tool for understanding and guiding what is going on in the other person and in the interaction. Therapists frequently get feel ings of anger, sex, loneliness, sadness and longing which can only be com ing from, or aroused by, the other person: that is, if reflection suggests that they were not there in the therapist before the meeting and there is nothing in the therapistís current life to explain their presence in the therapy session. These unexpected feelings may of course echo or stir some of the therapistís own deepest emotions; and that is where a training therapy is so essential, so that the therapist may be sensitive and alert to this possibility and not get the therapy muddled up with his or her own issues. On the other hand, the feelings should not be dismissed: their unexpected awakening may be giv ing a valuable clue to the other personís inner state and process, even if that is being either consciously suppressed or unconsciously repressed (that is, suppressed before reaching conscious awareness). The recognition by the therapist of such feelings in themselves can then be fed back to the therapee if appropriate, stored for future disclosure, or contained and used to guide and inform the interaction. It is like Casementís *On Learning from the Patient* (1985), except that in this case it is learning from oneself and from oneís own reactions to the other person.

A second type of counter transference, and the strict meaning of the term, is not this direct transmission, but refers to the therapistís feelings experi enced in response to the therapeeís active though unconscious transference to the therapist: they are a more indirect form. For instance, the person may see the therapist as a persecuting figure from the past, and by their behavior somehow evoke the relevant corresponding feeling in the therapist. Or they may feel perpetually rejected, and unconsciously evoke an urge to reject in the therapist, thus bringing about the situation which they fear, but which needs to be stirred into awareness so that it may receive the necessary atten tion and working through.

Where counter transference is especially valuable is that our experience of it varies according to the nature of the other personís disturbance: in that respect it offers the possibility of introducing order into the ways of working with the myriad problems and complaints which people present. Most important to me personally among counter transference feelings has been a maternal or parental feeling evoked by people who have been severely deprived in earliest infancy but who may not themselves be consciously aware of their deprivation, only of its consequences. This sort of parental caring counter transference is an invaluable gift in alerting us to the possibility that it is early deprivation that lies behind their experience. The resultant therapy may need to be very long term and intensive, and may require regression. If the therapist is not willing to enter such a long and demanding period of dependence then they have the opportunity of referring the person to someone who is. Trusting our counter transference feelings is acutely demanding, but it is both necessary and reward ing. To do so requires us to develop confidence in what we feel and courage in suggesting any possible reason for it to our partner in the therapy.

Listening Perspectives

The person who has worked most concentratedly on counter transference as communication of the underlying problem in therapy is Lawrence Hedges. His concept of listening perspectives (1983 et seq.) deserves far greater recognition and application than it seems to get, certainly in the UK but also in America. With this concept he brings meaning into the therapistís varied counter transference experience; and to this we now turn. His use of the word perspective allows for a certain overlapping of the phases in development to which it refers, but identifies the dominant level among the four which he delineates.

It was Lawrence Hedgesís analysis of counter transference in its many forms which shed so much light for me on psychotherapeutic interaction. At tention to it might help to ensure that people who come for therapy are given that which is most appropriate for their problem; and it might avoid them being sent to someone who by using the wrong approach merely aggravates the trouble. Here I give a brief outline of Hedgesís work; later in the book (chapter 6) I look at its application in day to day practice.

Hedges uses the term listening perspectives for the four levels in psy chotherapeutic work which he identifies because they determine the way in which we can best listen to the other person and to our interaction with them, and can identify what we may hear. He draws on the work of all the major psychoanalytic authors and clinicians up to his time; each has focused on some particular, but often fairly distinct, aspect of disturbance. Neurotic conflict, focused on sex and aggression, is associated with the name of Freud, who used verbal interpretation of the personís hypothesized unconscious workings as the means of therapy. Neurotic conflicts are seen to be a product of three person interactions (Freudís Oedipus complex), in which the child is held to become aware of both parents and of the relationships between all three, from about 3 years old.

After Freud came Kohut, who investigated the development of the self, with its narcissistic disturbances occurring at an earlier age, say 2 3 years, during the formation of the self. Therapeutic work with narcissistic distur bances has a large non verbal component, reflecting their earlier origin. Earlier even than that are the borderline troubles, placed in the early dyadic interaction with the mother, at the childís age of 4 months to 2 years. These were researched by workers such as Winnicott, Balint and Bowlby. They date from the stage of life when feeling is the primary mode of communication, with cognitive and verbal faculties not being fully developed. Work with people who have an underlying borderline disturbance can in consequence only be carried on effectively at a non verbal and holding level rather than through any more didactic approach.

To these three stages in development on which the first two generations of psychoanalysts did so much work Hedges adds something considerably more primitive, which he calls the organizing level. Here the infant is trying to connect with life, with their carer, and with the world in general; and to make sense of it all. It is the level of autism, of connection, of organization, of a growing integration, and of the most basic trust, during which our organizing principles take their shape. This perspective would take in the work of Tustin, Little, some of Balintís, and Hedgesís own, together with the observations of Thomas Ogden (1989) on what he calls the autistic contiguous position (*IJPA* 1989, 70, 127 140) in the terms of Kleinian metapsychology.

Breakdown in this very primitive area is termed by Hedges organizing breakdown. It corresponds to what in classical psychoanalysis is referred to as a psychotic breakdown, leading to a psychotic transference, then thought to be untreatable, being non verbal, primitive and not understood. Staying with the person in their confusion and, if need be, sharing it is a chief require ment of therapy at this level. Many practitioners, including Hedges himself (1994.1), feel that the use of touch may often be necessary for effective work (see further Galton 2006).

After years of working along these lines, I would suggest that there is an even more primitive level of disturbance in addition to these four: one more specifically physical; that is, the skin hunger and physical yearning to which I have alluded earlier. It may perhaps overlap with Hedgesís last mentioned level, but its features are specifically a lack of the experience of touch, of human warmth, of skin and body contact. Touch has been described as the foundation of experience (Barnard and Brazelton 1990); nothing can be more primitive and necessary. It might also be described as the foundation of attachment; it can itself bring bonding about. It is to be seen as one of the most elemental, physiological, requirements. Lack of food cannot be corrected completely; it can result in enduring bone and muscle deficiency.

Lack of touch can result similarly in hormonal and emotional deficiencies: possibly shown physically in the youthful appearance commented on earlier. It certainly leads to a lack of a feeling of solidity in life, and failures in at tachment and trust, while simultaneously giving rise to a constant yearning for its provision and to withdrawal from contact for fear of encountering fur ther devastating disappointment. It can lead to a boundless, lifelong (though usually concealed), yearning for tenderness; and this too can dominate a therapy.

The point of Hedgesís ordering of these various phenomena into his four recognizable perspectives or levels is that each of them results in a particular experience of the transference and counter transference in therapy, as will be taken up again in chapter 6. If we listen carefully both to the other person and to ourselves, especially to feelings as well as words, we can gain a price less perspective on the process in which we are engaged and can find help in knowing how to proceed: each level needs a differential response and way of working. The transference and counter transference tell us in particular whether we are working with the child in the adult, at the level of tenderness and innocence, or with the adult, at the level of passion, sophistication and maturity. It is usually the former.

Relational Psychoanalysis

It would be impossible to give any proper outline of developments in psy choanalysis in America without giving due attention to Relational Psycho analysis. Previous sections in this chapter have concerned Self Psychology and developments from it. Relational Psychoanalysis comes last only because its connection with Ferenczi means that it leads on to our own meeting with him in the next chapter: its origin, in the work of Harry Stack Sullivan, was actually earlier than that of Self Psychology. It is also a fitting conclusion to all the various preceding developments: it is likely to be the one which will provide the overarching structure for an integrative umbrella for all relational schools, whether of Self Psychology, Intersubjectivity, Listening Perspec tives, British Independents, or some modern Kleinians.

Some of the most outstanding workers and writers in the field of modern psychoanalysis spring from the soil of Relational Psychoanalysis. Its devel opment is absorbingly described in Emmanuel Ghentís foreword to Skolnick and Warshawís *Relational Perspectives in Psychoanalysis* (1992), and in the first chapter of Aronís *A Meeting of Minds* (1996). I have mentioned previously Greenberg and Mitchell as representatives of this school. The re lational position has been developed greatly by others since them too, notably Lewis Aron in the book just mentioned. He, together with Adrienne Harris, also wrote a land mark book (1993) acknowledging the legacy of Sandor Ferenczi, not only to Relational Psychoanalysis but to the whole of psycho analysis of whatever school.

Relational Psychoanalysis developed out of Interpersonal Psychoanalysis. This in turn had grown out of Interpersonal Psychiatry, which was founded by Harry Stack Sullivan (1892 1949). His experience in psychiatry made him impatient with Kraepelinís system of psychiatric classification which treated a patient as an isolated individual. Instead he adopted a much more social interac tionist approach, as Ronald Laing did later in Britain. Its development into In terpersonal Psychoanalysis grew out of Sullivanís interest in Freud. Sullivan had had a Freudian analysis in his days as a medical student in the early 1930s, but came later to criticize Freud for mistaking his own particular cultural context for a universal one. The development of Interpersonal Psychoanalysis was furthered greatly by Clara Thompson (1893 1958), who was Sullivanís associate. Both Sullivan and she, successively, were directors of the William Alanson White Institute of Psychiatry in New York, the home of the Relational School.

Clara Thompson also was a psychiatrist who had undertaken a Freudian training, but later, in consultation with Sullivan, went to Ferenczi in Budapest for further analysis. He provided a better match for their interpersonal interest. When she came back to New York, Thompson passed on the benefits of her analysis with Ferenczi to Sullivan, and he and she together founded the school of Interpersonal Psychoanalysis. It became a somewhat loose grouping of ana lysts who laid emphasis on the social setting of disorders and on the cultural environment. It was criticized strongly by more classical Freudians for being too social and superficial, and for not working enough with intra psychic con flict. Many of the graduates of the William Alanson White Institute did not feel at home with either an absolute socially slanted or an absolute individually slanted approach. They came to include analysts who were being influenced by Self Psychology, by the British Object Relations movement, and by modern Kleinianism. They therefore formed in 1988 the Relational track in psychoana lytic training (Ghent in Skolnick and Warshawís *Relational Perspectives*).

The underlying influence of Ferenczi remained strong throughout the transition of the school of Interpersonal Psychoanalysis to that of Relational Psychoanalysis. The chief contributions of the school to present day theory and practice are its stress on the total situation of therapy as involving a transference from childhood, the delineation of the early relational matrix as forming the structure of what is transferred, and the importance of the thera peutic relationship as the means of cure. The effect of the relational matrix is well illustrated by H. V. Dicks in his book *Marital Tensions* (1967), where he makes it clear that in a marriage there are six in bed, the six being made up of the marital couple together with their two sets of parents.

Since the founding of the Relational School, a steady stream of books and articles on relational themes has been published by its members and adherents. They form part of what holds out promise of an eventual unifying of the several schools of psychoanalysis which see relationship as the basis of psy chodynamic work.

EVERYTHING POINTS TO FERENCZI

Out of the developments in psychoanalysis in the US and in Britain as outlined in this chapter, there have emerged three fundamental elements in the structure of a more human psychotherapy. One comes specifically from Balintís work, one from Kohutís, and one is more general. The first is Balintís concept of the arglos state (of innocence) as indicating the thresh old of regression to the world of childhood; the second is Kohutís concept of narcissism and the reality of narcissistic wounds; and the third is the phe nomenon of counter transference. These three insights all help us to see the child in the adult facing us, and to behave towards them accordingly with understanding, appropriateness and humanity. They each make an invaluable contribution to working with the child in the analysis whose existence was first adumbrated by Ferenczi.

What has been happening, then, is the emergence of changed practice and new theories to take account of the shift of work to the earlier years of infancy, both in the setting and nature of the original disruptions, and in the discovery of the child or infant present in therapy through whom these can be worked with. It represents nothing less than the development of a new paradigm for psychoanalysis, for which the wheels had been set in motion by the figure behind it all, namely, Sandor Ferenczi. His influence, publicly sup pressed for so long, can be recognized and traced back in the work of the Brit ish Independents, and in these various streams of psychoanalysis which have developed in the US. The more one looks, the more his influence is there. He deserves his title of being the co founder of classical psychoanalysis, and the founder of its modern relational form.

Chapter Two

Touching Base

SANDOR FERENCZI

It was Sandor Ferenczi who laid the foundation for all relational work and who transplanted the roots of psychoanalysis firmly into the early years of childhood. The final building block in my thinking and practice was set in place when I came across the material about him in Balintís book *The Basic Fault* and then read one of the books containing his papers which were cited in Balintís bibliography. It was as a result of that reading that I came across the papers contained in his *Final Contributions to the Problems and Methods of Psychoanalysis* (1955/1980); I was drawn into a different world. This vol ume contains in particular his seminal paper Confusion of tongues between the adult and the child (1933), introducing the concept of the language of tenderness.

It was electrifying. Here was someone who had formulated the answers to all my strivings of the past twenty years, who had asked the same questions, and who had had the same doubts. He had shared my hesitations about eth ics and methods, my questions about the problems which people brought to psychotherapy and how to respond to them; and, what is more, he had written about it all at least sixty years before, and no one in the course of my training had mentioned either his writings or their author. As the reader may gather, I identify strongly with Ferenczi. Psychotherapy took on a new feel: an ex panse of discovery opened up with immeasurable benefit both to me and, I know, to those in therapy with me. It confirmed me in the work of regression, which I had already allowed myself to start.

Ferenczi was born in 1873, in the last days of the Austro Hungarian Empire, with its twin centers in Vienna and Budapest. Freud was established in Vienna, the senior capital; Ferenczi, 17 years younger, in Budapest. There seems to

19

have been a certain division of opinion and practice between these two centers within psychoanalysis from the earliest days, and it continued for many years, both in regard to analysis itself (Benedek, in Aron and Harris 1993) and in regard to supervision (Jacobs et al., 1995). It may well still do so.

Sandor had moved from his family home in North Hungary in 1897, and in Budapest became a consultant in psychiatry and neurology, as Freud had in Vienna. As psychoanalysts studying unconscious processes Freud and he shared an understandable interest in parapsychology. He had many medical and scientific publications to his name before he ever met Freud, and had himself in 1900 been sent Freudís *Interpretation of Dreams* for review but decided it was not worth the effort to comment (Stanton 1990). By about 1906 he had become more positively aware of Freudís work and increasingly enthusiastic about it: he wrote about it, lectured on it, and formed a wish to meet its originator.

When he met Freud, in 1908, the two men took to each other at once. They began a fruitful collaboration and intimate friendship, sharing, as Freud re corded in a letter to Ferenczi of 11 January 1933, an intimate community of life, feeling and interest (Falzeder et al. 2000). Thereafter, visits (largely from Ferenczi to Freud) occurred regularly, and both men appear to have taken it for granted that they would spend their holidays together (Brabant et al. 1993). That did not mean that they did not have some differences of opinion, even when on holiday (Dupont 1995, 186, n4; Fortune 2002, 8 9; Gay 1988, 189). Ferenczi, for instance, objected to Freud appearing to use him merely as an amanuensis; Freud complained about Ferencziís dependence. Here were seeds of later disagreements. In spite of that, a correspondence between them had begun which was to take place every few days. It was to last for 24 years and to yield 1250 or so surviving letters, of which more than half are Ferencziís.

Hoffer (1991, 465n1) comments on Freudís unmistakeable love and deep admiration for Ferenczi, and says that Ferenczi served as Freudís alter ego, representing the passionate and unrestrained side of Freudís personality. They clearly shared a deep mutual respect and affection. They complemented one another not only in founding psychoanalysis, but also in real life. The schism between them just before Ferencziís death was seen by Michael Balint in his obituary of Ferenczi as a tragic event of monumental proportions (Greenberg and Mitchell 1983, 182), and again, as a trauma on the psycho analytic world (Balint 1968, 152).

FREUD'S FRIEND AND CHOSEN SUCCESSOR

Ferenczi was a great man. It is tragic that he finally fell foul of Freud, who was stronger; and that Ferenczi and his works were in consequence banished and largely forgotten. This was the pattern of all of Freudís close relation ships with male friends: great closeness, followed by contrasting distance and hostility after some disagreement. Of their number, Ferenczi was the closest and most loyal. Originally he was a founder member of the psychoanalytic movement, and was one of its constant promoters and guardians. When he later developed variant opinions and techniques of which Freud disapproved, he was consigned to the psychoanalytic dust bin: rumors of mental instability gained currency, given permanent form by Ernest Jones (Maddox 2006).

Until that happened, for more than twenty years the lives of Freud, Fe renczi and their families had been to a great extent interwoven. When, in 1909, a year after they had met, Freud paid his first visit to America to give lectures at Clark University on the subject of psychoanalysis, Ferenczi went with him. It was Ferenczi who suggested the topics and who took such part in the framing and material of the lectures that it seems difficult to say exactly who was ultimately responsible for their shape (Freud 1933).

Ferenczi has a claim to be considered a joint founder of psychoanalysis: Freud had already used a goodly amount of Ferencziís work and a large number of Ferencziís suggestions in his earlier theorizing. There are, for instance, numerous and valuable acknowledgements to Ferenczi in Freudís *The Psychopathology of Everyday Life* (1901): these must have been referring to Ferencziís works before they had ever met (Brabant et al. 1993, 60, n5). Subsequently, as Freud (1933) said later in his obituary of his friend, a num ber of papers that appeared later in the literature under his or my name took their first shape in our talks. These were on autumn holidays together in Italy. They were succeeded by constant exchanges in their correspondence. If Ferencziís contribution had continued to be assimilated instead of eventu ally being extruded it is likely that psychoanalysis could have avoided many of its later defects and become a method of therapy of considerably wider application much sooner than it did.

Instead, Ferencziís work has had to be recovered, after a period in which the narrower Freudian interpretation of psychoanalysis had decades to develop on its own. Having rejected modification from the inside, it is now naturally considerably harder to modify it from the outside. The exclusion of Ferenczi with his findings about earlier years, about the potentialities of regression, about relationship, and about the child in the analysis brought a discontinuity into the development of psychoanalysis. Its classical expression ruled supreme but became fossilized and out of touch with advances in science and in con temporary culture. Now that Ferencziís contribution has been restored, the result is a discipline in two disparate parts, with classical psychoanalysis left as a historical specimen which has failed to evolve constructively. There could have been a gradual development through cross fertilization of the two into a unified model which would have done justice to both old and new, honoring the old for its fundamental historical importance and the new for the more human form which it now was able to take.

The closing of ranks against Ferenczi was an astonishing volte face. Freudís own daughter, Anna, described Ferenczi in a letter to Michael Balint as someone without whom the development of analysis is unthinkable (Aron and Harris 1993, 69); Freud himself called him a master of analysis who made all analysts into his pupils (1933). Ferenczi was also the first psychoanalyst to hold a professorial chair in psychoanalysis at a university (in Hungary) (Mart n Cabr 1997), and he was the founder and first president of the International Psychoanalytic Association. In addition he organized the founding of *The International Journal of Psychoanalysis* (Aron and Harris 1993, 1), though it is the name of Ernest Jones which appears on the masthead of each issue. He was, further, an original member of the Secret Committee formed at Jonesís suggestion in 1912 to protect Freud and the Cause (Gay 1988, 230), and he was marked out by Freud to succeed him in the leadership of the movement (letters from Freud to Ferenczi, 5 July 1930, 5 May 1932, and others, in Falzeder et al. 2000).

At the end, however, Freud disagreed with Ferenczi on the latterís varia tions in theory and in practice: in theory, about the role of trauma in the genesis of mental disturbances; in practice, about the need to re experience trauma rather than just remember it, and about the modification of psychoana lytic rules to bring about cure. Behind the disagreements lay the significance of the early years of childhood. No other point of view than Freudís was to be allowed (as had happened with Jung, Adler and Reich): in consequence, psychoanalysis became a truncated growth with half of its source of life cut off. The things latent in Freudís work which had been taken forward by Ferenczi became checked in their growth and ignored for years, while the more rigid features hardened. Hoffer says: If Sigmund Freud was the father of psychoanalysis, Sandor Ferenczi was the mother. Psychoanalysis lost its mother through Ferencziís untimely death in 1933 at a time when each man was profoundly disillusioned with the other. Psychoanalysis thus became a one parent child (Hoffer 1991, 466). By losing its mother in this way, psychoanalysis had for several decades only the acknowledged influence of the father in its development; though the continuing influence of the mother evidently continued unnoticed underneath it all, awaiting her full return.

The use of the word mother underlines Ferencziís complementary role in the founding of psychoanalysis, but it can be misleading. It is a metaphor reflecting a traditional stereotyped view of gender difference. Its use in this context refers to the exercise of the gentler, more emotional, traits which are often attributed to women as their exclusive possession, but are not in fact re served to them. They can be, and are, shown and possessed also by men. They were clearly shown by Ferenczi. We are all on a continuum: some men can be more tender and caring than some women; some women can be more aggres sive and confrontational than some men. It is a quality of humanity which is being designated by the use of the word mother, a quality of gentleness and care. In the particular case of psychoanalysis it connects also with work on the relationship between a child and the actual mother, and her demonstration or otherwise of these more tender qualities. In respect both of exercising the traits and of pursuing the work, Ferenczi was engaged in something that was missing from the work of Freud.

FERENCZI'S DEVELOPING WORK

As well as being Freudís closest colleague, Ferenczi had from the beginning had his own independent views; and there was constant tension between his loyalty to Freud and his own freedom. His dedication to psychoanalysis was such that he never ceased to work at it and to question and adapt. His experi ence of being analyzed by Freud had left him with questions, and his own continuing work left him with further questions: he worked with much sicker people and much earlier disturbance than did Freud. As the classical Freudian approach was not designed for this, Ferenczi tried to develop ways of work ing at the problems which arose.

Freud did not actually like the very ill: he went so far as to refer to them variously as rabble (Gay 1988, 529n), riff raff, and disgusting (Brabant et al. 1992, 85, l.1). Ferenczi on the other hand took on the most hopeless: his colleagues were accustomed to sending him their hardest cases knowing that if anyone could help them, he would be the one (Stewart 1992). This difference reflected the fact that Freudís interest was science; Ferencziís passion was heal ing. It echoed their personalities, too. Freud used methods which he considered suitable for a scientific enquiry, while Ferenczi was willing to adapt his methods until he found something which would suit the particular need of his patients.

This focus of Ferencziís formed the background for developments in his work after his brief analysis by Freud (in 1914 and 1916) and his army service in World War I (1914 1918). During the war, he had been director of the war neurosis clinic in Budapest, working with soldiers suffering from shell shock and related troubles. He tried to use the techniques of psychoanalysis with them, but found that free association, for instance, proved to be too slow for the numbers of patients involved, and it was unable to deal with the trauma of shell shock. He therefore set about trying to find fresh approaches and methods by which the difficulties could be overcome.

His Search

This search extended to the end of his life, and covered three main phases. The phases are generally labeled as those of active technique, relaxation, and mutual analysis (Bokanowski 1996); though they might be better described as those of activity, passivity and elasticity (flexibility), which are the names that Ferenczi gave to them on other occasions (Dupont 1995, 160). The latter set of names highlights his modifications in the role of the analyst.

The first phase, of activity, covered the years 1918 1926, and was one in which Ferenczi as analyst took a more active and directive role in the analysis, the aim being to increase tension in the patient so as to get things moving. Such practices were decried by classical workers, even though things like setting a termination date had been done earlier by Freud himself (Freud 1937). Ferenczi pointed out also that analysts already intervened actively by giving verbal interpretations: he was merely extending such activity (Ferenczi 1926/1994, 199 200). What was more important was that he found and ac knowledged that a more active technique did not always succeed: it didnít alter the analystís aggressive attitudes, and it tended to reproduce the original trauma from which someone might be trying to escape.

He therefore tried to replace that approach, in his second phase, with a more passive one, where the patient was encouraged to relax, though the analyst still remained in an authoritarian position. This issue of authority was to be tackled in his third phase: in the present one he tried in spite of the au thoritarianism to show towards the patient attitudes of permissiveness, flex ibility and frankness (Hoffer 1991, 467; Lomas 1993, x). Such attitudes were intended to promote re experiencing on the part of the patient. This was more than an intellectual remembering or a thinking back to the past: it meant bringing the past into the present and giving life to the emotions attached to the memory. Ferenczi also called this process reminiscence.

Important to this phase was the fact that he permitted regression, heavily frowned on as a dangerous indulgence by Freud and most others. Regression was what allowed the patient to go back to an earlier phase of life, notably to childhood, and to re experience events as a child rather than just recalling them in words. In spite of all this, Ferenczi still came to feel that the process was authoritarian and unequal. He said: One begins to wonder whether it would not be natural and also to the purpose to be openly a human being with feelings, empathic at times and frankly exasperated at other times. This means abandoning all techniqueí and showing oneís true colours just as is demanded of the patient (CD, 94).

This conviction brought him to the last of his three phases of adapting and developing psychoanalysis, extending from 1929 up to his death in 1933. It was the phase of elasticity, which focused particularly on the healing of trauma. It meant him being more flexible, to the extent of being open and honest about his thoughts and feelings, especially his counter transference feelings both positive and negative. It meant some self revelation; and it meant abandoning his position of aloofness and authority. It culminated with his ventures into mutual analysis.

The Question of Mutual Analysis

Here we are going to give some attention to Ferencziís exercise of mutual analysis. This is worthwhile to explore, first, because it led to various impor tant developments and insights within psychoanalysis, and, second, because it is used prejudicially by some in order to dismiss or overlook the most positive features of this phase of flexibility. These involved the dropping of the analystís remote and authoritarian mask and the permitting of a genuine emotional engagement. The classical reaction to Ferencziís ventures into mutual analysis also provides a particularly clear instance of the confusion of tongues between child and adult about which Ferenczi was to write so forc ibly in his 1933 paper.

Ferenczi said, Finally, it will come to the suggestion of mutual analysis (CD, 94). This marked the extreme, and concluding, part of his third phase. It was not an inevitable culmination. An analyst can be open, honest, frank and self disclosing without becoming an exactly equal participant in the analysis. The latter usually proves not to be helpful; the former certainly is. Ferenczi himself felt that mutual analysis had not worked, but he was still trying to improve on it: one of his last conclusions before he died was all in all, still no universally applicable rules (CD, 157). It was, nonetheless, a courageous thing to allow and attempt, though easily misunderstood, and it duly gave rise to the outraged reactions of more orthodox workers. A modern criticism of it, by a writer generally favorable to such pioneering work, is that Ferenczi con fused mutuality with symmetry: the therapeutic relationship may be mutual in that the partners are equal, but it is not symmetrical, in that their roles are not the same (Aron 1996).

The move into mutual analysis was perhaps not quite as strange as it may seem: the people with whom he practiced it were fellow therapists; and this was uncharted territory (Dupont 1995, xx xxii). One response to coming across uncharted territory is not to venture into it and to prohibit others from going there either, for fear of what might be found. Ferenczi was braver and more highly motivated than that, and was dedicated to finding any method which he felt might ease the suffering of his patients. He felt further that he himself had not had a proper training analysis to give him any precedent: he had to solve the problem on his own. He was a very brave man.

The mutual analysis that gives rise to most comment was with Elizabeth Severn, an American psychotherapist who was herself practicing in Budapest during the eight years of her analysis (Aron and Harris 1993, 105). She was also in touch with Freud. Ferenczi was led to consider, too, whether a greater mutuality might also be indicated in his work with Clara Thompson, the fellow analyst whom we have already met in the previous chapter as one of the founders of Interpersonal Psychoanalysis in the United States (Shapiro, in Aron and Harris 1993, 168).

Elizabeth Severn had been severely sexually abused in her childhood. She told Ferenczi during the course of her analysis with him that even in indulging her (as in his relaxation or passivity phase), he was not being fully honest about his own counter transference feelings (chiefly ones of dislike). This Ferenczi admitted, and tried to work at them so that they might not be a block to her recovery. Severn suggested the route of mutual analysis and Ferenczi accepted the challenge, acknowledging that his own analysis had not equipped him to deal with the feelings that he had. When he did so in mutual analysis, he found to his surprise that the analysis that had become blocked began to move again. This experience led him to emphasize the need for a full and rigorous training analysis for those intending to practice, which was not then the custom. His call was based on more than his experience with Elizabeth Severn. He spoke, too, from the brevity of his own analysis with Freud, and from the fact that he had himself conducted in earlier years what is considered to be the first training analysis [that of Ernest Jones in 1913] (Aron and Harris 1993, 1).

Although with hindsight Ferenczi came to think that his move to mutual analysis had been a mistake, from it there ensued, nevertheless, considerable benefit to psychoanalysis: chiefly this recognition of the necessity for a full training analysis for potential analysts. This later became a universal requirement. He also opened up the way to incorporating a greater equality and mutuality into psychoanalysis; and brought a realization of the importance of working with counter transference, which he had noted long before the famous paper of Paula Heimann (1950). One can see an echo of his use of mutual analysis, too, in the modern practice of co counseling. Perhaps what made Ferencziís work so controversial was first, its novelty and boldness, and secondly, the depth of disturbance in the people involved that made it such a tangled issue. New methods remained yet to be discovered to enable the tackling of such depths; but he undoubtedly started the process of discovery.

One particular aspect of Ferencziís mutual analysis with Elizabeth Severn which attracted Freudís criticism and angry wit was his permitting her to kiss him. It would appear that Severn went to Freud and unthinkingly told

him I am allowed to kiss Papa Ferenczi. Perhaps in fact she did it think
ingly, possibly in implied criticism of Freudís own distancing of himself from
patients I can imagine employing such covert aggression against a feared
figure myself. Freudís caustic reaction was that this would lead to petting
parties (letter from Freud to Ferenczi, 13 December 1931, in Falzeder et al.
2000; see also Dupont 1995, xv, and 3, n3). His letter seems to be totally un
comprehending: it would seem to be a clear example of the inability of some
adults to recognize infant needs, and the consequent misinterpretation of a
tender childlike relationship as a passionate adult one. This is the possibility
which Ferenczi deplores in his paper on Confusion of tongues (1933). It is
clear from Severnís words that she is speaking of an experience of tenderness
which had been lacking in her childhood, and that she is acting as a child
might with its father. Freud, on the other hand, understands it as an activity
between two consenting adults.

From all these years of testing out adapted methods, the two later phases (of
relaxation and flexibility) had the most enduring aspects. Out of them came the
discovery of regression on the part of the patient as the means of working with
trauma, and the exercise of greater openness and mutuality on the part of the
analyst. Both regression and mutuality later became the distinguishing charac
teristics noted earlier of the British Independent stream within psychoanalysis;
the latter at least is widely supported within American practice.

FERENCZI'S CRITICISMS OF FREUD

Freud may be well known for his criticisms of Ferenczi and his develop
ments, but at the end, Ferenczi came to criticize Freud too for the latterís
very different practices, and for his withholding approach. He came to think
that these were not the neutral approach that they claimed to be, but were
actually harmful, and repeated peopleís early traumas. He makes several
trenchant criticisms of Freud, his methods, and his attitude to patients in his
Clinical Diary (1995, xxiii, 184, 212). Freud, in his turn, criticized Ferenczi
for his supposed sexual freedom (Gay 1988, 578) and in particular for his
furor sanandi his passion to heal (Dupont 1995, xxiii; Hoffer 1991, 468).
Where Ferenczi might have been seen as providing a valuable complement
and counter balance to Freud, Freud himself increasingly came to see him as
a rival, challenger and subverter; to be banished and ignored.

Their differences centered on three distinct though interrelated things,
whose underlying implications were profound. The three things were the is
sues of abstinence, reminiscence (re experiencing), and trauma. The
disagreement about abstinence concerned the possibility, from Ferencziís

side, of this repeating an analysandís earlier trauma: he felt that analysts might unintentionally, in their very neutrality, be reproducing distant and damaging parental attitudes. The disagreement about reminiscence, or re experienc ing, concerned whether healing was always through verbal remembering, or whether it was through re living the original traumatic events. Ferenczi made the point that trauma cannot be remembered because it has never been con scious. It can only be re experienced . . . the painful memories remain rever berating somewhere in the body (and emotions) (1955, 278 279). Freud saw regression and re experiencing as indulgence. He doesnít seem to have been too keen on children, or at least on adults re living their childhood, however therapeutically necessary anyone else might have thought it. Children in his day were generally seen as small editions of adults, and were not considered to have modes of being and feelings of their own.

The third and central disagreement was about trauma. It involved the other two, abstinence being held likely to repeat the experience of trauma, and re experiencing being the way of healing it. The question was whether trauma is real (Ferenczi) or fantasy (Freud). Originally Freud had treated it as real: he had indeed started off by seeing it as the origin of neurosis, which he held to be due to some sexual trauma such as seduction (Freud 1896). Soon after that he came to feel that sexual trauma was an unconscious, almost arche typal, fantasy: the actual details were not so important (Hoffer, in Roiphe 1996). Various reasons have been put forward as to why in 1908 he changed his mind and withdrew his Seduction Theory to insist that fantasy was the prime cause of neurosis. His ambition of creating a universal theory of human psychology is suggested by some to have been the chief dynamic. The oc currence of fantasy is a phenomenon common to everyone and could be em braced within general laws; trauma is necessarily an individual experience.

Ferenczi, on the other hand, felt very firmly that trauma was a real hap pening. He traced the origin of most problems to a traumatic experience such as a shattering deprivation, or a massive assault, in oneís earliest life; and in this he came up sharply against Freud. Ferenczi said, No analysis can be regarded (at any rate in theory) as complete unless we have succeeded in penetrating to the traumatic material (FC 1955, 120). This was the conclu sion which he drew from his experience of analytic working. It meant that the origin of most psychopathology other than any which has its roots in physiol ogy or genetics is external, not internal. It arises initially from impingements on the child from outside, not from their inner dynamics.

Personally, I do not see that trauma being the origin of later disturbance, even though it is an individual experience, militates against its being part of a human psychology of universal application: interaction, however many variables it may introduce, is seen nowadays as an inescapable part of scien tific inquiry. Fantasy would enter the mix immediately after the occurrence of trauma, as the sufferer tried to make sense of the latter. This would then elaborate the effects of the trauma, and the relative contributions of the origi nal event and of its elaborative fantasy would need to be disentangled from one another and from their interaction.

Freud, in contrast, continued to emphasize fantasy and internal reality as the true object of analysis. He continued to work in an atmosphere of absti nence, with no modification to accommodate the experience of trauma, and, furthermore, in a manner which might re evoke it. Many believe that his failure to hold by his original findings of sexual seduction in fact did great harm, in allowing society to deny such happenings, and in permitting analysts within drive theory to ignore them (see Miller 1985). Finally, his emphasis on fantasy carried with it his rejection of Ferencziís stress on trauma, in spite of the latterís arguments and evidence, and finally resulted in his rejection of Ferenczi himself.

Alongside these theoretically based disagreements there also arose in Freud an increasing distrust of Ferencziís ways of working in which he was adapting established psychoanalytic technique to new ways of meeting the challenges of his work. Freud was fearful for the effect of this on the Cause (of psychoanalysis) which he felt had been built up over the years by him, Ferenczi and others with so much care and struggle.

THE FINAL SPLIT

The final split came with Ferencziís paper Confusion of tongues between adults and the child (1933), written for delivery at the Congress at Wies baden in 1932. Ferenczi had given it to Freud to read in advance. The content of the paper will be dealt with more fully in the next chapter. Freud demanded that Ferenczi keep silent about it until he (Ferenczi) had reconsidered it. It is difficult at this distance to see what Freudís vehement objection was. It is a highly perceptive and profound paper (Bokanowski 1996, 519), but it went against Freudís view of the different roles of fantasy and reality in relation to childhood sexual abuse, and it emphasized sensuality and childhood over sexuality and maturity.

The effect of Ferencziís differentiating between sensuality, the language of childhood and tenderness; and sexuality, the language of adulthood and passion, is what this book is about. That differentiation would have shaken one of Freudís most fundamental beliefs about the driving force of life, sug gesting that it might be connection (relationship) rather than sex (drive). It further opened up the whole area of the earliest years of life which had not figured in Freudís version of psychoanalysis: he held that disturbances arising in those years (including things then recognized as forms of psychosis) were unanalyzable. He had a blind spot about maternal interactions; and Ferencziís work and enthusiasm possibly made him fearful.

Relations with the mother were indeed central to the differences and division between Freud and Ferenczi. Freud did not and would not deal with his own relations with his mother, as Ferenczi pointed out to him. Ferenczi felt angry, too, that Freud had not dealt with his (Ferencziís) negative transference to him in his early analysis. Freud thought that he had, but he understood the term to refer to negative aspects of the father transference. Ferenczi, for his part, meant the negative maternal transference, which was foreign to Freud, and there were not then the tools to work with it (see Bokanowski 1996). It was that area which Ferenczi had begun to open up; but Freud himself wasnít open to it.

It was the failure to include this phase of life and its dynamics within the first fruiting of psychoanalysis that impoverished it and made it only a half therapy. Incorporation of the maternal aspects of early life and the discovery of their effects would have held within it the potential of a greater wholeness. Ferencziís uncovering of the importance of the mother child link and of the early and continuing life of the child, an inquiry later augmented and ampli fied by the work of others, has lain behind much of the subsequent history of psychoanalysis. It is perhaps significant in this respect that Winnicott, who did so much in this area of the mother child relationship before the re discov ery of Ferenczi, had possibly unconsciously tapped into this buried source in that he was supervised by Melanie Klein, and she herself had been analyzed, over a period of seven years, by Ferenczi, though there seems to be a singular lack of mention of this in much of the literature.

THE IMPLICATIONS OF TRAUMA IN INFANCY

The clash that occurred between Freud and Ferenczi over the nature of trauma was what brought their differences into the open. Ferenczi was repeating what Freud himself had rejected many years earlier. How to respond therapeutically to the effects of early damage is still a living issue in psychoanalysis (Hoffer 1991). The question is whether the consequences of trauma are to be handled more effectively by refusing a patientís urgent requests and expressed needs, or by meeting them. Freud, and classical Freudians subsequently, held and hold that to accede to patientsí requests risks precluding genuine resolution of their distress. Ferenczi, on the other hand, held that to refuse them risks repeating the original trauma. A clinical illustration of this issue is contained in chapter 4, in the section on   confrontation and collaboration.

One question that does not appear to be addressed in relation to the issue is why meeting the patient's needs should be considered per se any worse a so lution than refusing them: it seems to be taken as a self evident fact, whereas one reason for a patient's distress might simply be that their requests are never met. The prejudged rightness of refusal seems to be rooted in an assumed and unquestioned attitude of disapproval and hostility, akin to the taboo on ten derness; as if anything smacking of childhood is to be ruthlessly suppressed. I remember my own shock, having been brought up under such a regime, when I heard my son in law say to his son in response to the latter asking for something more than he already had, of course you can, darling.

Freud worked with human development from the age of four onwards, con centrating on the father, on triangular (oedipal) relationships, and on unearthing neurotic conflicts: Ferenczi worked on the earlier years, on the relationship with the mother and on deep trauma, which needed a more mutual setting to resolve it. The controversy that erupted between Freud and Ferenczi, said Boschan (in Roiphe J, 1996, 136a), represented a dramatic enactment of the very issues at stake: Freud's attempt to stop Ferenczi from presenting his Confusion of tongues (1933) at Wiesbaden can be compared to a father disavowing what the son experiences as traumatic, dismissing it as a child's fantasy.

In spite of the attempts to exclude Ferenczi's insights, they were bound to re surface at some time as culture changed, science advanced, child develop ment was researched, and people everywhere took further the exploration of the origins of disturbance and the possibilities of healing. The move inaugurated by Ferenczi then sprang up again and returned to fuller strength, joining up with these newer findings which he himself had done so much to initiate. By that time it was too late to meld harmoniously with the old: it resulted in the unre solved mix of theories such as that which Greenberg and Mitchell uncovered, especially those where relationship rode uncomfortably in harness with the older, more surgical, approach based on a now outdated drive theory.

It was given to Ferenczi to see bits missing from Freud's work but latent within it, while at the same time contributing to and adhering to the basic tenets of that work. Because of the split, these bits remained undeveloped in Freudianism. They included the role of the mother, the interactional aspects of the therapeutic encounter, the need for respect for the other as a subject, the necessity of openness and honesty, and the constant presence of a child in the analysis. In other words, Ferenczi had begun the movement back to the earlier years and the dyadic relationship between mother and child which the second generation of psychoanalysts (Kohut, Balint, Winnicott) brought into the open. It was he who set the paradigm shift in motion.

It is notable that it was only after 1938, the year in which Freud died, that anyone was able to differ markedly from him and yet remain within the psychoanalytic movement. This was the time when, for instance, Klein, Fairbairn, Winnicott and Balint in Britain, and Sullivan in America became engaged in controversy and discovery: it was too late for integration to be possible, so an uneasy truce prevailed, and the developing streams continued to run in parallel with each other and the old.

Most of all, Ferenczi was prepared to adjust both his theory and his practice to find more effective methods of working. He was ready to experiment and innovate, to change tack, backtrack and set off again if any particular approach didnít work. He was above all flexible, and did not feel rigidly bound to a preconceived set of rules if they did not appear to be achieving their purpose. Most of all, in his emphasis on interaction, openness, honesty and mutuality, he paved the way for psychoanalysis to focus on and make use of the qualities and processes which lie at the heart of ordinary human communication and relation ship. He laid the foundation for a more human psychotherapy.

It would appear that in many ways he was a man ahead of his time. His views of science, humanity, relationships and childhood were breaching the limits of those currently dominant around him. Those latter views have now developed and provide more appropriate ground for Ferencziís methods to take root: his time has come. As Maddox (2006, 211) says, Freud did not, and could not, appreciate that Ferencziís technique . . . was based on a new philosophy.

It may well be that Freud nevertheless sensed at some level when he read Ferencziís paper on the Confusion of tongues, that, in dwelling on the real ity and universality of early trauma and discovering the continuing presence of the traumatized child in an analysis, Ferenczi had opened up a new and earlier world which would shift the foundation of his own lifeís work. Clas sical psychoanalysis only took into account later happenings and dealt with oedipal, conflictual, three person situations. Kohut and Winnicott were to confirm independently that happenings before this were more fundamental happenings at the level of the development of the self and in two person relationships respectively. The hypothesized Oedipus complex would not even occur in its classical form if earlier difficulties had not been resolved. Thus Kohut said that the presence of a firm self is a pre condition for the experience of the Oedipus complex (1977, 227). Winnicott added that in the 1920s, everything has the Oedipus complex at its core . . . the anxieties belonging to the instinctual life at the 4 to 5 year period in the childís relation ship to the two parents. . . . Now, innumerable case histories showed me that the children who became disturbed . . . showed difficulties in their emotional development in infancy, even as babies (1965, 172). This new world was going to require a different model.

Chapter Three

Two Languages

THE DIVIDE

Ferenczi had been such a loyal supporter and friend of Freud that one may well wonder at his relegation to outer darkness being so absolute. Some of the extinguishing of him was of Freudís doing (Gay 1988, 586); yet, while the split itself may have been due initially to the two men themselves and to things unresolved in their relationship, its perpetuation seems to owe quite a lot to calumny spread by Ernest Jones. The calumny referred to Ferencziís supposed mental aberrations towards the end of his life: their nature was unspecified. In contrast, a reading of his *Clinical Diary*, covering the last year of his life, from 7 January to 2 October 1932, shows that there were no such aberrations: his sanity is amply demonstrated. Among other things it demon strates his continuing solicitude for Freud.

Jones got the words about Ferencziís mental aberrations from Freud (Gay 1988), but this does not seem to be enough to explain Jonesís active suppres sion of Ferencziís work. It was easy to dismiss Ferencziís contributions as being the outpourings of a diseased mind; but it gives the impression of being an argumentum ad hominem: if you donít like the message, shoot the mes senger. It has been suggested that Jones was possibly jealous about his own analysis: he had had Ferenczi, while Ferenczi had had Freud (Aron and Harris 1993, 6). He certainly seems to have been jealous of Ferencziís friendship with Freud, and of the formerís place in the ruling clique of psychoanalysis (Mad dox 2006). It smacks of rivalry between two contenders to the throne (like the rivalry between Melanie Klein and Anna Freud in Britain some years later).

Freud did say wounding things about Ferenczi in a letter to Jones after Fe rencziís death in 1933 (Gay 1988, loc.cit.), yet he also wrote an obituary for him in the same year in which he paid him great tribute (Bokanowski,1996, 521a).

33

He would appear to have felt very ambivalent. Besides penning that obituary, Freud again wrote about Ferenczi in 1937, sometime after the latterís death, in his paper Analysis terminable and interminable (1937; Sandler 1991). There he speaks at length of the vicissitudes of the analysis of a certain man, who had himself practised analysis with great success (Freud 1937, 221; Sandler 1991, 8). This was Ferenczi: Freud had not managed to get his friend out of his per sonal life, in spite of his extrusion from the mainstream of psychoanalysis. He went on in that paper to mention Ferencziís work in attempting to shorten the duration of analytic treatment. No doubt it is desirable [to do this], he says, and after referring to his own abandoning of hypnosis as a suitable instrument for this purpose and no substitute for that having yet been found, he goes on to say, from this point of view we can understand how such a master of analysis as Ferenczi came to devote the last years of his life to therapeutic experiments, which, unhappily, proved to be vain (1937, 230; Sandler 1991, 17).

At the same time the paper testifies to the deep division between the two men arising from an inability to bring into the arena of debate the profound is sue that lay between them. That issue was the part in later disturbance played by events during the period of the mother child dyad. The issue remained unconscious and unverbalized. Analysis terminable and interminable seems to represent Freudís fear at never being able to supply what Ferenczi had needed in his analysis. What this was, Ferenczi himself was to find later through his work with others, namely, attending to the contribution of the mother towards disturbances in later life. It is significant that Freud writes of Ferencziís continuing need as to do with an instinctual conflict rather than with a longing for love: the concept of such an unresolved yearning of earlier origin seems to be foreign to Freud.

The phrase analysis interminable in Freudís paper means just what it says. It expresses the fear at the center of the Freud Ferenczi controversy. With hindsight this can be seen to be concerned with the analysis of pre oe dipal troubles, involving a maternal transference, to which Freudís classical technique and his own blind spot were not suited. The fear attached to it was that the patientís problems might never be resolved, and that the analyst might get caught up in them and in an endless dependence (see further chapter 9). That might indeed be the outcome if the methods applicable to later arising neurotic conflict were to be applied without modification to earlier needs, be cause with those methods these needs are never either faced or met, and they become ever more urgent on account of that. It is not necessarily so if other more appropriate methods are used methods which Ferenczi was discover ing. Freud in the end was angry at Ferencziís failure to bow to his wishes that Ferenczi keep quiet about his findings, and he disapproved strongly of the direction Ferencziís work was taking.

Ferenczi in consequence was forced into the shadows, not only by Freud and Jones, but also by his other analytic colleagues. He formed a threat to them with his dropping of the analystís defenses, and with his uncomfortable interpretations of analytic attitudes, both of which developments were an out come of his discovery of the world of deficit in child development. As Judith Dupont says in her introduction to Ferencziís *Clinical Diary*,

> Ferenczi emphasizes the hypocrisy of certain professional attitudes of ana lysts their denial of countertransferential feelings that are uncomfortable or contrary to their ethics. He considers such practices to be traumas inflicted on the patient, likely to revive the very traumas from the past that the analysis is supposed to cure. This was a situation Ferenczi himself had experienced, not only in his role as analyst but also as an analysand and a member of the analytic community. (1995, xix)

With the suppression of Ferenczi went the suppression of his realization and demonstration that early damage could be a possible area for analytic work: a possibility which was up until then unrecognized and even denied. It could be done, Ferenczi found, by the creation of a particular quality of relationship between analyst and patient. Ferencziís work had therefore to be rediscovered by others, decades later, which then cleared the air for the rediscovery of Ferenczi himself.

Freud and Ferenczi together could possibly have formed an integrated psychoanalysis of the widest appeal and application, but only if there had been immense modifications in the classical Freudian model. They did form such an integrated partnership at the beginning; any deep differences between them did not rise to the surface until later. Ultimately they came to represent complementary but contrasting aspects of the human life span and its prob lems, which called for similarly complementary methods of work within an integrated overall model. Freud does not in fact seem to have seen the pos sibilities, needs and nature of work with the earlier years. His psychoanalytic work had been overwhelmingly with adults and late developing problems. Ferenczi, while originally working with the same, had been led by his expe rience to discover disorders earlier in development, of a different nature. In working with those, he had also found that while there might appear to be an adult in front of the analyst or therapist, there was in effect a child, for whom the classical approach needed to be modified.

Their work seems to a surprising extent to have reflected their own indi vidual personalities, reinforcing the idea that anyoneís practice of therapy is an expression of their own individual life experience. Unfortunately they were unable to coexist in an evenly balanced partnership, and a split devel oped. Such splits are of course one of the things which psychoanalysis claims to be its sphere of corrective work. In this case, the two men complemented each other almost perfectly but sadly failed to meld. Freud needed his friend for a more complete and effective psychoanalysis, but failed to be sufficiently adaptable to accommodate him or to see the need to do so.

The result is that at present we have within psychoanalysis two contrasting approaches to emotional illness which have developed so differently as to make them incompatible even though some practitioners try to hold them together. The problems and populations to which each is applicable are quite distinct. Classical psychoanalysis, with its confrontational, distant, critical attitudes, is not suitable for working with the earlier years. Nor does it appear to be really suitable for any human encounter without considerable modification.

Nowadays most, if not all, of those who come for psychotherapy are served better by a model based on Ferencziís work. Hysterical conditions, which Freud chiefly worked with, are not generally reported in contemporary cul ture: this is a widely acknowledged change. People coming for therapy today have earlier and more diffuse damage; they suffer from a deficit in develop ment rather than from neurotic conflict; they create a maternal transference and counter transference; and they often need to re live their earliest child hood situation. These are the people whose states are variously termed narcis sistic, borderline and psychotic (organizing), or who have undergone some other early trauma. For them the neurotic transference thought by Freud to be essential for psychoanalysis was deemed to be impossible to achieve. He appears not to have seen the possibility of any other sort.

What is needed is an overall superordinate system of psychoanalysis spacious enough to include within it both sets of life problems and both ap proaches to their solution. The caveat has already been entered in relation to this that classical drive theory needs modification in theory and in practice to bring it into conformity with modern sciences, both human and natural. Freud and Ferenczi needed something bigger than both of them: a larger vision. The situation feels like that between the Republic of Ireland and Northern Ireland, or between England and an independent Scotland, where a greater entity such as Europe might overcome their differences sufficiently to give a basis for cooperation. The integrative umbrella is most likely to be some form of relational understanding: it appears to be widely accepted that many of the various major schools of psychoanalysis are already moving towards this.

This also touches on the question of motivation, classically thought to be something to do with instinctual drives: now, to do with emotion. What is needed is a satisfactory unitary theory, applying equally validly to every part of human life: one which will replace drive theory (Freudís hydraulic tension reduction model), and subsume object relations within a higher order theory, such as one which has integration as the basic motive. This urge to integra tion would need to include the forming of relationships, and also embrace the search for meaning, or trying to make sense of life. The best overall treatment of motivation to date, written from a Self Psychology and Intersubjectivity standpoint, is that of Lichtenberg et al. (1992); except that for some reason they do not include an urge for integration and meaning as one of their moti vational systems; perhaps because it is of a higher order than the others which they identify, and might itself be their integrating principle.

TENDERNESS AND PASSION

We need now to look in more detail at some of Ferencziís concepts. What happened to him and to his insistence that there could be differing approaches to psychoanalytic work might be said to have happened also to his valuable, original and profound hypothesis that there are two languages in psychoanaly sis. Both the hypothesis itself and one of the languages became excluded. The two languages referred to are the language of tenderness, and the language of passion. They are described and distinguished in the last paper which he wrote before he died: Confusion of tongues between adults and the child: the language of tenderness and of passion (1933), which we shall look at more fully later in the chapter. The language of tenderness belongs to a child; the language of passion, to an adult.

Tenderness in Ferencziís usage refers to the pre oedipal phase of experi ence: it focuses on such things as sensuality, and snuggling close. We can elucidate more of what he meant by looking at the German word which he used in his original paper, for which tenderness was Balintís chosen translation into English. The mother tongue of both Ferenczi and Balint was Hungarian, though Ferenczi wrote his later papers mostly in German. In this instance the German word which he used was Z rtlichkeit (Stanton 1990). Z rtlich means loving, and the meaning of Z rtlichkeit, therefore, is in the area of loving ness, fondness, tenderness. The word innocence might be equally good: the quality of innocence is well expressed in Rycroftís book *The Innocence of Dreams* (1979, 7), where it means not knowing, not hurtful, having a core which is by its very nature sincere; or, as Suttie (1935, 50) says, There is no criticism, so that goodnessí and badnessí are non existent. This is the age (or the momentí) of innocence. Chambersí Diction ary has among its entries for innocence being a child, which points to the state before the child is wakened to adult passions. It recalls and parallels the word arglos, which Balint translated as innocence and which he used to denote the state into which a patient entered at the start of regression, marking the possibility of the new beginning (chapter 4).

The words tenderness and innocence express the two poles of a mother child relationship. Tenderness is the quality of a mother in caring for and responding to the innocence of a child; maternal tenderness, corre sponding to child like innocence before they learn adult ways. At a tender age means at the age of innocence, where sensuality is the physical mode. Tenderness and innocence together represent the ambience of childhood and the mother child dyad and encapsulate the full meaning of Ferencziís general use of the word tenderness : it is this atmosphere which Ferenczi sees as needing to be reflected in an analytic sharing in which the child in the adult appears in the analysis.

The contrasting meaning of passion, which translates the German word Leidenschaft, is adult, oedipal and genital. Leiden means to suffer, and seems to have become transformed into the meaning of passion in the same way as these equivalent English words. Its sense lies around passion, fervor, heat. It enters into life with later development, and belongs to the world of neurotic conflict, genital sexuality, and the adult. Tenderness and innocence belong to the child. Premature imposition on a child of the adult language of passion shatters the childís innocence and comes into profound conflict with their natural language of tenderness.

The implications of a focus on the world of innocence and tenderness when working with the child in the analysis is given in Confusion of tongues. This paper is itself firm testimony to the clarity of Ferencziís mental state at the end of his life, whatever Ernest Jones was to say later. The suppression, or perhaps more accurately the repression, of his work is acutely the situa tion in respect of the language of tenderness, of childhood. Repression is used deliberately: it means that it was forgotten because it was threatening, both to Freud and to the psychoanalytic movement. Freudís was the adult language, the language of passion: his focus was not on childhood per se but only on its part in the development of passion, of adult sexuality. Children were seen as little adults.

In the development of passion, on this view, the chief function of the lan guage of tenderness is to form the basis of, and to phase into, the language of passion, held by most to be by far the more important language in adulthood. The language of tenderness is not seen as having independent significance. Yet some people do not ever reach the integrated adult stage and attain the sphere of passion undisturbed (via the Oedipus complex, as Freud put it). If their needs have not been met at an earlier stage, they can get stuck there, as mentioned in chapter 1. Both psychoanalysis and psychotherapy (probably all of the latter, but certainly psychoanalytic psychotherapy) often completely miss this point. Especially is this so with some analyses conducted according to the old drive theory, or classical, model: such an approach would indeed seem always to hold this danger. It can cause more damage than it cures. This is possibly due not only to the misinterpretation of innocence, but also to an underlying attitude of hate, foreign to a child seeking understanding, infusing the classical approach (see Suttie 1935).

Classical psychoanalysis is just not applicable to people whose develop ment has been traumatized at some stage before adulthood. Its understand ing of the problem and its verbal approach to healing it is not adequate. The trauma usually, if not always, occurred before the development of language. The cure of people, though, was not Freud's main aim: his was more one of detached scientific inquiry. He accused Ferenczi of being unbalanced over this very issue, of being driven by a passion to heal (which we might think is what it should all be about, and a worthwhile sort of passion to have). The language of tenderness thus remained ignored in mainstream psychoanalysis and in therapies deriving from that, even though it is the language which belongs to this early stage of life where so much damage occurs and where people can become arrested in their development. Ferenczi warned that the language of passion is actually dangerous if applied to someone living in therapy at this earlier level of tenderness, and that it can reproduce an original trauma. The languages get confused.

From the start, his warning would seem to have fallen on deaf ears. The danger seems not even to have been noticed by some of his most distinguished immediate colleagues. Both Freud himself and Melanie Klein analyzed their own children: this impacts as a highly intrusive, indeed incestuous, action in relation to one's own children. It is extremely muddling of boundaries: the two levels would seem to have become totally tangled. The introduction of adult passion where childhood tenderness should prevail is furthermore a ma jor objection to other work of Melanie Klein. Her writings show that she em ployed adult language, images and sexuality in her interpretations of the play and inner thinking of children with whom she worked. These are concepts which we may take leave to doubt are actually those of children, but which are forced on them by a powerful adult in a manner which might otherwise be described as a form of rape. Mrs. Klein appears to have been distinctly unethical in this, forcing intimate adult interpretations onto a child's mind, and offending their na ve humanity.

The importance of the fact that we are often dealing with a child in therapy, and need to be careful to work at the child level, using the language of ten derness as Ferenczi put it, thus was not taught in training courses, nor was the name of Ferenczi mentioned. While Ferenczi himself may have made a partial comeback in that there are now books and conferences about him and an admiration for him, the recovery of this vital contribution of his is not com plete. His work can still be ignored, as it was in the three training programs of which I had experience, and as it is largely to this day in at least one program with which I am well acquainted. This is an impoverishment of the whole of psychoanalysis and of psychoanalytic therapy. Ferenczi needs to be restored to his place of pre eminence together with Freud in the establishment of psy choanalysis. Further, his emphasis on working with the child who is present in every analysis needs to be accepted as the basis of effective and appropri ate work particularly with people suffering from early damage, but also with all people, whatever the origin of their difficulties.

Psychoanalysis has developed in the years since Freud in the direction of working with earlier years and the mother child dyad. This is where Ferencziís work and writings were pointing, and the development which they were initiat ing. He reached this stage after many years of continuing and developing work within the older model. His insights therefore provide a basis for a suitable theory to undergird appropriate practice in both the old and the new areas of work. For a long time the new areas struggled to find any accepted expression within the classical Freudian fold: the theory then current was not adequate to the task. The fact that we are more often working nowadays in the realm of childhood, and need to employ the language of tenderness, calls for greatly increased recogni tion of and emphasis on Ferencziís work. The language of tenderness, the basis of childhood, is fundamental both to life and to therapy: it needs to be honored in both and to be given a proper placc in the practice of the latter.

THE CHILD IN EVERY ANALYSIS

To understand the importance of recovering the sense of this language, it is necessary to go back a bit and start from what Ferenczi had to say about the phenomenon of child analysis occurring within the analysis of adults, and then to follow the development of this line of thought in his last few papers. It was all a part of his conviction that the earliest years with the mother were formative in much of later disturbance. In view of the confusion of tongues between Freud and Ferenczi themselves on this point, it is of great interest that the dates of the two last central papers by Ferenczi which we are about to look at coincide with the dates of two of Freudís later papers, Female sexuality (1931) and On femininity (1933). In these papers Freud shows some awareness of the role of the mother in early development and of the possibility that we must retract the universality of the thesis that the Oedipus complex is the nucleus of the neuroses (1931, 226). He then dismisses the possibility (Van Heute 2005).

Ferencziís remarks about child analysis are contained in his paper Child analysis in the analysis of adults (1931), published two years prior to Con fusion of tongues. This is on how childhood experiences are, given the right conditions, automatically re played during the analysis of an adult. The physi cal setting for the development of these conditions is provided by the dyadic enclosure within which psychoanalytic work is carried out. We have only to provide the right atmosphere within that setting for its development, or rather perhaps, we have only to ensure that we are not preventing it. In Confusion of tongues (1933) he takes the theme further, and makes it more specific.

In the earlier paper, Ferenczi questioned the sharp distinction made up to that date between the analysis of children and that of adults, the two being conducted usually by different groups of people, using different techniques, and in modern days (2009) having distinctive training. He himself was in the stream that worked with adults, though he had encouraged and supervised the work of others with children (such as Melanie Klein and Margaret Mahler). He had nevertheless come to notice in his practice of adult analysis, through his attempts to modify its technique in order to help more intractable cases, that as he did so, and as he adopted a more accepting attitude towards them, there was a spontaneous movement in them towards the re living of child hood. What started as the analysis of an adult became a child analysis. The patient became more na ve (i.e., childlike, new born) in their speech and in other expressions. This is what was identified later by Balint (1968) as the arglos state. Confrontation of any sort immediately and completely blocks the emergence of the frightened child.

If instead the analyst could respond to the patientís move and accompany them into a warm acceptance and responsiveness (instead of a cold withhold ing), it encouraged the person to go further into their childhood experience and to allow themselves to recall and re experience, usually quite unexpect edly, events which had been traumatic in their effect. These will have been for the most part completely forgotten consciously, but will have remained to form the basis of their subsequent lifetime disturbance. The re experiencing then led to healing. Ferenczi himself described the need for this re experi encing as follows: one has no right to be satisfied with any analysis until it has led to the actual reproduction of the traumatic occurrences associated with the primal repression, upon which character and symptom formation are ultimately based (FC 1955, 131). Re call of the event with its buried but still living emotion is what is needed.

The process of re calling or re experiencing is not easy: the buried event comes to the person with all its original force, and affects the therapist simi larly. It only happens if the analyst is himself sufficiently childlike in his ap proach, and does not ask questions which at that stage of life a child would not understand, nor offer interpretations which are far from the childís ex perience in whatever situation had been recalled. This was evidently behind my own analystís suggestions that language in therapy should be as childlike and as earthy as possible: those are the grounds of a childís experience. Once recalled, the traumatic experience, with its emotions, its consequences and effects, then has to be worked through thoroughly for any relief to become established and long lasting.

In order to work with this analysis of the child, Ferenczi adds, It is im portant for the analysis that the analyst should be able to meet the patient as far as possible with almost inexhaustible patience, understanding, goodwill, and kindliness. (FC 1955, 132). These are what a child needs and can un derstand. Not only a child: it is an approach which is likely to get through to the most hardened adult, and one to which an adult can respond just as much as can a child (cf. the account of the Special Unit at Barlinnie Prison by Jimmy Boyle in *A Sense of Freedom* [1977]). It can be an extremely demand ing task, in analysis as in life, powered partly perhaps by the therapistís own inner dynamics harboring a need to act in such a potentially vulnerable way, but also by what Ferenczi termed a kind of fanatical belief in the efficacy of depth psychology (FC 1955, 128). He goes on to say this has led me to attribute occasional failures not so much to the patientís incurabilityí as to our own lack of skill (FC 1955, 128). With this, I would whole heartedly concur.

The Fundamental Place of Trauma

Ferencziís emphasis on the unexpected appearance of a child in an analysis is closely connected to his insistence on the centrality of trauma as the origin of later disturbances. In his paper Confusion of tongues between adults and the child (1933) he says, allow me to report on some new ideas which this more intimate relation to my patients helped me to reach. I obtained above all new corroborative evidence for my supposition that trauma, especially sexual trauma, as the pathogenic factor cannot be valued highly enough (161). As we have seen, trauma was one of the main issues on which Ferenczi and Freud diverged (though Freud did nevertheless continue to have a place for it [1937]).

Ferenczi was firmly convinced that the origin of psychopathology lay in some actual overwhelming historical trauma that had happened to the person when a child. He came increasingly to believe that the incidence of such external trauma was very high. Trauma does not have to be sexual in nature: any abuse, whether sexual, physical, verbal or emotional can give rise to it, as can severe deprivation. Ferenczi said in a letter to Freud written on Christmas Day 1929 (Falzeder et al. 2000), 1. In all cases in which I penetrated deeply enough, I found the traumatic hysterical basis for the illness, and 3. . . .

psychoanalysis engages much too one sidedly in obsessional neurosis and character analysis . . . the cause lies in the overestimation of fantasy and the underestimation of traumatic reality in the pathogenesis (376). He pointed out also the possibility that there can be a resurgence of the buried experi ences of trauma during psychoanalysis.

By trauma, Ferenczi meant the occurrence in a childís life of an event too overpowering either to be coped with or assimilated (FC 1929.2, 121). It is something too big for the childís undeveloped emotions to absorb. It therefore overwhelms the childís defenses, with the consequence that emo tions are frozen, recall of the event is repressed and some sort of split within the victimís personality is brought about. This is not abnormal: it is a natural coping mechanism to enable us to deal with any event which threatens life or sanity; but it can have enduring and harmful results if not remedied in some way. The traumatized part of the self can be split off, either vertically, as in the development of a split or multiple personality, or horizontally, by repres sion into areas of the brain outside the range of our attention. From there, both because of its own continued though buried existence, and because the rest of the personality attempts to avoid any repetition or stirring of it, it continues unseen to exercise a malign and limiting influence on the personís development. The most extreme form of the response is dissociation (split personality) (Mollon 1996).

In emphasizing the widespread occurrence of trauma, including ones of sexual provenance, Ferenczi was making a vital point. The fact of trauma underlies the contrast already noted between conflict theories of psycho pathology and deficit theories. Trauma gives rise to such a deficit in a personís development: it is only the after effects of this, where the child tries to make up for or defend against further pain and confusion, which give rise to conflict. Kohut was implicitly making the same contrast in his move from classical psychoanalysis to Self Psychology, focusing on nar cissistic needs rather than on neurotic conflict. Only a deficit model does justice to the fundamental reality of there being a traumatized child at the heart of every analysis.

The fact that trauma is the origin of later disturbance is also clearly at the root of Ferencziís ideas about regression, about re call and re experiencing, and about the approaches used and attitudes required in therapy. Ferenczi continues in his letter to Freud of 1929 to say: 4.The newly acquired expe riences naturally also have an effect on details of technique. Certain all too harsh measures must be relaxed (376). The reality of trauma has far reaching consequences for practice.

Ferenczi thus made us aware that in therapy we are most likely to be talk ing about someone who has been traumatized; and that trauma reduces the person to the level of a child, to the age when the trauma happened. This is part of the foundation for his work on the confusion of tongues. The use of one of the tongues or languages, namely that of the adult, of passion, was likely to repeat the trauma: the use of the other, the child language of tender ness, is more likely to make it possible to release the person from the traumaís continuing power.

The Wise Baby

It is worth digressing here briefly to note also what Ferenczi saw as one significant consequence of trauma which shows up in later life as well as in therapy. He mentions certain phenomena of splitting which he had ob served in his patients when they were in a childlike state. If the patient felt deserted in the analysis, it seemed to result in a split in personality in which one part of the patientís personality adopts the role of father or mother to the rest (FC 1955, 135), trying thereby to undo the traumatic experience of abandonment.

These observations led Ferenczi to recall his concept of the wise baby, which he had mentioned in an earlier paper of 1923 (The dream of the clever baby, [FrC 1926/1994, 349]; though, in that paper it has a rather different meaning to his recalling of the concept in 1933). The phenomenon can be recognized in the way people talk about themselves; in the way they report having dreams of looking after a wounded or needy child; and in the way in which some are driven even as children to look after others, including their own parents. This is a practice which they are likely to continue into adult life, some becoming therapists. Thus we have the concept of the Atlas per sonality, where children take on adult responsibilities from a very young age (Vogel and Savva 1993). Cozolino (2004, 181) observes a pathological caretaker may be a perfect child, an Aí student or loyal friend on the outside, but an empty, sad and lost child on the inside. Alice Miller (1987) too has remarked that some children who are seen as unusually talented may have developed in this way: they look functional but they feel empty and devoid of vitality. A child who may appear to be an adult is still only a child under neath.

Such a child does not rebel, but instead searches for others who need nurturing. They then either identify with that other and give them the care which they wish they had had, as an indirect means of giving it to themselves; or they see the other as the wounded child and care for them as if they were the childís mother. As is often evident in various types of interaction, persecutory and exploitative as well as deprived, the person (whether therapist, therapee, or anyone in ordinary life) can play the part of both poles in turn of their original bi polar relationships. History repeats itself.

To explain the concept of the wise baby, it seems   and I cannot do better than to quote Ferenczi himself   as though, under the stress of imminent danger, part of the self splits off and becomes a psychic instance self observ ing and desiring to help the self, and that possibly this happens in early   even the very earliest   childhood   (FC 1931/1955, 136). Working with people who have experienced this split is similar to working with sufferers from any other trauma. The analystís behavior is required to be   rather like that of an affectionate mother,   taking back the childís assumption of care for itself. Since   even in analysis, this tender relation cannot go on forever,   there is bound to be disillusionment and disappointment for a person in this sort of therapy as much as in any other. Thus there will also come about spontane ously the situation of frustration (or many such situations) which was Freudís main tool; except that in Ferencziís approach this too needs to be met with understanding rather than withholding or ignoring.   We have to take great pains and show much tactful understanding in order to bring back reconcili ation even in these circumstances, in contrast to the lasting alienation of the same situation in childhood   (FC 1931/1955, 137). Such a response will in its turn result in the personís growth towards independence, and answer Freudís and othersí fear of an outcome of eternal clinging.

CONFUSION OF TONGUES

This brings us to the last of Ferencziís published papers   Confusion of tongues between adults and the child   (1933). It is subtitled   The language of tender ness and of passion.   The paper builds on his previous writings, especially those relating to child analysis as occurring in adult analysis, and to trauma as the pathogenic agent. The paper angered Freud greatly. As recorded briefly ear lier, he asked Ferenczi not to read it as planned at the Wiesbaden Congress of the International Psychoanalytic Association in September 1932, but Ferenczi went ahead   only to be greeted with rejection by his friend, and the eventual result of his reputation being besmirched and his memory suppressed. The rejection was such that Freud refused to shake Ferencziís hand when they next met, offending against the universally accepted norm of greeting throughout Europe, which exists especially in lands sharing German culture.

As a piece of innovative writing (which Freud otherwise encouraged in his followers) and of clinical observation and adventurous theorizing, it is dif ficult to see what could be objected to: the paper is a great exposition of his subject, true to life, powerfully heuristic, and consonant with modern experi ence of psychotherapy. It could only be objected to if it went against treasured dogmas or shibboleths of Freudís, such as the primary place of fantasy and the use of abstention in psychoanalytic work: this it evidently did. It was enough to ensure its condemnation; though, as I have suggested earlier (chap ter 2), Freud possibly sensed most deeply that it was moving psychoanalysis into a different world, branching out from his own creation.

The paper describes how adults and children speak different languages of love and closeness: the language of passion and the language of tenderness. The former belongs to the adult world of sexuality, genitality, sophistication, denial, guilt, suspicion. The latter relates to the universal childhood need for acceptance and openness, for closeness and warmth, to sensuality. Adults can, however, mistake this for genital sexuality and seduction, and react to it with passion, causing unbearable trauma and evoking immeasurable guilt in the child; the adults then, frequently, deny their part in it. The premature forcing of genital sensations has a . . . terrifying effect on children; what they really want, even in their sexual life, is simply play and tenderness, not the violent ebullition of passion (Ferenczi 1929.2, in 1955/1980, 121).

To repair this experience of forced imposition followed by denial, and to re spond to the childís need for warmth, Ferenczi holds that there is a need to pro vide a warm accepting relationship in therapy. Many who came to him needed to be allowed to regress to a childlike relationship with the therapist such as might have existed before their experience of trauma, regardless of whether that trauma was of invasion or of deprivation. They needed to be allowed to experience the warm, close, non threatening tenderness for which they longed, without it being misunderstood and treated as a search for passion.

Freud didnít agree with Ferenczi. The disagreement largely had its origin in the lack of analysis in Freudís day already noted of the motherís role in a childís early life and in the therapeutic transference. Ferencziís work made possible the supplying of this lack. Up until then the possible part that the mother might play in the genesis of disturbances had not been known, recognized or worked with: it was Ferenczi who realized its absence, and who opened it up to later gen erations until it now forms the major aspect of therapeutic practice. However, the immediate effect of Freudís disagreement was to close the possibility off. Ferenczi, in living example of what he himself was saying, met blankness, rejec tion, coldness and withdrawal of love: and died. As Erich Fromm (1935) was to say (quoted in Bacciagaluppi 1993), Ferencziís premature death was a tragic end to his life. Torn between the fear of a rupture with Freud and the realization that a departure from Freudís technique was necessary, he did not have the inner strength to pursue the road to the end (Aron and Harris 1993, 187).

Ferenczi at the last nevertheless remained true to himself. He made his choice: he read, and published, the paper. In this he had, rather oddly in view of Jonesís later public attitude to him, the support of Ernest Jones: Jones thought it would be seen as strange if the President of the International Psy choanalytic Association was not permitted to present a paper (Maddox 2006, 212; Stanton 1990, 50). Ferenczi was, though, not forgiven by Freud, and died. It is possible that his death, together with his long final illness, was at least partly a psychosomatic reaction to Freudís rejection of him: he himself felt that it was. He felt that his health needed harmony with Freud (Falzeder et al. 1996; CD 1995, 212), as it had, earlier, needed harmony with his mother (Bokanowski 1997). He had experienced his mother in his early life as forbid ding, destructive and difficult to please.

REALIZING THE INSIGHTS

In his Confusion of tongues paper Ferenczi is dealing with an increasing rep etition by patients in his daily psychoanalytic practice of traumatic events. It led him to believe that insufficiently deep exploration of the exogenous factor leads to the danger of resorting prematurely to explanations often too facile explana tions in terms of dispositioní and constitutioní (FC 1933/1955, 156). His attempts to explore the traumata by means of his previous psychoanalytic tech nique involving abstention and interpretation did not bring the release that he had anticipated and hoped for. For this originally he blamed the patients, as was customary. However, when the situation persisted he began to look at himself and his own possible part in it, and to listen to what his patients said to him.

He gradually came to the conclusion that patients identify themselves with their analyst, rather than contradicting or opposing him (or her). They repress any anger, hostility or criticisms that they feel, and only express these if they are given special permission or encouragement to do so. It is therefore a diffi cult task to become aware of what patientsí actual feelings or criticisms might be, not only because of the analystís reluctance to hear but also because of the patientís reluctance to speak.

Ferenczi came to feel that a great part of this repressed criticism was di rected towards professional hypocrisy. Analysts greet the patient with polite ness and promise to give them their undivided attention, but conceal their deeper feelings (FC 1933/1955, 158 ff.). When he introduced greater honesty into the situation, admitting his lapses of attention and some of his less favor able reactions (some of which might now be called counter transference), he found that the atmosphere cleared considerably, the patientís anxiety less ened, and the situation became more resolvable.

He considered that what made the difference was admission of the analystís insincerity or error. This served to set the patient free. It was an experience which people of that time, and still to a great extent now, may have been denied by their parents. The discovery revealed to him that the previous analytic attitude and posture had run the danger   and frequently fallen into it   of reproducing a situation very similar to that which in childhood had led to the personís illness: that is, of traumatizing the patient and then denying all responsibility for it and blaming whatever happened then or subsequently on the patient.

It was, in other words, reproducing a situation of trauma. Ferencziís definition of this as an occasion where something emotionally overpowering had happened to the child included the observation that its occurrence and significance were then denied by those to whom the child turned for help; who might sometimes be the adults responsible for it in the first place (FC 1933/1955, 162 163). It was in consequence no wonder that when the same thing happened as a result of their   therapy   the patient could not do anything other than repeat the symptom formation exactly as they did when their ill ness had started. He also uncovered the significant finding, now generally ac cepted, that the original agent in trauma was usually a member of the childís family or someone well known to them (Balint 1969).

Ferenczi found further that a more open, honest and intimate relationship brought him additional corroborative evidence for his hypothesis that trauma was the pathogenic factor. He saw such trauma happening in interactions between adults and children when an exchange may start on the level of ten derness but assume erotic (passionate) forms. When the adults are themselves emotionally disturbed in some way (and who isnít), they may mistakenly interpret the childish play as if it were expressing the desires of a sexually mature person, and respond accordingly.

If this occurs, it is difficult to imagine the state of a child after its occur rence. Reactions which one might ordinarily expect are paralyzed by anxiety: the anxiety also compels the child both to submit to the outrage and to take responsibility for it. They feel confused and split   innocent and blameworthy at the same time. They are overwhelmed by the event, saturated with emo tions which they are not able to understand or process. These emotions as a result remain submerged, distorted, convoluted, immensely compressed, seeking expression in any way possible, usually by means of the body. More, the perpetrator frequently behaves as if nothing had happened; and they, together with any other adults to whom the child speaks of the happening, may deny its reality, leaving the child even more unsupported, full of doubt of themselves, traumatized and split.

Ferenczi deals with this almost entirely in terms of sensual play between adult and child, and the untoward developments which may follow the precocious super imposition (each of his words is chosen very carefully) of passionate and guilt laden love on an immature as yet guiltless child (FC

1933/1955, 164). This undeveloped state of the child he terms the stage of tenderness. It is disrupted by the violent intrusion of passion. This gives rise to the Confusion of tongues. He extends the concept to the parallel imposition of passionate punishment on a childís playful misdeeds when the childís harmless intentions are interpreted by an adult in terms of the latterís thinking and projections. This too results in a splitting, and can result in the childís identification with the adult way of seeing things, whereby the child absorbs a sense of towering guilt for what started off as innocent play.

The same identification can happen when a child sees suffering in an adult if the child comes to feel or is made somehow to feel responsible for the suf fering and for putting it right. All three happenings passionate love super imposed on a childís longing for tenderness, passionate punishment inflicted on a childís desire for play, and passionate suffering seizing on a childís wish for harmony all lie behind splitting of the personality, in which one part re mains innocent and undeveloped; one part is converted into the wise baby developed beyond its years; and a third part is banished beyond awareness. All of them are residues of the longing and yearning for tenderness; that is, for the warm and innocent holding, being and acceptance which is a childís birthright.

It requires emphasizing too that trauma can be wider than this, even though it is extending Ferencziís focus. Its origin need not only be an assault from outside. If the need for a warm, close and sensual relationship is not fulfilled in childhood, whether or not specific physical or sexual abuse occurs, it can set up a yearning which can continue as an underlying need into adulthood. This calls for recognition also as an instance of trauma, and needs to be pro vided for through therapeutic regression (cf. FC 1929.1/1955, 106). Deficit and trauma are very close: a fundamental need has been expressed by the child, if only by his or her existence, and it has been denied by those closest to them.

It should not be overlooked that while trauma and the confusion of tongues are described in terms of a childís early history, they were brought to Ferenc ziís attention by his reflecting on what happened during analysis. It was there that the child was discovered again. His experience resulted in his conviction that an identical trauma, with all its effects, could be imposed on a patient (the child in the analysis) by the confrontational yet withholding manner of the analyst. Further, he concluded that interpretations were offered to the pa tient at the level of passion, when they related to things which happened and were being recounted at the level of tenderness. Adult interpretations were forced upon the child: the result was trauma reproduced. We need always to be aware of the child in the person with us.

A NEW BIRTH

The period of Ferencziís writing of these papers feels like the period preced
ing the birth of a child. It expresses a new body of psychoanalysis, emerging
out of the earlier oedipal, adult, work. The period was accompanied by con
siderable birth pangs, with the sad and painful dispute between Ferenczi and
Freud chief among them, ending with the death of the mother. This was
paralleled very curiously and inconsistently during these very same years in
their correspondence by Freudís repeated insistence on Ferenczi assuming
the presidency of the International Psychoanalytic Association, as the only
person in whose hands he felt the future of psychoanalysis would be safe.
Ferenczi eventually refused, on the grounds that he wished to pursue his
research, which was finding out what might be, rather than preserving what
was. The presidency went to Jones instead.

Chapter Four

Ferenczi's Legacy: The Difference It Makes

Ferenczi gave birth to, if he didnít altogether determine, the paradigm shift in psychoanalysis. The mysteries of human development, disturbance and dynamics that lay unexplored beyond the work of Freud were bound to at tract later investigators wanting to leave no stone unturned. It is not surprising that similar discoveries and shifts should have been made in differing parts of the world independently yet more or less concurrently. The work of Kohut in America on the Self does not seem to have been directly related to the work of Balint and Winnicott in Britain, yet they inaugurated closely related developments. Behind most advances, apart from that of Kohut yet affecting his successors, lies the form and influence of Ferenczi.

Ferenczi was the first to move away from Freud while still maintaining the central principles of psychoanalysis. Although he was a dedicated practitioner of Freudian psychoanalysis, he was nevertheless open to seeing that Freudís approach needed modification in both theory and practice if it were to be more generally applicable and effective. He left a fourfold legacy. First, there is his courage in leaving the beaten track in order to make new discoveries. Secondly, there is his uncovering of the two languages of psychoanalysis, that of the adult (passion) and that of the child (tenderness). Thirdly, there are the accompanying developments within the practice of psychoanalysis itself, such as the vital part played by the relationship, the need for mutuality and equality in the interaction, the place of trauma in early life, the use of regression, the constant presence of a child in the analysis, the importance of counter transference, and the need for rigorous training: all these are crucial elements in modern practice. Fourth, there is his personal influence on other analysts, and, through them, on each of us.

We have already seen Ferencziís influence on the early Freud. His interac tion with and influence on Freud continued to the end, even if Freud came eventually to reject what his friend was saying. After Ferencziís death, too, Freud (1937) made as we have seen more than one warm acknowledgement of him and his work. In addition, Ferenczi was the first analyst of Melanie Klein and encouraged her in her work with children. He was the analyst too of many of those who emigrated from Central Europe to Britain and America before the Second World War. Of those in America, Mahler, Gedo and Ro heim were among those who had been his analysands: his greatest influence there, though, was through Sullivan and Thompson and the emergence of the Interpersonal and Relational schools of psychoanalysis. His impact can also be seen strongly in the school of Intersubjectivity that developed out of Self Psychology.

In Britain, Ferencziís legacy was brought firmly into psychoanalysis through the British Independent group, and particularly through the work of Michael Balint who had been both his analysand and his colleague in Hun gary. When Balint emigrated to Britain in 1939, by the Ferenczi familyís wish he brought Ferencziís papers with him. He then continued, elaborated and broadened Ferencziís work by means of his own; and edited the transla tion of the remainder of Ferencziís papers into English (some already existed in English from earlier years). Further to this, he translated Ferencziís *Clini cal Diary*, which was edited for publication in 1995 by Judith Dupont, Mi chael Balintís niece. Though he translated it about fifty years ago, he had to delay its publication because of the aftermath of the rift between Ferenczi and Freud. He also had to wait until the death of Anna Freud to make possible the publication of the correspondence between her father and Ferenczi (Aron and Harris 1992, 9). Balintís work with these documents makes it possible to see clearly Ferencziís influence on all relational work in psychoanalysis. Andre Green indeed calls him the father of modern psychoanalysis (Brabant et al. 1993, xxxv, n14), where the metaphor in this case refers to Ferenczi as the originator of Relational Psychoanalysis, rather than as exercising qualities traditionally attributed to the male of the species.

The aspect of Ferencziís work which I would stress at this particular point is not so much his discovery of the relational possibilities of psychoanalysis: the contrast of that with the Freudian stress on the isolated individual is al ready widely disseminated through the movements mentioned in the preced ing chapters. What I wish to pinpoint here is Ferencziís accent on the gentler aspects of the work, which enabled it to move into engagement with earlier years of life than those believed possible by Freud. This especially applies to his revealing of the presence of a continuing child in therapy, a traumatized child.

I think that Freud must have perceived that this meant the end of his dream that his version of psychoanalysis might be a universal theory of human psy chology and a universal method of treatment. That must have been why he was so shocked. It would have been better if his followers could have recog nized this too. Some later workers, such as Winnicott and Balint, expressed their unease and disagreements, but they had in general to contain their dif ferences within an overall expressed allegiance to his teachings. Their fate might otherwise have been the same as that of Ferenczi: permanent exclusion. One wonders if that would necessarily have been a bad thing: the radical dif ference between the two approaches might have become established earlier; and having broken free, the newer dynamic might have been able to find less esoteric and more generally acceptable approaches.

THE NEED FOR A NEW WAY

The underlying theory of classical psychoanalysis and its resultant practice are both unsuitable for and inapplicable to conditions of deprivation and trauma. The former belong to the world of neurotic conflict. Until the classi cal drive model is repudiated clearly, its underlying pessimism, hostility and authoritarianism will continue to dominate psychodynamic work and to affect its outcome, risking further damage to the already highly vulnerable: its ethos of confrontation is not conducive to the practice of a human psychotherapy.

Drive theory, the Oedipus complex and neurotic conflict belong to special forms of a comparatively late stage of life. It is inappropriate to apply them generally to an earlier stage and a different form, when linguistic, emotional, cognitive and relational abilities are none of them fully developed. This is applying adult language and understanding to a child stage of life, or the lan guage of passion to the era of tenderness. It is in the stage of tenderness and childhood that the inner life of people with early damage is formed, and in which it continues. If the person in therapy should nevertheless appear before us as an adult, we need to remind ourselves of Ferencziís finding that there is still a child inside, and that the fundamental processes of therapy and analysis are of such a nature as to evoke this child. What is needed is a theory and practice which takes the child in the adult into account, and respects the level of tenderness still dominant within.

The two models of psychoanalysis, old and new, adult and child, are in compatible as they are. Because they deal with a human life which is unitary there needs to be a theory of human dynamics developed out of those two models which will be equally unitary and applicable to all stages within that life, even if it relates to different age levels in slightly different forms. Such an integrated unitary theory can then be reflected in the practice of psycho analysis and do more justice to its purpose.

A new model is more likely to be based on the later findings of Ferenczi taken together with contemporary scientific work than on the early meta psychology of Freud. That is, it is more likely to be a child appropriate, relational model rather than an adult, individual, one, with an underlying theory of motivation which takes integration and relationship into account as basic goals, as touched on in the previous chapter. The child appropriate model can always be adapted for use in therapy with an adult by means of a greater use of words and symbols and a more sophisticated understanding of motives. A child needs more of a pre verbal approach, consisting of more emotion, more physicality, more holding (though we might be surprised as to how much of those an adult also might need). With an adult there can be a higher proportion of cognition to emotion, while still preserving simplicity, warmth and respect.

American workers, especially those of the Interpersonal tradition, seem to have been better able to acknowledge the radical divide between the two systems of psychoanalysis more openly, perhaps, at least partly because Fe renczi, in distinction to Freud, had been their inspiration from the very begin ning. They are more willing to declare a dividing line between their emphasis and focus of work and those of Freud, even while acknowledging their debt to the foundation he laid on which their later developments have built.

Freudís original methods and theories are now decades old, formulated during a different era of scientific knowledge and previous to revolutionary social and developmental discoveries. He changed his theories himself sev eral times within his lifetime, but was not prepared to allow them finally to be developed and modified by the work of others. He accepted radical con tributions from Ferenczi in earlier years, but when they appeared directly to affect the basis of his own work he drew the line. Ferenczi was intellectually and therapeutically the equal of Freud, and provided an essential complement to the latterís paternalistic, scientific, objective attitude: in Ferenczi there is more of a concern with real aspects of life, with interaction, with healing, with relationship and with the child.

Once the world of infancy and childhood was opened up in this way, it brought with it discovery of the realms of trauma and deprivation, of regres sion within therapy as a means of dealing with those, of the predominance of deficits in personality rather than conflicts, and of the basic necessity of working with emotions. The need for someone in therapy to have some sort of emotional connection to what they bring out of their unconscious if they are to experience genuine change had been there in Freudís work (Strachey 1934): in practice any emotional emphasis would seem to have become buried in words, and, to judge by the literature, often in extremely lengthy, complex and intellectual interpretations.

Words are indeed the main characteristic of Freudian psychoanalysis. Emo
tion comes into its own with Ferenczi. Freud was left hemisphere; Ferenczi,
right hemisphere. Both are needed; but the verbal emphasis backed by an
unscientific motivational theory runs into a dead end when most radical dis
turbances are pre verbal in origin and motivated quite differently. Especially
is this so when its metapsychology is built around a death instinct which leads
in practice to hostility (Suttie 1935). It is further aggravated by ignoring the
reality of the child and displaying an impatience with childlike things. This
was the current attitude in Freudís (and indeed Ferencziís) day, and no doubt
played its part in militating against recognition of what Ferenczi was saying
about the child in the analysis.

A response suited to an adult is not applicable to a child, nor is treating the
child as a small version of an adult. It is muddling the two languages. The
child has never been an adult, and cannot fully understand the complex or
the abstract or the grown up things (though they may frequently understand
more than the adult likes to think). A response suited to a child, on the other
hand, is applicable also to an adult: we have all been children, and can all
understand that world if we allow it. One of the great truths reinforced by
psychoanalysis is that there is still a child in any adult: that adult can therefore
easily grasp the childish, the simple and the physical if encouraged suitably
to do so.

Ferencziís observation of the child at the heart of analysis thus brings with
it the question of how to respond to that child, and what methods are appro
priate for meeting their needs. At the same time as discovering Ferencziís
work and insights I was also in my practice discovering the relevance of his
findings and the urgency of applying them. The most fundamental need that
such a child can bring is a longing for the supply of the tenderness that was so
often missing in earlier life. This can be unrecognized by practitioners within
the classical drive model. For them the trouble is neurotic conflict, and the
remedy, a detached working at it in the therapy until a hoped for resolution.
Unfortunately the earlier need does not get resolved by this procedure. It
merely gets more deeply buried under further pain; yet this type of therapy is
often taken to be the only one there is.

It does not have to be so. There is an alternative. It recalls the Irishmanís
comment when asked how to get to some distant place I wouldnít start from
here. However, like his interlocutor, at the moment we have to. Ferenczi
tried to find a better model. Others have had their part in finding one too, but
apart from Suttie (1935) have not been sufficiently direct or open in challeng
ing the continued reliance on the old. They may well have persevered dog
gedly with the development and interpretation of their own work in order to
get at least something done, but raising oneís head above the parapet had not

proved to be a good idea. Ferenczi's work, and my own experience within my second training analysis together with my supervision with Harold Stewart, confirmed my growing feeling that there must be an alternative.

I have written this book because of my own experience. My experience of psychoanalytic psychotherapy was both as practitioner and participant: some of it was highly damaging. I have also written because of my discovery that Ferenczi had many years previously provided the means of avoiding the damaging part of the experience; and because of my outrage at the treatment accorded to him by Freud and his followers. I feel that his insights are still not given the clinical importance that they merit, in spite of the renewed stress put on them by those later workers who have recovered them. They are left to be discovered more or less by chance.

It is an urgent task to get Ferenczi's attitude to psychoanalysis more onto center stage, to be at least on an equal footing with Freud's. There is a tell ing paragraph in Ferenczi's paper Child analysis in the analysis of adults (1931): Neither he [Freud] nor I dream of suspending our collaboration be cause of these differences in method and in theory; for on the most important principles of psycho analysis we are in perfect agreement (127). In spite of being written before the schism between them, the latter part at least remains true. We shall look in the next chapter at what these most important principles might be.

I see Ferenczi therefore as representing a side of psychoanalysis whose suppression leaves a partial discipline. What is left expresses Freud and his paternal judgmental approach: it omits the more traditionally maternal attitude of Ferenczi. This could be expressed succinctly as the difference between confrontation and collaboration. One half, if not three quarters, of human nature is excluded: not only is the feminine half omitted as compared with the masculine; but strictly Freudian psychoanalysis is also in danger of leaving out childhood in favor of adulthood, and the child who is always pres ent in any analysis is ignored. Ferenczi corrects the imbalance, in favor both of women and of children; and in a way that benefits all humanity.

THE ORIGIN OF CONFRONTATION

It can easily be observed that the classical Freudian approach using drive theory leads to an aggressive or confrontational stance: one has only to read its literature, let alone experience its practice. By confrontation I mean not a gentle firmness pointing out some difficulty, but a critical, aggressive and demeaning attitude which makes the other person feel held in contempt and wanting to fight back. There is an inherent parallel between the division into

drive and relational theories, and that between confrontational and collabora
tive practice. Drive theory is impersonal and does not take account of the
person to whom (or against whom) it may be directed. It reflects a radical
rift between two modes of being. This basic weakness at the heart of Freud's
theories makes it difficult to apply them in a manner that can convey under
standing, concern and respect to the other person.

The situation is aggravated by Freud's (and others') view of reality as be
ing something objective, outside us, which with education and insight can be
discovered. The Freudian idea was that a therapist or analyst owns perception
of this objective reality, with which he or she can judge the other person.
The other needs merely to be informed of the reality: their own perception
is invalid and must yield to the superior authority of the analyst. Freud on
at least one occasion actually refused to continue the treatment unless his
interpretation was accepted by the patient. This concept of objective reality
is one of the things which is criticized by Stolorow and Atwood (1992, 92)
from within Intersubjectivity: they point out that each of us has access only
to a subjective reality. The belief that there is something unchanging to be
perceived outside us is indeed not upheld by modern psychology (Spinelli
1989). The task of therapists is to understand and to share people's subjective
realities, whatever they may be.

The point about confrontation has been made before, from inside the main
stream psychoanalytic movement. In *The Origins of Love and Hate* published
two years after Ferenczi's seminal paper on Confusion of tongues, Ian
Suttie (1935) wrote about certain errors and prejudices in Freud's original
theories and attitudes. They chiefly concerned Freud's authoritarianism and
paternalism, and in particular the hate that lies behind his theories of aggres
sion and the death instinct. Suttie attributes this to a great extent to the already
mentioned neglect of the mother in Freud's work. He distinguishes Freudian
metapsychology, in which love is denied, from Freudian practice, in which
love is actually on occasion stated to be the active agent in psychoanalytic
cure. He sees the metapsychology as being founded on a totally false basis.
The practice mercifully to some extent contradicts it, but practitioners are left
to be confused by the contradiction.

The hatred underlying classical psychoanalytic theory is demonstrated
by many instances already cited in this book, and also in the general tenor
of publications deriving from that approach whereby hostility and aggres
sive confrontation are presented as the order of the day. They are usually
unquestioned, taken for granted as the approved way to work. Suttie (1935)
characterized the Freudian way of working as reflecting hostility, and Schafer
(1997) characterized the Kleinian as reflecting suspicion (quoted in Mitchell
1997, 138); and that is in keeping with my own reading and experience. It

is amply shown as well in Freudís attitudes to and comments on his patients and on sick people in general. In my own first training analysis I remember my classical analyst rebuking me one day for not behaving with him as two chaps working together. If the quest is conducted in an overwhelmingly critical, judgmental and authoritarian manner by one of the parties involved it is not likely to be seen by the other as a genuinely mutual or companionate venture.

The division between hate and love, confrontation and collaboration, points up the difference between impersonal discharge and the search for connection. It touches on the contrast between withholding and pastoral mod els of healing, and between scientist and humanistic understanding of the person. If the two streams could be held sensitively together, people seeking psychotherapy might be more likely to find an approach that suits them and their disorder best, rather than having to make do with something impersonal and unsuitable. Fortunately, I found the alternative just when I needed it. By changing my analyst, and giving up that particular classical form of training, I was able to enter a totally different experience. From the stultifying despair depicted by Stolorow and Lachmann (1980), I was able to enter into a world of hope. Growth remained painful, but at least it was growth, not a mortifying cul dc sac. I hope that in my turn I have made that alternative available to others, through both practice and teaching.

Confrontation and Collaboration

The difference in approach between confrontation and collaboration can be illustrated by examples. One comes from my supervision with Dr. Har old Stewart. I was engaged in therapy with someone who would now be described as being borderline. My experience with the person puzzled me hugely, and previous supervision had been no help. When I moved to Dr. Stewart, I asked him if he could tell me why this person bothered to come to me for therapy. As far as I could see nothing was happening, and I often felt extremely sleepy in the sessions, fighting to keep awake; yet the person was absolutely faithful, regular, unfailingly punctual, and never missed a session. Harold Stewart said that if they werenít seeing me they would either be in a mental hospital, or dead. That gave me encouragement in a lonely task, and the heart to continue and to recognize that what I was experiencing was the natural consequence of working at a deep level with someone who presented so vaguely. It would have been of no help at all to have attacked the person for being so negative: it required sitting with them with endless patience, sharing the negativity and despair until something inside them moved. The sleepiness was a result of the personís emotional repression: there was no life in the air. That person went on later to become a therapist themselves.

A further example is given by my experience with a young woman who had been sexually abused as a child. It was with her that I first noticed some thing that others also have commented on, how physical features of trauma are recovered first, long before emotional and verbal memories. Unconscious movements of the body mirroring the original situation, recall of the furnish ings or other physical features of the setting, and acute awareness of the time or weather, come first. They are recalled in the form of neutral observations imprinted on bodily memory: there is no emotional memory. Extreme distress makes the person dissociate themselves emotionally at the time from what is happening: it is the only way to survive. Gradually other things follow the physical recall, to form a cumulative verbal and emotional memory of the event (Fraser 1989).

I do not know the exact details of what had happened to this particular per son: to have asked directly would have been an intrusion equivalent to the origi nal, and a damaging inhibition of the unfolding process. Certainly it included some form of oral violation; in consequence, visits to the dentist were a source of terror. There were also difficulties with eating, which were to prove fatal. She stopped coming to see me when she became seriously ill and incapacitated with her digestive problem: both she and I felt it had its origin in the abuse. My chief regret now is that I was so bound by rules of professional technique and propriety that I failed to visit her in her home when she was dying. I was aware that she was seriously ill, but I did not know that it was terminal: maybe know ing that would have enabled me to break through the rigid rules of training. I also regret that in spite of a collaborative therapy she did not feel able, or did not wish, to let me know that she was dying. I was, on the other hand, greatly touched that before she died she had asked that I should speak some words at her funeral. Unfortunately I failed to get there due to a mistake in the location; but during the therapy she had given me some marigold (calendula) seeds, which thereafter brought me a vivid reminder of her each year.

The reason I have recalled this person is that because of her trauma she was naturally very sensitive to intrusion. One day she began to look both frightened and angry. On my inquiring whether something had happened she asked if I would fold my legs back under my chair, which was facing hers. Stretching my legs out brought me into her space and aroused terrifying feel ings from her past ordeal. It was a simple if inconvenient request, and one which I found it hard always to remember; but I drew my legs back and tried to avoid any such subsequent transgression of her boundary.

I mentioned this episode in a seminar with a classical training body, and was greeted with a cry of outrage. I was told that I should have refused, so that the young woman could learn that she could not expect to be treated forever as someone special. She would have to come to terms with the reality that life was like that. The fact that such a confronting response on my part would undoubtedly have put an end to her therapy, if not to her life, did not seem to matter so much as the refusal of her request and the frustration of her needs as required by classical theory. This is a particularly clear practical example of the issue mentioned in chapter 2 about refusing or acceding to peopleís requests.

It seems obvious that sheer humanity should prevail in such an instance, whatever psychoanalytic theory might dictate: as indeed it should also in other less serious instances where a warm human response is indicated rather than a blank inhuman rudeness and rebuttal. I refer to things like the prof ferring of gifts, the answering of questions, and the returning of greetings, in study or in street. All these things are frequently of supreme importance, sensitivity and significance to the person concerned: they can be, and should be, discussed further in therapy sessions following such occasions, where their meaning can be thoroughly explored.

The more humane and collaborative model of practice is of particular relevance when earlier damage and deprivation are concerned. Some with a stronger core may be able to withstand, or put up with, aggressive confronta tion. They might, I suppose, even enjoy fighting and arguing, not that that will help the process much. People with early experience of trauma do not have this adult strength: inside they are still the wounded child, looking for love. What is more, since most people who are in any way disturbed suffer from some measure of this inner fragility, and it will also arise even in dif ficulties that may develop later, this means that such a collaborative approach is relevant to all.

This is especially so when the damage is so severe as to lead to the group of disturbances called narcissistic, borderline, organizing, or psychotic. A notable feature of all of these is that they have their origin at various stages of early cognitive development, often before the advent or use of words. Any therapeutic approach such as the classical Freudian which uses exclusively words and verbal interpretation, regardless of any confrontational ethos, is not likely to touch the depths. An approach open to love, to silence, to en gagement, to relationship and to holding is more likely to make contact.

THE SENSITIVITY OF PEOPLE ON THE BORDERLINE

While everyone involved in therapy could benefit from a change in practice to a gentler and more interactive approach, it is crucial for those suffering from early disturbances, and absolutely crucial for people on what is called the borderline (chapters 1, 4, 6). Ferenczi made the initial discoveries about the difficulties that can attend the search for tenderness in early life, and the damage if the search for it is wrongly responded to then or later. A failure in this early essential interchange is one of the things which I take to lie behind a diagnosis of borderline. It is difficult to find a clear explanation of what the word means: it is usually left to the context. It is not obvious what it is the borderline of: whether of health, of sexuality, of psychosis, or, as I believe, of being able to exist at all. It is usually seen as being due to some break down in the dyadic relationship with the mother or primary carer. The best ordinary description that I have seen is that of Dr. Frank Lake (of the Clinical Theology Association), where he speaks of it in terms of dread and of trans marginal states, where a baby has been driven to the edge of endurance, yet has to hang on (1981,1986). Neither of these is dealt with well within psycho analysis, though fear of falling might have some relationship to it.

To cope with an adult world without the foundation of a sound childhood can be well nigh impossible, achieved only at the cost of repressing oneís deepest needs just as they had to be repressed in childhood. It seems to be equally impossible for those whose rearing was more benign to understand the world of those for whom it wasnít. This applies to therapists as much as to anyone else. They seem time and time again to be frightened by the intensity of need resulting from early damage; they interpret it in terms of later distur bance, and attack it. Such lack of empathy for the situation is what may give rise to the manifest suspicion of closeness, which leads in turn to a fear of dependence, contempt for the weak, and further rejection of those who have never yet known acceptance.

When I started practicing as a therapist I worked with almost all who came to me for help (something else which I discovered later I held in common with Ferenczi). The underlying complaints were hazy, vague, and difficult to define. They appeared to reflect more of an underlying unease with the person themselves than any specific disturbance. Many people were to all outward appearance mature adults holding responsible jobs: only they knew and in the privacy of therapy allowed me to know that they were broken and dis integrated inside, just managing to hold on to life and to competence. I still have a copy of a cartoon pasted inside the cupboard above my desk: it shows someone hanging by their fingertips to the edge of a cliff. The caption reads Right now Iím working on a fascinating project STAYING ALIVE. That was to me a poignant image of many of those with whom it was my privilege to work.

It was in reading Balint and Ferenczi that the cloud of unknowing sur rounding people with such a concealed background began to dissolve. Those practitioners were describing exactly what my therapees were showing in their therapy and in their accounts of life. Together the writers showed how working with people on this borderline of life is one of psychotherapyís most challenging tasks. It demands a costly emotional engagement between the two participants and a deep commitment to the therapee on the part of the therapist (the reverse commitment happens more naturally, given the special circumstances of the encounter). It frequently involves going back through the earliest days of life and experiencing the rawest of raw emotions without any of the usual later sophisticated defenses. If one is to help people who are deeply damaged, this sort of involvement, however costly, is essential. Christopher Bollas says in connection with his extensive discussion of regres sion and dependence that the analyst and analysand have to let themselves go somewhat mad together (1987, 254). I have preserved memory of that phrase because it is so true.

Involvement takes time: a lot of time. *The International Journal of Psycho analysis* once had an article which suggested that for the solving of a fairly limited problem, therapy might take about three to four months, while for a change in character, it might be three or four years: and this is borne out in experience. A change in basic personality, on the other hand, (i.e., a change in the way one is able to see the world and react to it), a true metamorphosis, which is what requires the work of regression and is essential when one is working on the borderline, takes much longer: it is more likely to take ten years or more. Sometimes much more.

Coping with Trauma

Ferenczi had grown to feel that most people who came for analysis had suf fered from some trauma as the origin of their pathology: trauma includes deprivation. Michael Balint followed him in accepting this; he also sought to develop the understanding of it and to find ways of working with its re sults. In my turn I found it true that people had suffered trauma of various types in their early lives I cannot think of any exceptions. This underlines the important part that people and events external to us play in the genesis of emotional illness and disturbance, rather than worries or conflicts of en tirely internal origin. Experiences of trauma always include the essentials in Ferencziís definition of it (1929.2, 1931): that it happens within a pre exist ing relationship, and that the sufferer feels totally alone. The result of this is an inability to comprehend or cope with the violent emotions aroused, such that victims are overwhelmed by them, and there is no one there to help. Traumaís chief characteristic is that its content is emotional, not just a physical accident.

In consequence of this it is inevitable that those who have suffered from early trauma do not, and cannot, present with a readily identifiable problem. Trauma brings natural protective and adaptive mechanisms into play and the events are banished before conscious processing can be allowed. The suf ferers have never been enabled to talk about it or to verbalize it. It usually happens so early that they do not have the power of language in the first place to enable them to express it in words. Emotions are shattered, unmet, uncontained and finally repressed, only to reappear in the victimsí bodies. What people who have suffered early trauma do present with is therefore very vague: as Ferenczi said, the real cause of their distress has never been conscious, and never before been put into words. This vagueness is actually an indicator of the depth and early date of damage, as also of the intensity and length of the reconstructive therapy likely to be required. It frequently is presented together with a history of an extensive variety of physical illnesses in childhood and a similar variety of present day demands for medical atten tion and operations: these are the physical signs of unconscious turbulence, as Ferenczi also observed.

Elsewhere he said too, such persons have actually remained almost en tirely at the child level, and for them the usual methods of analytic therapy are not enough (FC 1929.2/1955, 124). What is needed for cure is emotional recall of the situation into the present, or its re living: there is then some pos sibility that it can be symbolized (put outside us into words) and tamed. With the modified methods used by him, Balint, and others since, the therapeutic relationship can become a situation in which people are enabled to return to childhood and face once again the reality of their past experience. The thera pist may often find him or herself cast in the role of the persecutor: more comfortably, in that of the rescuer. Transference and counter transference then refer not just to the two individuals involved but, to use Balintís image of primary love as being like the air around us and upholding us, they refer to the whole setting: childhood itself comes alive again; and this time it carries a hope of healing. The whole analytic relationship becomes a repetition of the earliest family scenario; and the two people create a new entity.

The reality of trauma is at the root of the need for regression; and it is in the work of regression that the need for the exercise of tenderness becomes most acute. Trauma and deprivation are two sides of the same coin. In both, the child can be faced with a situation too big to cope with, which has to be dealt with by repression and splitting, accompanied by denial of the body and of their emotional and physical needs: there is no one there to help or ease the pain. Working in the sensitive area of those very early years is where the two languages of tenderness and passion are so markedly different. How to sup ply the lack of tenderness without straying into the passionate is a question which constantly arises, and which is addressed later in this book. It was this question which informed so much of what Ferenczi did and wrote, and which forms a significant part of his legacy to us.

If it is a problem to work with tenderness without getting passionate, it is also a problem for those not engaged in such work to understand it at all and not to read into it their own interpretation, which is almost invariably from a passionate viewpoint. The first to interpret it thus was of course Freud, in his reaction to what he was told about and by Ferenczi. Another, though not with respect to Ferenczi, was Klein, who, as we have seen, forced her adult interpretations of child experience on to the children with whom she worked. Although initially analyzed by Ferenczi and encouraged by him in her work with children, she seems to have carried into that work a prejudice for the pas sionate, adult, world. Freudís treatment of the erotic transference suffers from the same distortion (see chapter 6). To separate the two, the worlds of child and adult, of tenderness and passion, of sensuality and sexuality, is difficult but it needs to be done if people stuck in a damaged world of childhood are to be helped to grow away from it.

Working with Regression

The practice of regression would seem to be specifically a concern, and a contribution to psychoanalysis, of the British Independents. Harold Stewart (1992, 111) says the concept of therapeutic regression is absent from the literature of both the Kleinians and the Contemporary Freudians (the two other groups within the British Psychoanalytic Society). He also says (1993) that regression to dependence . . . is a naturally occurring phenomenon that the analyst allows to occur, which is what both Ferenczi and Balint had found. On the part of the therapee, regression happens spontaneously. On the part of the therapist, I do not know whether the ability to allow it can be learned, or whether it depends on having a particular personality. I certainly found that I was drawn into it by my own individual background, and that I was able to understand and tolerate the more extreme demands that the work put upon me by the fact that in the other personís behavior I could recognize my own.

Everyone with whom I worked intensively had difficulties which involved deficient care in their first two to three years, as well as that deficient care ly ing behind any associated difficulties which occurred later. By then the stage had been set for a locked in character, a truncated personality and a rigidly unhelpful view of the world. Others, who required less intensive work, had had a firmer foundation and suffered from restrictions which were more superficial and recent: they therefore took less time to fulfil the tasks of therapy. No one came whose problems seemed to be only or indeed at all of oedipal origin: as I have indicated earlier I have difficulty in identifying quite what this refers to, so I might have been missing something that to others, trained in that way, was glaringly obvious. If it was, they never managed to communicate what it was to me. Peopleís problems in my experience had developed earlier, and had only been aggravated by the appearance of more figures on the scene. In other words, they were dyadic in origin rather than triadic or triangular.

The people with whom I joined in long term and intensive work thus owed the origin of their difficulties to the stage before the oedipal, to the two per son (dyadic) stage of life, which concerns the relationship between the mother (or other primary carer) and the child. A babyís experiences are always within a relationship. This immediately makes the dyadic setting of long term one to one psychotherapy potentially ideal for re living that original two person relationship and for the repair of whatever damage might then have occurred. Potentially, because the repair calls for humanity, acceptance, patience, co operation and respect; just as one might hope a child would find within its earliest bond. These are the features of a collaborative type of therapy rather than a confrontational one. The re living and countering of the trauma in their life needs a carefully honed human situation to effect it, with a therapist who is finely tuned to their needs and does not unthinkingly pursue a course which can only aggravate the original problem.

For completeness of treatment of this topic, I need to add that Balint (1968) and Stewart (1992; 1996; also in Aron and Harris 1993) both make a distinc tion between malignant and benign regression. Balint associated malignant regression with gratification by the analyst arising from conflict needs (de manding something from the analyst, at a more developed level), and benign regression with recognition by the analyst arising from self needs (seeking something missing in themselves). I am not sure that one can separate the two sets of needs so sharply: the latter probably underlies the former, and the conflict needs might in fact themselves be triggered by the analystís ap proach if using that sort of model. Stewart (1993) for his part says Ferenczi, in his time, did not understand the real malevolence of severe hysterics, with their borderline or almost psychotic personalities (262). Apart from ques tioning the use of the word hysteric, I wonder if both Balint and Stewart are not just labeling as malignant a regression that went wrong, and benign, one that went all right.

From my own experience, I would say two things. First, a regression can indeed feel, and become, malignant. One to which I was party did, but it was, I believe, the result of extreme intensity of need on the part of the other person rather than malevolence, and it was furthered by the particu lar interaction between the two parties. It is the analyst or therapist who holds primary responsibility for that interaction and, like Ferenczi, I feel that it is probably usually, though certainly not always, our lack of skill that is at fault if it goes wrong. It underlines Ferencziís call for an effec tive training analysis; and also calls for good supervision. It requires very close attention.

The second thing I would say is that malignant regression, if it occurs, could be something to do with the fact that as a result of trauma emotions have been buried, and are not accessible. The only thing that remains real is the physical, and physical expression. The traumatized person needs to be helped to find emotions once again, and thereby to discover alternative ways to interact that lie behind the physical. This remark perhaps needs for its understanding that malignant regression usually seems to refer to a regres sion in which physical gratification of the other person becomes a violent and destructive demand.

I may give the impression that regression is a continuous long term state: on the contrary, as Balint and Bollas both make clear, it is more like entering into and emerging from a state that repeats itself in every session; that is, from session to session, and within each session. People may surface from it for a discussion or explanation or interpretation: indeed in ordinary regression they have to emerge from the state at the end of every session in order to resume their everyday life. It is frequently excruciatingly difficult and painful, but they manage to do it nevertheless.

Entering Regression

It seems in place here to say something about the onset of regression, which has been mentioned earlier once or twice as being a recognizable stage in a therapy. Balint used the word arglos to identify the state into which a person enters. It was marked for him by particular signs: the person may, for instance (in my experience, always) become closely attached to the therapist and very dependent on them. In . . . regression the patient allows the infantile part of him to be lived through in his analysis while his adult part can still function in the outside world and enable him to lead a responsible life in the world (Bosanquet, in Galton ed. 2006, 40).

The German word arglos roughly means innocence. It is unfortunate that Balint chose to use strange new words for several of his vital concepts: the result is that their basic nature, their beauty and their simplicity are obscured and our attention is diverted away from the concepts to the words themselves. It makes him somewhat difficult to read. His description of the arglos state (see chapters 3, 6) is remarkably similar to Freudís description of the beginnings of transference love (1915, 162). In that paper, I think that Freud, without real izing it, is actually talking about the personís move into the level of the child, but he treats it throughout as an adult happening. The move is in consequence never allowed to occur, and the person is treated throughout as an adult.

For Balint, the arglos experience subsequently phases into and pervades the period of the new beginning, when re growth becomes possible. Balintís aim in making use of this state, contrasting with classical psychoanalysis, was to provide a setting where an atmosphere of primary love could develop, and regression could take place. His guidelines for creating this atmosphere make three points: first, for the therapist just to be (not to intervene or interpret); secondly, to accept all material (not try to organize it); thirdly, to accept the regression and create a climate in which both parties can tolerate it mutually. It means providing the time and milieu for a regression to occur; not doing anything otherwise to promote it but allowing it to develop, avoiding any interference that is not absolutely necessary.

THE NEED FOR RELATIONSHIP

Increasingly over the years I have realized that I am not alone in seeking a more collaborative and considerate approach in psychotherapy. Many others, almost from the very beginning, but often working in comparative isolation, have experience of work with such deeply damaged people, and from their accounts of their work clearly use these more suitable ways of working. They find that the old ways of looking at this sort of work and trying to understand it are neither applicable nor helpful. It needs the new paradigm. This they and I have come to recognize as a relational way of understanding and of work ing. It is not surprising that it should be so: the origin of peopleís emotional damage is within relationships of one sort or another. It makes sense that the remedy should come from within a relationship too. One cannot engage with an emotion in isolation.

The truth about the need for relationship was there from the beginning, but it was obscured for a long time by the reductionist scientism of Freud and his followers. The phenomena of transference and counter transference arise from relationship, but the significance of that was overlooked in earlier work. Recognition of its centrality came about later: in Ferencziís work; in the object relations movement in Britain, above all in the work of Balint and Winnicott; and in the work of the continuing Independent tradition in British psychoanalysis. It seems, however, to have been left to Americans to formulate the approach most clearly: people such as Kohut, Greenberg and Mitchell, Stolorow and Atwood and their group, and Hedges, amongst others, as we have seen in chapter 1.

An automatic consequence of working in a dyadic relationship such as psychoanalysis is that it brings out the unfulfilled and unresolved need for tenderness where this has not been met in earlier life. I suppose that this might be another way of saying that regression takes place spontane ously: the need for tenderness could be its trigger. Tenderness should be the response, not cold remoteness. It means that although we appear to be working with adults we are actually working with the child in them, which is what was identified by Ferenczi: and we respond to that child. Ferenczi accordingly realized the need to respect our therapees as we would a child, with all their potential, their sensitivity and their responsiveness to love; as also their reactions of devastation and self protection at any hint of rejection, dismissal, misunderstanding or misattunement. The path of tenderness is a demanding path to follow: a loving foster parent would recognize it.

In sum, many people who come for therapy lack sufficient experience of tenderness (Ferenczi), of primary love (Balint), of primary parental preoc cupation (Winnicott), or of fulfillment of their narcissistic needs (Kohut). Whatever it might be called, they are each aspects of the same thing, though maybe at slightly different levels. What those people seek in therapy, whether they know it explicitly from the beginning or not, is to be able to return to childhood and grow their way once again through its tangles, accompanied this time by someone who allows them to hold on to them and who has been through it themselves. They do not need to be attacked and criticized and made to feel that their desperate state is all their own fault.

The Taboo on Tenderness

I have mentioned Ian Suttie in connection with his finding hate at the heart of Freud's metapsychology, arising from the latter's commitment to his pos tulation of a death instinct. He also dealt extensively with the social, cultural and psychoanalytic taboo on tenderness, especially in relation to men; a taboo which might have a lot to do with the critical attitude often shown towards sick people. Tenderness and childhood both seem to be viewed with suspi cion in classical psychoanalysis, even though they form an important part of its subject matter. Suttie sees the taboo as related to an overall prejudice against childhood (1935, 95), and interprets its origin as a desperate attempt on the part of therapists (and everyone else) to preserve our defenses against a longing for something on which all of us have lost out to some extent. To show tenderness risks unleashing the repressed forces of our own need and yearning. Even such an apparently neutral practice as the touch involved in massage can release untold depths of yearning in someone who has lacked

tenderness and touch in their early life. The touch of massage can create at
tachment and trigger the longing for more. Child carers too are warned not to
cuddle deprived children in their care as it unsettles them (i.e., it is liable to
open up a hidden well of yearning). While eventual privation of this type of
love in childhood as one grows is recognized as inevitable, the longing for it,
if it has not been adequately met by then, remains so painful that the whole
conflict is forced out of mind and fiercely defended against. We return to look
at this longing further in chapter 9.

Unfortunately Suttie died at a young age, just before the publication of
his book, and was unable to take his work further. Like Ferencziís, Suttieís
contributions seem subsequently to have sunk into partial oblivion, and, again
like Ferencziís, also need to be recovered: they are very relevant for a human
psychotherapy. He was, significantly, an admirer of Ferenczi, and his wife Jane
was one of Ferencziís early translators (1926/1994). As Dorothy Heard (1988)
says in her introduction to the second edition of Suttieís book, it is likely that
Sandor Ferenczi influenced the way that Suttie developed his ideas (xxii). It
is puzzling and thought provoking that two men had similar ideas at much the
same time, both of them picking up the lacuna in Freudís work and thinking:
one of them was Freudís closest friend and collaborator on the Continent of
Europe, the other was a comparative newcomer to psychoanalysis in Britain.

Suttieís book was published in 1935 yet he wrote on the same theme as did
Ferenczi whose Confusion of tongues was published in German in 1933 but
not in English until 1949, long after Suttie had died. Ferencziís first mention of
tenderness, though, is a little earlier, in his paper The problem of the termina
tion of the analysis (1927), yet this was not published in English until 1980.
In that paper he has a comment which is still valid: After the naughty, defiant
child has fired off all the shots in his locker in vain, his concealed demands for
love and tenderness come naively into the open (84). A further mention occurs
in his paper The unwelcome child and his death instinct (1929.1), which was
published in both German and in English. There he refers to an ill disguised
longing for (passive) tenderness (104). Possibly Suttie could have seen or
read that paper, and might even have been present at the XIth International
Psychoanalytic Congress held at Oxford in August (1929), where Ferencziís
next paper The principle of relaxation and neo catharsis (1929.2) was read.
It enlarges on the theme of tenderness and contrasts it with passion: What
[children] really want, even in their sexual life, is simply play and tenderness,
not the violent ebullition of passion (121). He develops this theme as we have
seen in his next paper, Child analysis in the analysis of adults (1931), and
deals with it fully in Confusion of tongues (1933).

In his own book Suttie hardly mentions Ferenczi: he attributes (1935, 75)
to Ferenczi the saying that it is the physicianís love that heals the patient. It

must be said that this is surprisingly similar to one or two of Freudís remarks on the subject, for example, in a letter to Jung of 6 December 1906 (McGuire 1974, 13; quoted in Aron and Harris 1993, 56). Suttie was perhaps reflecting the spirit of Ferencziís work in contrast to that of Freud. In spite of that he doesnít list Ferenczi in the index. Suttieís work therefore either represents a mysterious synchronicity with Ferencziís, or he was diffusely aware of the latter, possibly through discussions with his wife Jane who had translated Ferencziís earlier papers but whose connection with Ferenczi and his work remains unexplained. That awareness could then have acted as a guide and reinforcement for his own thinking. Bowlby, in his foreword to Suttieís book, links Suttie working in London with Ferenczi, Hermann and the Balints working in Budapest. It may have been reciprocal influence rather than synchronicity which caused it, but it is of considerable interest that issues of relationship, of the place of the mother, and of tenderness in the practice of analysis were being aired so early in different parts of the psychoanalytic world.

Dorothy Heard, in her introduction, and John Bowlby in his foreword to Suttieís book, both see Suttie as one of the earliest object relations theorists: Heard records (in Suttie 1935, xxiii) that Bacal (1987) regards Suttieís work as representing an epistemological break with the traditional psychoanalytic theory of his day and as anticipating the work of the other, later, object rela tions theorists (see chapter 1 of this book). That is the break which underpins the focus of this chapter; the new paradigm for psychoanalysis.

The significance of the epistemological break (or paradigm shift) cannot be overemphasized, for either theory or practice: it reflected the preparatory workings carried out and published by Ferenczi. Suttie draws attention to the striking contradiction between psychoanalytic work executed according to the classical method of idealization of passive technique and disavowal of all responsibility and the saying attributed to Ferenczi and quoted above it is the physicianís love that heals the patient. The old classical psychoana lytic attitude is encouraged in its confrontational and aggressive approach by the underlying influence of hatred; it is discouraged from being collaborative or gentle by the taboo on tenderness. In order to make the transition to a dif ferent way effective, we have to be prepared both to demonstrate love and to break the taboo. In moving thus from one model of psychoanalysis to another, we need to consider what might be the essential things that determine whether or not any particular form of psychodynamic work can be called psychoana lytic. What is it that defines psychoanalysis?

Part Two

APPLICATION

Chapter Five

The Essentials

HIGHER ORDER PRINCIPLES

The essentials of psychoanalysis to be identified here are those which are vital to clinical work; that is, they operate at the practical, basic level. They belong nevertheless within a higher order framework of more pervasive all embracing principles. The requirements to conform to humanity and to science have already been identified as such super ordinate parameters; but within these there are also, first of all, the intended goals of psychoanalysis, and, secondly, guides for its conduct, to be considered before we come to the practical issues of its day to day content.

In regard to guides for conduct, the prime need for respect has already been identified, and, following the insights of Ferenczi, the need to allow for the presence of a child in the person in front of the therapist (and in the therapist too).

In regard to the goals of psychoanalysis, there are two, very closely related to one another. First, there is the aim of furthering integration in the life of the person concerned; secondly, there is the search for meaning, or making sense of life. These two will help to promote healing. It reflects an underly ing conviction (and assumption) that all symptoms and behavior have some underlying meaning and purpose; that it all makes sense somewhere (Home 1966). Finding that meaning and purpose will automatically bring about greater integration. The loss of purpose and of meaning is a frequent present ing problem; and the wish to recover them an excellent motivator. If people believed that there was some meaning to their problems, however concealed that meaning might appear to be, and that they were willing to search for it, that usually served as sufficient reason for me to accept them into therapy.

The remaining foundation pillar of psychoanalysis, and one which can eas
ily be overlooked or taken for granted, is the setting in which it takes place;
that is, the necessary setting of a relationship between two people. That, too,
is part of the higher order framework, within which the essential clinical
aspects and processes find their mutative function. It is within these varied
over arching principles and guidelines that the practical clinical work of psy
choanalysis and psychodynamic therapy is carried out.

ESSENTIALS AND INESSENTIALS

The identification of the two languages of psychoanalysis, against the back
ground of so many and varied schools and approaches on both sides of the
paradigm shift, has raised the question of what exactly it is that constitutes
psychoanalysis or psychoanalytic practice? How can the new emphases claim
to be a continuation of the old, to share the same name and to do the same
work? Is it a particular sort of training that determines it? Is it belonging to
a particular body? Is it subscribing to Freudís teaching? Or is it working ac
cording to certain principles which have developed during and since the time
of Freud, and which have become clearer with each new development?

I believe that it is the last; and I consider that an analysis of the field of
psychoanalysis reveals four fundamental emphases. These owe their origin
and fundamental nature to Freud, but have also been greatly developed and
refined since his day. Any approach which holds to all four of these essen
tials is entitled to call itself psychoanalytic: any other approach is not. These
four are: working with processes that are normally outside consciousness
(awareness); the recognition of the phenomena of transference and counter
transference in human interaction; a commitment to the central importance of
childhood to all of subsequent life; and the vitality of the physical especially
as expressed in the emotions. Above these is the overall criterion and quint
essential requisite for effective and caring work; that is, respect for the other
person. This last is the most essential of all, the lack of which immediately
rules out certain approaches and practitioners, however orthodox they may
otherwise appear to be.

Sometimes psychoanalysis is spoken of as if its essence can be captured in
non essentials, in things at the periphery of practice; in requirements such as
membership of a particular training body, the frequency of therapy, the use
of a couch, adherence to Freudís basic rule (of free association), the prac
tice of interpretation, or sticking to the fifty minute hour. The question has
become more immediate in the UK with the emergence of the College of Psy
choanalysts. This body seeks to widen the use of the term psychoanalyst

beyond membership of the British Psychoanalytic Society to all those who consider that psychoanalysis is what they practice and who are recognized members of psychoanalytic psychotherapy training bodies.

Whatever the precise importance of the various non essential characteris tics just mentioned, I see psychoanalysis as defined rather by the four main principles of practice set out before them; that is, by dynamic principles rather than static rules. If those criteria are present in any psychotherapeutic work then it can deservedly be termed psychoanalytic. Whether someone practic ing according to those principles would necessarily wish to be known as a psychoanalyst is a different question. The term has been historically appropri ated by practitioners of the classical method within a particular exclusive pro fessional body and has been given thereby unfortunate dogmatic overtones. It may lead to some misunderstanding therefore as to what others who might bear the same title but who are of a different persuasion actually do; though it might be a good idea to emphasize the wider meaning before the word gets completely absorbed into the narrower sense. Otherwise, as Neville Syming ton (2007) has commented, it may be necessary to find a different name for the new psychoanalysis.

ENGAGING WITH UNCONSCIOUS PROCESSES

The first of the clinical essentials is belief in the existence of a reality outside our immediate consciousness. Unconscious processes is a better way of referring to this than to call it the unconscious : the latter implies that it is a location rather than an active process. Awareness of such processes dates from long before Freud: his part was to make the study of them his life long work (Whyte 1978). Modern psychology has no quarrel with the concept, though it might speak of it more in terms of awareness or of attention, as in Levin's *Mapping the Mind* (1991/2003, 20, n3). In that book Levin says the study of unconscious mechanisms is the study of the clinical correlate of neuronal sys tems, most of which function automatically (i.e., out of our awareness).

The existence of processes outside our awareness but nevertheless part of us and affecting our behavior was accepted even in ancient times. It was Descartes who created a problem with the concept, in that he equated mind only with conscious thought (Whyte, 26ff.). Freud became alive to its possibilities through hypnosis: he was already interested in parapsy chological phenomena, and seized every opportunity of investigating them. What was more important for Freud was not mere belief in unconscious activity but his major premise about it, which is that unconscious mental contents seek expression. This forms what has been called the big ques tion of psychoanalysis (Rychlak 1973, 216, 222); that is, the question of motivation why we do what we do. Freud saw the seeking expression in terms of impersonal energy seeking discharge any old how: many prefer to see it nowadays in terms of motivation directed towards integration, (i.e., in terms of teleological factors [as did Adler]; see chapter 3). We act to produce order, to fulfill a purpose or to achieve a goal.

Stolorow and Atwood (1992, 33) fine tune the concept of our unconscious processes in the light of modern psychoanalytic work by suggesting three types. These are first, the pre reflective unconscious, or the organizing principles of life, our underlying values, which we take in with our motherís milk, and which we are largely unaware of as we absorb them. Secondly, there is the dynamic unconscious, whose contents are denied and kept out of awareness because they are threatening, disturbing or painful (equivalent to the Freudian concept of repression) these are things which have at some time been conscious but whose subsequent awareness we guard against. Thirdly, there is what they term the unvalidated unconscious, consisting of things like aspirations and longings which have never evoked an accepting response and which therefore have been allowed to lie dormant (similar to Bollasís (1987) valuable concept of the unthought known). They omit, however, a fourth type of unconscious content, pointed to by Ferenczi, which is the traumatic unconscious, consisting of things, events and memories which have been split off or dissociated as a result of unmanageable trauma: this is a more radical exclusion than that of repression.

Accessing unconscious processes is the task of therapy, because they are usually what mess up our lives. Ways of accessing them need separate atten tion, but may be indicated here briefly as comprising things like following feelings, studying dreams, and unraveling the meaning of bodily symptoms and sensations and of slips in speech and behavior (Freudís parapraxes). These ways include the use of words, as in the course of employing that prized psychoanalytic tool free association. If followed in Freudís original sense of the phrase, this would be one form of the following feelings al luded to a few lines back. Since Freud, it has however come to be interpreted as saying anything that comes to mind, but that is a distortion of what he actually wrote. His expression was *freier einfall*, which means something more like uncensored irruption ; that is, the breaking through into awareness of something not foreseen, rather than saying everything that comes to mind. The latter might only (and sometimes does) result in ceaseless and rather meaningless chatter, frequently indulged in as a defense against anything unforeseen.

The threads of our life are semantic threads. Experiences are linked by meaning; the meaning is given by the particular emotions felt. That is the value of free association of the genuine sort, and of following the feeling of an experience or a dream. It can be a most valuable instrument. Feelings can lead to forgotten happenings which are unconsciously associated with one another. Follow the emotional smoke is a ruling principle of psychodrama. It means exactly the linking mentioned above, where a feeling suddenly brings to the fore some related but unattended event, and both together reveal the warp and woof of our individual lives.

This is a valuable way, too, of looking at dreams: not to look at the symbols occurring in the dream as if there were a dream dictionary telling their meaning, but to ask what was the feeling of the dream? Then to ask the person reporting it can you stay with that feeling? Try just to let it be in your mind. Let yourself enter into it: where does it take you? Or, what comes into your mind with that feeling? Only the dreamer knows what the dream and its varied bits may have been about usually a mix of a residue from the preceding day, plus long standing emotional problems still being worked out. Freud is often quoted as saying dreams are a royal road to the unconscious. In fact, he didn't: he said something rather more humble and sensible, namely the interpretation of dreams is the royal road to a knowledge of the unconscious activities of the mind (1900; 1953, SE V, 608; 1976, PFL 4, 769). There is usually little that is very direct about it.

There are in addition to these ways of accessing unconscious processes such things as the use of metaphor (see chapter 7); taking note of body language; being sensitively open to the communication of emotion; working with the transference and counter transference of perceptions, expectations and emotions; being alive to contradictions; and being aware of the different levels at which communication may be taking place. Abreactive techniques are sometimes used in medicine though not normally in psychodynamic work: they are only of use if material thus released is thoroughly de briefed and worked through carefully over as long a time as it needs to elucidate its meaning.

TRANSFERENCE AND COUNTER-TRANSFERENCE

In tandem with attending to unconscious processes, the second essential of clinical work in psychoanalysis is the use of the phenomena of transference and counter transference. Working with the transference has been a sine qua non of psychoanalysis from the start. It would seem to have become a phenomenon cloaked in mystery; but is on the contrary an ordinary and universal psychological occurrence which is perfectly understandable in terms of modern theories of perception. These see it as based on our urge to make sense of and impose order on our environment. It is the active construction of reality: we interpret things according to what we know and expect. What we expect depends in turn on our previous experience of things, of bits of ourselves and of our reactions (often seen in other people), of our interactions with people from our past, and of the emotions evoked by various situations.

Very simply, we apply a filter of anticipation to our sensory input, such that sensations pass through a screen of expectations to become our perceptions of reality, or *phenomena* (Spinelli 1989). Psychoanalysis takes this ordinary phe nomenon of perception and makes it one of its chief tools of exploration. Breuer thought that transference, whereby a patient saw him as a figure from their past, was a barrier to treatment: Freud fortunately saw it as an adjunct, and by this profound insight made it a foundation of the psychoanalytic method. The most important and deeply rooted of our expectations come naturally enough from our childhood, and for that reason are often unconscious. It is as if we are look ing at the world through childhood tinted glasses.

Transference thus provides a means for exploring the way in which a person sees life; it provides the material that makes up our inner representa tional world. The other personís inner representational world is what thera pists need to enter if they are to understand those with whom they work. The other personís inner world is their psychic reality, their belief that the world is made as if it were how they see it. Our psychic reality, formed largely of unconscious assumptions, is what then determines behavior. Psychic real ity seems to be another way of saying phenomenon, or the world as we see it. I havenít seen this said before, but it would undoubtedly seem to be so. If it has not been said before it is perhaps another example of the closed world of psychoanalytic thought, where there is little cross fertilization with other disciplines: if it has, then I have failed to notice it.

The trouble with our perceptions is that the structures which we impose upon reality are often formed incorrectly and furthermore applied inappro priately; in consequence they lead to the problems which bring people to seek help. These ingrained perceptions are transferred from one situation to another one which they do not match hence the term transference. In offering help to sort such situations out, therapists believe that therapy will be a microcosm of peopleís ordinary everyday world, and they practice it in a setting which promotes such transference and throws into relief what they need to know. It brings about the interaction which Freud called the transfer ence neurosis, where the therapist is seen through the eyes of the therapeeís earlier world.

When this occurs it is a sign of hope. Through it we can see the presupposi tions which peopleís past experience has imposed upon them presupposi tions about people, about relationships, about the world and about events in it such that those assumptions, rather than reality, have come to rule their lives. It follows that the more important the therapist can be to the person, the more likely it is that strong feelings will be evoked, important past situations will be re created, and restorative things can happen. That is why psychoanalysis emphasizes aspects of encounter which help to encourage the re emergence of these early feelings and not to block them, things such as the frequency of therapy, and details about its conditions and setting.

Roughly corresponding to the four sorts of unconscious processes outlined in the last section, four sorts of underlying material may serve as material for transference to a situation in the present. First, there are the organizing principles of life which we absorb in childhood. These include particular at titudes to people and events and particular ways of reacting to them, which affect both perception and emotion thereafter. These attitudes and reactions may no longer be appropriate in later life but they have become rigid and fossilized such that it is extremely difficult to alter them without insight as to their origin. They belong properly to a time that lies in the past, but they come to be felt by the analysand as the present. They can hopefully be recognized, initially by the analyst, as not matching the actual present or, if they are ap plied personally to the analyst, as not matching his or her actual person. The analyst in the latter case might ask a simple question such as I wonder who that is? to make the point. The more focused and developed of these reac tions were the dominant aspects of transference for Freud.

Intimately connected with the organizing principles there is the wider aspect of those early unconscious processes, that is, the whole atmosphere of life and of childhood in which these principles were laid down. This is written about extensively by, for example, Christopher Bollas in Britain and the Intersubjective School in America. Under the influence of this facet of transference, the whole therapy becomes the arena of childhood, and what the Intersubjective School terms vividly the original relational matrix of the person becomes activated. This global expression of transference arises especially where regression takes place in the therapy.

The second sort of transference which arises corresponds to the second sort of unconscious process identified by Stolorow and Atwood, and to repression as defined by Freud. That is, transference reflecting the processes of the dy namic unconscious, where, in order to maintain such equilibrium as we have managed to preserve, we seek actively to shut out from awareness memories of people, things and experiences which have been damaging to us in the past. Transferences of this sort can be revealed by, for instance, the avoidance of certain topics, the unquestioning expectation of inevitable outcomes, irratio nal prejudice against certain people, and the carrying out of oddly evasive and self defeating behaviors. An alert therapist will pick these up.

A third type of transference is the whole array of unfulfilled hopes and longings which the same authors termed the unvalidated unconscious. These buried ambitions and yearnings are triggered off to rise to the surface when the person, in a suitably accepting therapeutic atmosphere, perceives some hope at last of their fulfillment. This can give rise to an intense attach ment between therapee and therapist, where the latter is seen as being the fulfillment of all the formerís dreams. Fourth, there is any hidden underlay of radical dissociation, mistrust, hurt and abnormal sensitivity which might be the result of trauma. Any sensed similarity of setting, person, memory or feeling may be enough to set off once again the emotions, defenses and the often extreme reactions associated with the trauma.

For Freud, transference referred only to the second type of unconscious process. Fosshage (1994), in a formative article, sees the extension of trans ference mentioned (organizing principles) as relating to a model of dis placement, while the third type of process (the unvalidated unconscious) relates to a model of organization. The displacement model refers to the generalized transfer or displacement of happenings of the past on to the pres ent; the organization model refers to the ongoing attempt to find what was lacking and integrate it into the whole. The organization model would also appear to apply to such part of the displacement model as refers to the imposi tion of previous experience on to the present in the hope of creating some sort of order. The purpose of this would be to make of the present something that we can understand, and that we therefore know, or think we know, how to deal with. The two models illustrate the move from drive (individual) theories to a more relational understanding. Freud may be thought usually to be an undiluted individualist, but his emphasis on transference actually introduced into his intrapersonal world of drives an interpersonal dimension: it referred to something that happened between people. He was more relational than is sometimes thought (see Reisner, ch.13 in Skolnick and Warshaw 1992). Others since his day have taken these more relational aspects of transference much further forward; especially through their development via the related fields of counter transference and intersubjectivity.

The organization model is perhaps similar to the cognitive behavioral ap proach to therapy, except that the latter appears to ignore the strong anchor ing of perceptual organization in the emotions, and overlooks the consequent need to release and re experience these restrictive chains by means of a more dynamic therapy which works with the emotions.

It is important to stress again that not all transference is unreal or unhelp ful: it is a natural phenomenon with adaptive significance. It is when it is inappropriate to the present person or situation that it becomes a hindrance. It is, in the nature of things, whether real or unreal, at the root of all our be havior. When these roots can be discovered it gives the chance of modifying those that need to be modified.

Counter-transference Again

Counter transference is complementary to transference. It refers to the therapistís reactions to the therapee, particularly those brought about by their interaction: we looked at the various forms of it in chapter 1. It too reflects or dinary human processes of perception, projection and emotional communica tion sensitivity to it can be developed by awareness and training. Together with transference it provides an absolutely essential mode of exploration in psychoanalysis.

Three examples must suffice. The first two are examples of the direct com munication of feeling and of the therapist being used as a container for such hidden feelings. One is that I used to get strong sexual feelings of arousal when seeing a particular person. These feelings, so far as I could make out, did not come from me. I wasnít feeling randy beforehand, and the arousal was not directed at that person. They worried me until my supervisor told me that it might be the therapeeís repressed sexuality which I was experiencing. Sure enough, it transpired not only that the person was not currently active sexually but that they did not wish to talk or think about it. They tried to eliminate it from their lives, by a very powerful act of dissociation, but it was still there strongly under the surface, and it was this buried feeling that I was picking up.

The second example was when I felt sad, to the extent of tears coming to my eyes. The other person was showing no sign of emotion at all at the tragic story that they were telling: I think that they were actually smiling. I was only able to feed back a tentative observation to the tune of there seems to be some sadness around, an observation which could then be either accepted or denied. I have had both results occur, though in the latter event people did frequently later get in touch with what had been so hidden, to the point of denial.

The third example concerns sleepiness. This I suppose could be described as my response to something that the therapee was doing in the situation even though unrecognized by them. Transmission of repressed feeling and of the mechanisms used to deal with it can result in it. If my sleepiness was not initially on my own account, I came to recognize with the help of supervision that it invariably meant that the other person was cut off from, and actively if unconsciously, suppressing their emotions: it signified an almost total lack of life in the session (see also Cozolino 2004, 141). The only thing to do was to feed that feeling back at an appropriate moment if one occurred. This had the twin advantages of avoiding actually falling asleep and also usually of allowing the other person to get in touch with the feelings they were repress ing. On two occasions my experience was of having to fight continuously and desperately against sleep. It was a real struggle, as if a tremendous force was pushing me down, and I had physically to shake myself repeatedly in order to stay awake. The two occasions were with two separate people, who were each in a period of deep regression in their therapy, and who were, completely unconsciously, trying to prevent either me or them getting in touch with emo tions too horrible to endure. It was an active force, which might, I suppose, in an earlier cosmology, have been described as the devil.

I take up some other important aspects of the use and usefulness of coun ter transference in the next chapter, in the section working at non verbal levels.

THE CENTRALITY OF CHILDHOOD

The origin of transference lies in human nature: the origin of what is trans ferred lies in childhood and the earlier years. The two, transference and childhood, are practically inseparable. It was Freud who realized that we see our current life through the eyes of childhood and the past. Sometimes it is particular things, sometimes the complete atmosphere, sometimes particu lar events, sometimes a longing for things that hadnít happened, sometimes fears of what had: they are all informed by the emotions, expressed or unex pressed, which we experienced at the time. This web of experience forms the framework which we set on life, and provides the matrix into which we fit all our relationships. The centrality of childhood is therefore the third essential tool of psychoanalysis, given extra urgency with the shifting of the focus of so much psychodynamic work into that period of life.

Childhood became all the more important for Freud by his realization of infantile sexuality, which occurred in conjunction with his abandonment of his seduction theory. We may welcome the first, while deploring the second. Even if we do not accept his particular interpretations of the course of child hood and the dynamics of child development, we can accept nevertheless that childhood and its events are of supreme importance throughout life. Child hood therefore often comes up in therapy; or, more accurately, it is there all the time, as Ferenczi saw so clearly. Freudís original discovery of its impor tance has been augmented and strengthened by Ferencziís later explorations. Freud uncovered the bearing of childhood on later life; Ferenczi discovered that not only did it influence that but it also actually re surfaced in an analy sis. It was a present reality, not just a past determinant.

We need in consequence to be aware of childhood all the time. It is not that it needs to be addressed explicitly in every session and in every therapy, as if that is all the work that is required mere recall of it is not in itself neces sarily helpful. It does, though, need always implicitly to be borne in mind, and to be addressed if reference, spoken or unspoken, is made to it in the context of the difficulties of present life. It needs then to be brought forward into the forefront of therapy and addressed both as past and present. As a result of that, its continuing relevance and power can be grasped, defeated if inappropriate, or welcomed and assimilated openly into current life if benign. Even if childhood is not formally in the open or being addressed, we need to remember that there is always a child just under the surface, and temper our approach accordingly.

Peopleís use of language can often point to this hidden child. For instance, use of the words silly and stupid, which people in therapy frequently re peat about themselves or about things they say, is an unerring indication that they are talking about childhood. They are words which adults use to children to characterize words or behavior which the adult wishes either to dismiss or to disapprove but which to the child were probably both necessary and sensi ble. The child may at the time have outwardly accepted the adultsí rating, and may indeed duly repeat it; but inside they still feel misjudged. Other words and phrases which adults around them might have used but which could not have been part of the childís own vocabulary at the time can point to similar confusion. They either donít match a childís experience or they donít match a childís language development.

The tempering of our approach in response to (and in encouragement of) the surfacing of the child is one of the things that suggests the necessity of using child language where possible in therapy. It is because childhood provides the basic template for the understanding of life that we are likely to revert to the language of childhood when a situation or expression brings us close to childhood experience, whether we recognize it openly or not. This language is physical and earthy. Following on this is that hearing this sort of language helps someone to get into their childhood experiences. We pick up the echoes. It is the reason for the therapistís language to be as simple, direct, earthy and child like as possible. It makes all the difference in the world to describe a childish tantrum as diarrhea rather than a well formed motion rather than to cloak it in long circumlocutions. The hearer knows immediately what is meant and is helped to see the outburst in a more fundamental light.

At the beginning of the book I mentioned that my therapist told me early on that the longer he went on the more he realized the dominant effect of child hood on present experience. At the time I accepted the remark with unex pressed skepticism (an excellent example of my reaction to dogmatic adult remarks in my own childhood). I thought it was special pleading; but as time progressed I came to see its truth more and more. I hope I have passed it on to others in my turn. In particular, the importance of our childhood perceptions lies not in what really happened, but in how we saw it, that is, in the mean ing of what happened, or the meaning that we attached to what happened. That fundamentally means the emotional significance that it had for us. Its importance lies further in the fact that the influence of those perceptions and emotions does not go away, but continues to affect our behavior from beyond our awareness throughout our later life.

Theories of Child Development

Perhaps this is a good place to say something about theories of child de velopment. Two things, really. One is that Jungís theories have been justly criticized as lacking power in therapeutic work because he did not have any consistent theory of child development. The second, and distinctly related to that, is that having some theory of child development helps us to identify what stage of life someone is referring to or living out in therapy. They also make us aware of the relevant levels of verbal or emotional development that might apply to that stage.

Freudís psychosexual stages of development provide one such theory. They are provocative and interesting, hypothesizing that as a child grows the libido moves from one erotogenic zone of the body to another; but I did not ever find that they served to illuminate anything of the vicissitudes of peopleís lives. A great edifice has been built on the foundation of those stages, with various types of psychological development being attributed to each, such as the oral personality and anal personality, the latter being sub divided in turn into things like anal compulsive, anal retentive, and the like. These diagnoses seem little more than descriptions of straight for wardly observable and describable characteristics, but with a critical edge to them; and I have never found them useful in therapy or clinical work. If they ever had significance, it belonged to the classical drive theory era of theorizing. They are reductionist, biologically based, and make little refer ence to interaction.

People have indeed produced theories of development covering almost every aspect of life, physical, moral, social, cognitive (Piaget) and spiritual. Of them all Eriksonís (1950) presentation of stages of psychosocial develop ment is preeminently useful for any sort of relational therapy. It is a dynamic theory, the stages representing our interactions with other people as life pro gresses, together with the outcomes of those interactions. They can help in identifying the sort of crises that might have occurred in a personís life, the underlying reason for them, and at what age or stage of life they might have occurred. One of our psychiatrist lecturers in psychology said that Eriksoní's stages were so well drawn that particular psychiatric diagnoses fitted par ticular stages to such an extent that he had only to inquire a patientí's age to identify the likely diagnosis.

Even more relevant would be a setting out of what might be called psycho emotional stages identifying dominant emotional crises at each of the phases of life, together with their recurrences at later phases when similar crises re cur. This would enable us to relate them both to character and to their likely appearance in the course of a therapy. The precise nature of that appearance would depend on whether their discovery, expression and resolution earlier in life had been benign or malign. The sort of psycho emotional events of which I am thinking are pivotal crises like trust, attachment, separation, loss, and others. The critical occurrence of each of these can be placed in one or other of the psychosocial stages, as also, according to the above psychiatrist, can the various types of breakdown. They have each been written about, and worked with, separately, but they need integrating into a consistent overall pattern if the variety of human experience permits it. Josephine Klein (1987) helpfully orders in this sort of way the contributions of varied psychoanalytic writers to the developing achievements and crises, emotional and otherwise, of different stages of life as it progresses.

EMOTIONS AND THE PHYSICAL

I have least in quantity of words to say about this particular legacy of Freudí's as the fourth essential of psychoanalysis not because it lacks importance but because it is so basic and all embracing. It is the bedrock of life. The physical is as vital to psychoanalytic work as it is to life itself. This is chiefly just be cause it is there and because it is all pervasive and fundamental, especially as the seat of emotion. Freud usually referred to it as sexuality, but his use of the term is closer to what we might now refer to as physicality ; that is, the fact of having a physical body with all that is associated with it the totality of our sheer body ness, with its sensitivity, its sensuality and its sexuality. Early sexuality, to which Freud referred so much, would better be called sensuality. It is not the adult genitality which is the meaning we generally attach to the word in our day. Life starts with feeling; and Freud is stressing that our being has its origin in being bodily, earthy, incarnated. Lifeí's roots are in the body: we are embodied beings, not walking minds. That is one reason why it is so important that in psychotherapy we use suitably earthed language, in order to stay in touch with this ground of our being. That also is the reason why the use of metaphor is so effective: it touches our physical substrate, connecting it up with the mind, as it was in the beginning.

Freud rooted his emphasis on the body and things physical in his drive theory, according to which our human motivation was determined by im personal drives, which were entirely physical and underlay all action. That theory sees the rooting of drives in instincts rather than in emotions. It is different now. Affect (emotion) is seen as the major factor motivating human behavior, and as the central motivational construct for psychoanalysis (see the quotations from *The International Journal of Psychoanalysis* of 1995 and from Stolorow, Atwood and Brandchaft [1994] on page 15 of chapter 1); yet the emotions are, above all, also physical in origin.

The significance of the body in therapy is thus now supremely in regard to the emotions, which arise from and are part of our physical being. The word emotion is from the same root as the word motivation : both are about what moves us. They are physical words; and they show the absolutely fun damental role both of the body and of the emotions in human life. A life lived without emotion lacks purpose and dynamic, and this is presented by many people as one of their main problems when they come for therapy. They feel no motivation or purpose. It can show up in their therapy later on, as men tioned a little previously, in a feeling of sleepiness and lifelessness pervading sessions, as well as in a general felt lack of purpose and meaning.

When emotion is pushed away in this manner, and especially when events occur too early in a childís life to be put into words and there is no conscious means of encoding it, it becomes stored unconsciously, out of awareness, in the body, thence to emerge as headaches, other psychosomatic disorders and various outcroppings of bodily sensations. Everything that is of sufficient significance to move us but is not acted on is stored in the body: nothing just disappears. These physical, or psychosomatic, symptoms can say a lot about the origin of the particular events which might have caused them. For instance, it is possible to ask people suffering from headaches if they can say any more about what sort of headache it is, and exactly where in the head it is felt. Sometimes it may be experienced as an overall splitting headache, when the person is in two minds about something. Sometimes it is located at the surface of the frontal lobes, where it points to a confusion of thought. Sometimes it is felt as being located deep within the lower center of the head, near the hypothalamus, where it points to deep emotional conflict and clears when the emotional problem is identified and verbalized.

Emotions are central to mental health (which might be better described as emotional health). All psychiatric disorders can be described in the language of emotions; of their expression, their repression, and their recrudescence; and all psychiatric diagnoses can be expressed in everyday emotional terms (cf. Bentall 2004). Within psychiatry, psychotropic drugs are used to control the emotions, and to keep them suppressed if they are beginning to surface. This is a mistake if people want to live their own lives. What is most needed, instead, is an opportunity for emotions to be recognized and accepted in a safe setting for people to be helped to learn how to express them and to act on them appropriately just as one might hope would happen for a child within a family, but often doesnít.

Freudís emphasis on aspects of human biology, on sexual development, and on childhood all highlighted this physical basis of our life, though he didnít make sufficient distinction between child and adult experience of the physical: they are, as Ferenczi pointed out, at different levels. The physical is lifeís ground that both gives it shape and roots it in the earth. In the beginning it is one with mind, as it is at birth; but the connection becomes contradicted or distorted as soon as experience enters in. Some of Carl Rogersís work (1967) is based on the failure of our brains to match the experience of our organism: a split develops. The body tells us things about our total make up, things that may be ignored or not known by the mind. This is the basis of the therapy known as bioenergetics. One example of such a split is the way noted before in which survivors of sexual abuse frequently reveal their forgotten experience by their bodily movements and gestures, another is the way in which oneís eyes can sometimes give a quite different message from oneís words.

For all these reasons, we need in therapy always to bear the physical in mind and to be alert to any allusions to it, for instance to the use of child language, to the expression of the physical in metaphor, or to body language itself. The bodily, the concrete, the earthy, these are what are basic to life and to experience (Barnard and Brazelton 1990): our language and our practice need to reflect this fact.

THE OVERALL SEARCH FOR MEANING

The central purpose of using and adhering to these four essentials of psy choanalytic work is to recover buried emotions, so that movement may be restored to life and a sense of meaning recovered. This is their raison dí tre. They serve the superordinate purposes of integration and meaning with which we started this chapter. I learned this first from my early supervisor Dr. James Home, of the Group Analytic Society, who wrote for psychoanalysis an im portant paper on the topic, The concept of mind (1966) (a title the same as that of Gilbert Ryleís earlier book [1949] of more general reference). It ad dresses the problem of mind and body; mind and brain. Homeís starting point was to try to answer the question What is psychoanalysis about? because he felt that much of its language made it incomprehensible.

In his paper he suggests that mind is the meaning of behavior. Mind is not something separate from the rest of us but is the connecting thread of our life, being the result of our reflecting on our experience and our behavior. If we lose a sense of meaning (and continuity) then we are prone to breakdown, illness, and somatic complaints. If we can recover it, we regain energy and purpose.

Home points out that behavior is a special word: we donít speak of the behavior of inanimate things, only of live entities. We speak of activity in relation to inanimate objects, of behavior in relation to animate ones. This is because behavior has meaning; activity does not intrinsically do so. Guntrip is another who points out (Hazell 1994, 251) that meaning belongs only to animate beings: it constitutes their subjective experience, and is their interpretation of their own behavior and of that of other living beings in terms of their aims and purposes. We are always searching for meaning as part of our search for order and integration.

We therefore usually speak of behavior as something which has meaning, and call it disordered if it appears not to do so. To that meaning we give the name of mind. Brain is a thing; mind is a quality. The workings of the brain give rise to mind. Brain goes with activity and facts, mind with behavior and meaning. Mental, or emotional, upset is then an upset in meaning, where things have gone wrong and have become unassimilable and incomprehensible, where oneís self image has been contradicted and sense has departed from life. Mental or emotional health is when our life has good meaning for us. It is the task of therapy to help people to find meaning again; then they can take charge of their lives once more and fulfill their purpose.

Psychodynamics or at least psychoanalysis does not always show very clearly that this search for meaning is at its heart: it can obscure it especially when its language is unclear, obtuse or full of specialist jargon or mystique. We need to hold on to the fact that the search for meaning is at the heart of psychodynamics and not allow it to be extinguished by professional jargon. We are not uncovering emotions for their own sake, nor to provoke an out pouring which leaves no one any the wiser. We are trying to help people to find the meaning of what has happened and is happening to them, or of what they think happened and why they might think it; and by that means to restore their sense of having some power and control over their own lives and to en able them to find constructive ways of dealing with difficulties.

Chapter Six

Theoretical Implications

NECESSARY CONSEQUENCES

If we seek to use the four essential tools of psychoanalysis within the overall search for meaning and taking into account Ferencziís insights, there are several consequences. In the next three chapters I try to tease out some of these. For the sake of clarity of presentation they are each somewhat roughly allocated to one of three categories which form the three chapters. These are, first, theoretical implications regarding some basic aspects of psychoanalytic work, which largely concern its ethos; secondly, practical issues which are mostly concerned with the setting and procedure of therapy so as to facilitate communication within it; and thirdly, clinical insights affecting how the face to face interaction may proceed. All three chapters concern the day to day practice of a relational psychoanalysis working with the fundamental discov ery by Ferenczi of the presence of a child in the analysis.

The consequences follow chiefly from recognition that the work is car ried out within an acknowledged relationship which itself forms part of its focus. It involves using the power of this relationship, establishing a setting of mutuality and respect, having an open and honest exchange, facilitating the recovery and expression of emotion, loving the child, using appropriate language, and avoiding methods which might interfere with any of these. The tools to explore and promote all these are provided by the four elements which we have identified. A distinct advantage of concentrating on the dy namic essentials of practice rather than on theoretical requirements and rules is that it gives greater freedom in regard to inessentials, such as those touched on at the beginning of the previous chapter.

THE NEED FOR RELATIONSHIP

Relationship is the essential framework within which clinical practice is car
ried out. Modern psychoanalysis has come to recognize this relational basis
largely as an outcome of Ferencziís work. His uncovering of the reality and
importance of the relationship, and his adoption of it as a tool, represents
a crystallization of his modifications of classical psychoanalysis. It was an
essential complement to the uncovering of trauma and the practice of regres
sion, but rather more than that it is a vital part of psychoanalytic work at any
level. Unlocking the power of relationship meant the analyst permitting him
self or herself to enter into an emotional engagement with the other person
so as to form a personal bond, thereby creating the atmosphere of acceptance
and respect that might form a vehicle for change. Acceptance and respect are
qualities which are needed for any mutual human interaction, but they are
above all necessary for the promotion of growth, whether it be in family life,
in therapy, or in any other area of human exchange. Emotional engagement
is vital when there is a child present in the analysis of the adult: it is the me
dium for a childís development, as non engagement or over engagement may
have been the medium earlier for a childís stunting. In many instances the
emotional commitment of the therapist is crucial to any chances of recovery
which the other person may have.

In classical psychoanalysis, with the analystís abstention and holding back
from any interaction other than verbal interpretation, the power of the (absent)
relationship is frequently shown in its frustrating consequences. The   patient
reverts to childish ways of coping with the frustration, to opposition, anger,
and stroppiness. It appears sometimes that it is the analystís intention actually
to provoke such behavior and then to leave the   patient   to solve the prob
lems which it brings. The person was not able to do this in its first occurrence
in their lives, and they need particular help with a corresponding situation in
therapy. Instead, they are left to learn that   life is like that   tough! Such an
approach not surprisingly provokes a malignant regression to the oppositional
ways of a painful and resistant childhood in which children have been left to
cope on their own with the anger and despair from which they seek release.
The experience can result in what has become known (incorrectly; see the
last section of this chapter) as   the negative therapeutic reaction,   meaning
a fierce reaction by the   patient   against the analyst; but it owes its birth
not to the patientís resistance, on which it is traditionally blamed, but to the
analystís provocation.

An active relationship on the other hand in which the analyst is part of a
cooperative striving to work through the situation and feelings carried over
from childhood, has a power for good, a power of adaptability, and a power

for growth. The regression in such circumstances is benign. The frequent finding of outcome studies that the curative factor in psychotherapy is non specific and appears to rest in the therapist rather than in any theoretical stance or practice, bears out the essential importance and energy of the relationship formed between the two participants. The stronger the relation ship, the more likely it is that feelings belonging to past strong relationships will be evoked. This then makes it possible to look at what is happening in the present, to identify inappropriate reactions and their past causes, and to foster the development of reactions which match the new situation. In this, psychotherapy is like any other human relationship, and the same processes take place in it as in any other. It can form a microcosm of the personís world and of their relationships outside therapy; and is both an indication of the nature of the personís original relational matrix and an arena for the forging of a new one.

Since the main aim of psychoanalysis or psychotherapy is to help people to get into touch with their emotional life where power, purpose and meaning are contained, it is fairly clear that a relationship is needed as the instrument for this it is in relationships that emotions reside. It was in relationship that our attitudes and convictions were first formed; and it is within an appro priately strong bond that they can be re called and re formed. Especially is this so when the relevant relationship was the dyadic one between child and mother (carer). The two person dyadic situation of therapy has the potential to echo this and to hold out the possibility of change even at this most forma tive level.

Balint pointed out long ago (Gomez 1997, 123 124) that classical psycho analysis is based on the principle of interpretation leading to insight, rather than on relationship leading to maturation. This might seem to imply that the latter is a new form of therapy; but as Balint points out elsewhere, it is actually already there contained in the old. Freud emphasized the phenom enon of transference: whatever else it may do or be, transference belongs to relationship, as a happening between people. It was never followed up from that viewpoint, but was treated as a phenomenon occurring inside only one of the participants. The present day emphasis on relationship is only drawing further meaning out of something that was already there in germ, and which Ferenczi was instrumental in establishing as the basic setting of psychoanaly sis in spite of all attempts to stop him.

The Therapeutic Relationship

This prompts further thinking about the analytic or therapeutic relationship in particular. It cannot be too highly stressed that it is (or needs to be) a real relationship: it is not simulated or artificially engendered. It develops naturally. It grows out of the encounter with one another of two people as subjects. It involves genuine emotion which by its nature cannot be cut off at the end of a session. This emotion is the vehicle of healing. It is especially brought into active life and power in the more child centered interaction pres ent in the analytic encounter, but because it is real it will always continue, though at a different level, through any other meeting of the two people. I suppose that most therapists and therapees do not normally meet one another on other occasions than the analytic sessions, so that they are unable to ex perience this permanence of feeling or test it out. In therapeutic communities and during analytic training the parties do meet in other settings and can either bear witness to or deny its continuance in those other settings: I would be surprised if they can deny it.

The fact that psychoanalysis started from a position of requiring a with holding and abstaining analyst whose emotions were kept out of the interac tion may tend to make the later emphasis on the relationship sound forced and artificial, and the emotions engendered as unreal and for the therapeutic purpose of the session only. If so, this would fly in the face of honesty, reality and substance: it is essential that the relationship is real and the emotions are felt and known to be real and enduring.

The need for the emotions between the two parties to be genuine does carry a cost. It requires careful working through at the end of a therapy, with recognition of the difference between its context in the therapy rela tionship and in ordinary life. Usually it has felt to me that while the feeling may endure, the context is no longer suitable for subsequent meetings. Just sometimes the emotion may be so strong as to transcend the difference in context, and make it possible to spread from therapy to embrace the whole of life. A further cost of emotion being genuine is that the therapist is go ing to suffer if the therapy is terminated suddenly, such as by the death of a therapee. He or she cannot just dismiss it as a happening that does not engage them deeply. I felt as if I was experiencing the death of a child when someone whom I was working with in a therapeutic community died unex pectedly; the emotional bond between us was vividly alive, and was cut off before either of us was ready.

The difference in the attitude to emotion between classical and the more re lational psychoanalysis has its roots in the significantly different approaches which Freud and Ferenczi had to the analytic relationship. Freud had a complete separation between the analytic and the non analytic. He could be remote, abstinent, a blank screen in analytic sessions, and friendly, with tea, walks and shared holidays with the same person outside them. He did not consider the latter to be interfering with the analysis. Ferencziís model, on the other hand, was that the total relationship between the two people was what mattered: the analytic and the non analytic were one. The process be tween them was always in progress: mutual emotional engagement was what occurred, and had to occur, in analytic sessions and by the nature of it could not then be cut off in encounters outside the sessions. The difference in their views shows a quite different approach to the nature of analysis; and a lack of clarity about it seems to have been behind some of the misunderstanding that arose between them.

Ferencziís attitude towards analysis is on a par with his perception of the need for genuine emotional engagement with the other person. For effective analysis there cannot be the split between analyst and analysand hypothesized by Freud.

MUTUALITY

The setting of relationship means that psychotherapy is in its essence a shared endeavour, where both parties contribute to the outcome, even though not in quite the same way. This mutuality was contradicted by the principle of abstinence. While it might be felt initially that it is the therapee who needs to be persuaded that the work is mutual, so also very often does the thera pist. Withholding is not an option. To quote Neville Symington (2007), a clinical technique can only be effective if the person of the psychoanalyst is available to the other (348). There follow the words if the person of the psychoanalyst is concealed behind a fa ade, then the patient has no chance of developing his own personhood. The capacity to be a person develops through interaction with another person.

Earlier consideration of abstinence concerned its suitability particularly when dealing with trauma, but ultimately its use must be questioned in any interaction that professes to be human. Mutuality raises the issue of whether the blank screen is a useful, permissible or proper concept at all; it also involves consideration of whether it is in fact ever possible for the analyst to remain uninvolved. If he or she is present, is there not bound to be inter action? Classical theory espoused abstention in the belief that thereby the analyst would not affect the inner workings of the patient. On the contrary, abstention, or even unintended silence, has a considerable effect: they are both themselves actions within the overall encounter. There is in addition the scientific finding to be taken into account enshrined in the Heisenberg Uncer tainty Principle, which says that interaction is inevitable in any observation, however supposedly neutral: this would be even more so where human beings are involved on both sides of it.

The clinical consideration is a separate, and ethically more important, is sue. That is, whether it is proper or helpful for the therapist to seek to remain apart. This point has been cited in our looking at the fundamentals for thera peutic practice. It has been stressed on several occasions that the analystís or therapistís silence and withholding may often repeat for the analysand or therapee an earlier lack of involvement or responsiveness on the part of those around them which has already contributed to their present distress. Repeat ing it can be felt to be merely persecutory, and seen as a form of cruelty. It is neither helpful nor useful. Another consideration is contained in the work of many writers who have emphasized the potential of creativity residing in the emotional meeting of two people. If change is to occur, there has to be an in teraction of the two persons as subjects to one another. Koestlerís (1964) *The Act of Creation* suggests that this occurs when two contrasting viewpoints impact on one another.

This is, for me, related to the highly creative suggestions made by various practitioners about the nature of the therapeutic interaction, where, from the encounter between the two persons, the emergence of a third entity is seen as part of the therapeutic and indeed life process. This third party goes by various names, but it is especially significant in having been identified by workers in several distinct branches of psychoanalysis which otherwise differ markedly. There is, for instance, the selfobject of Kohut (1971), the transitional object of Winnicott (1951, in Winnicott 1958), the transfor mational object of Bollas (1987), the analytic third of Ogden (1994), and the X phenomenon of Symington (2007, 61): they all point to the coming into being within the therapeutic event of a new entity which was not there beforehand, and which, as the seed of a new creation, contains within it the possibility of growth.

The province of psychotherapy is in consequence the new field created by the interplay between the two subjective realities of therapist and thera pee, or, the mingling of their two inner representational worlds. The intersubjective field is something not there before the interaction, which brings into life things that are not there without it (Ogden). This is what Ogden calls the analytic third (1994, **75**, 1, 3 20). In regression therapy, I think it possible that this could be seen as the emergence of the child in the analysis, which becomes the locus of growth and the vehicle for change.

Donna Orange (1995), a leading intersubjectivity worker, has this fur ther to say: intersubjectivity views psychoanalysis as the attempt of two people together to understand through dialogue one personís organization of emotional experience by making sense together of their intersubjectively configured experience that is, of the new things that arise between them. The other is seen, as in any other truly mutual human interaction, not merely as the object of anotherís needs or perception, viewed from outside; they are experienced as a separate and equivalent center of self, from the inside. Someone once commented in a therapy group, He speaks to me rather than at me. To me or with me are different from being spoken at. There is an inner engagement between the two people: between the I and the Thou. The system thus formed, namely this intersubjectively configured experience, is what creates the something new in the room. It takes us undeniably into the concept of psychoanalysis or psychotherapy as an interaction, a mutual engagement, and a generative relationship between the two people involved that brings into being something new created by their encounter.

With this in mind, the question of the propriety of the analyst trying to keep out of the interaction is settled. To do so obviates the whole purpose of the enterprise. Fortunately, whatever the earlier beliefs about abstention, it was not able to prevent growth. As referred to earlier, studies have shown that the outcome of therapy has depended not so much on particular techniques but on the more human interactions which this particular technique was supposed to circumvent.

Besides these considerations about the necessity of involvement and in teraction for the processes of therapy, there are also more general reasons based on humanity for insisting on engagement. There is, first, a sense that observation alone is not an appropriate procedure for a human interaction: it makes the other person into an object. Secondly, psychoanalysis and its set ting promote (if they donít actually provoke) interaction; it is false as well as counter productive to pretend that they donít. It doesnít deceive anyone to act as if there is no interaction nor counter transference and as if this will not affect the other person. Ferenczi was the first to perceive this fact (CD 1995). To hold back in this way is, moreover, to withhold a shared experience that might otherwise help the other person, preventing them from attaining the richness of a fully human encounter. The present day rise within psychody namics of the concept of intersubjectivity carries with it the unavoidable im plication of mutuality. The therapeutic interaction has become more ordinary, without losing its uniqueness.

Mutuality is therefore a contemporary issue in most streams of psycho analysis. Levineís (1994) remark about the focus of psychoanalysis having changed in recent years from a focus on the mind of the patient to the inter active dimension inherent in the relation between analyst and analysand has already been quoted (see page 12). This present day concern with mutuality appears in most modern schools of psychoanalysis: in the American Rela tional School, in the Inter subjective Group and in the movement of Listen ing Perspectives, in the work of modern Kleinians, and in the work of the

British Independents. Harold Stewart is reported as saying that the emphasis on mutuality is one of the most important theoretical differences between the Independents on the one hand and at least some Contemporary Freudians and Kleinians on the other and that since the 1930s mutuality of working with a patient has perhaps been one of the British Independentsí clearest technical characteristics; though by no means avowed by all of them (see also Rayner 1991, 287 290).

Lewis Aron, in his book from the American Relational stream, *A Meeting of Minds: Mutuality in Psychoanalysis* (1996), clarifies possible misunderstand ing by pointing out that mutuality does not mean symmetry. The interaction is not symmetrical: there is a real difference between the two parties in the ana lytic encounter, both for the sake of the work and ultimately for the sake of the other person. There must be mutuality, but without the interaction having to be symmetrical. Mutuality in this context means rather the showing of some sort of basic respect for the humanity of the other and an acknowledged sharing in a common task. Neither of these aspects requires symmetry. How to maintain the distinction is an open question, left to us to solve for ourselves.

One thing is sure: mutuality means above all, emotional engagement and involvement. We must be emotionally engaged with the other person if we want to be effective; and we must also be able to be separate, if we do not want either to be exhausted, or unable to discern what is taking place. Only by costly emotional and deeply personal engagement can we hope to be of any real help to the damaged and struggling individuals who come to seek it, and who look, perhaps without knowing it explicitly, for some resolution of both their conflicts and their deprivations in a fully human encounter.

One characteristic of the mutual encounter in modern psychotherapy is that we are working with a concealed child in the person before us. The child both wants to emerge, and must emerge, from hiding if their needs and hurts are to be worked with constructively, and the ambience of the therapy needs to be such as to promote and encourage this. This has to be kept at the back of our minds even if we are dealing with later hurts which appear to be amenable to verbal expression and discussion. It takes center stage when we are dealing with those earlier troubles which start long before that period, when words are not what are needed.

WORKING AT NON-VERBAL LEVELS

This brings us back to the work of Lawrence Hedges (see chapter 1) and its contribution to practice. His teasing out of the clinical issues of working at earlier levels of disturbance, in particular at those which essentially concern the child in the analysis, is invaluable: it is an almost infallible guide. We saw in the earlier chapter that he delineates four levels in the work of psy choanalysis, or four distinct foci of attention. The first is Freudís centering on neurotic conflict, which has to do with fairly adult disturbances. In therapy associated with this level, the important means of inquiry is by verbal interac tion between therapist and client, and the agent of change is verbal interpre tation. The other three levels reflect the advance epitomized by Ferenczi in identifying the child in the analysis.

Thus at the second level, there came the work of Kohut and Self Psy chology in the US, which concentrated on narcissistic disorders, or distur bances in the sense of self. Thirdly, at much the same time, there came the work in the UK associated with Winnicott and Balint (and with Mahler in the US), which arose out of their work with the early mother child dyad. The difficulties that can arise here are specifically those called borderline disorders. Finally, work developed more recently on the earliest stage of life, where the difficulties arising are termed either psychotic (in a more medical model) or organizing (from a more humanistic point of view). At this earliest level, just staying with the person in their confusion is a first requirement of therapy.

Each perspective, or level, is recognized by Hedges as finding a distinctive expression in the therapy, which determines its language and atmosphere. I am also suggesting (see chapter 1, 15) that there is an even earlier level, relat ing to the deprivation of body contact, which may require even more definite physical response. The key point for practice is that each perspective or level gives rise to a particular experience of the counter transference; this is what suggests not only the dominant issue for therapy but also the approach or lan guage called for to meet it. Hedges deliberately chose the word perspective for his concepts as being more dynamic and less mutually exclusive than level : they may overlap. As long as we bear that in mind, it is convenient to use the two terms interchangeably.

To look at the differing forms of counter transference which mark each of the perspectives, we shall reverse the levels as they have been introduced above and re order them in their developmental sequence. At the first, we are working at the organizing perspective or level, that is, at the time when an infant is trying to establish connections and to make sense of what is going on in and around them. Working at this level we may in therapy ex perience the person as desperately but flounderingly trying to make contact with life. This can produce a sense of disconnection if not of chaos in our selves which echoes that in the other person. We are left wondering what on earth is happening, and can feel considerably disoriented by the end of a session.

Secondly, at the borderline level, which represents the childís early attempts to merge and to form attachments, the therapist frequently either feels pressured into an identity of being with the therapee or feels strongly parental towards them and called to provide endless care, verging on a symbiotic state   or both. Within this perspective we are asked to deal with merger, trust, separation and dependency issues: failure to be one with the therapee in whatever state they are at this level can cause immense hurt and rage; and an inability to recognize what is happening can bring about equally deep and mutually uncomprehended distress in the other person. On the other hand, it is possible that the therapeeís demands can buy into our own needs, which might mean that we so enjoy sup plying what is asked that we keep the other person dependent and hinder their growth, like a clinging mother. It is therefore most urgent, for the sake of the therapee, to be aware of this type of situation and of its counter transference.

Thirdly, at the level of narcissistic problems, concerning the development of the self, we are likely to find that verbal interpretation does not always work, and indeed can make matters worse. It may cause an offence of the nature of a narcissistic wound, whose depth and source is difficult both to recognize and to fathom (see further at the end of chapter 8). At this level, we are working with the mirror and idealizing transferences and can expe rience the other person, through our counter transference, as single mind edly seeking the missing bits of themselves needed for the establishment of their independent self. In consequence the therapist can feel used, and totally ignored as a person in their own right: bits of us only are wanted. This reflects our serving as a selfobject for the therapee whose purpose is to provide some essential missing function until the structure of the self is strengthened sufficiently not to need it or us in this particular way anymore. The experience can be puzzling, boring, irritating and hurtful, just like oc casions when we might feel we are being taken for granted or not wanted for ourselves in ordinary life.

At the perspective of neurotic conflict, the fourth and most developed level, we experience in contrast a fairly adult interchange. We feel more as if we are confronted by an adult trying to achieve mature solutions to problems within a mature relationship, with whom ordinary verbal or symbolic interaction is most appropriate, and verbal interpretation is a sufficient tool to resolve the difficulty. Finally, the use of the word perspective for the four phenomena leaves open the possibility that more than one of them may be in view at any one time, which requires great sensitivity in detecting the presence of those that may be the less obvious.

The Difference between Levels

As a broad general division, there is a very marked difference between the counter transference at the first three levels (organizing, borderline and narcissistic) and that at level four (the neurotic): this division is of critical importance. As we move back from level four to the others, in the way that psychoanalysis did in its historic development, we move from verbal to non verbal, from conflict to deficit, from particular aspects of character to a personís total situation, and from symbolic expression to something more concrete, physical, feeling and tactile.

This clearly parallels Ferencziís division of languages in Confusion of tongues. At the first two developmental perspectives and much of the third, we are at the non verbal, deficit, level, the level of the language of innocence and tenderness; at the fourth, that of neurotic conflict, we are at the level of the language of passion, though even then a language of some tenderness might be called for on purely human considerations. There is no call to sus pect people of malevolence unless they show it unmistakably.

People at the three earlier levels are helped less by verbal interpretation than by holding, containing, being and the emotional atmosphere of the ther apy relationship itself, and by the use, if words are used, of those appropriate to the stage. Work at any of these earlier levels, but especially at the most primitive, is almost certainly going to involve a very long term commitment on the part of both participants in the therapy. Consideration of work and counter transference at the even earlier level, where simple human contact is what appears primarily to be needed, is left to the concluding chapter of this book.

The level at which we experience, or, the perspective from which we see someone through our counter transference can thus help to direct the way in which we work with them. Balintís finding of there being two levels of ana lytic work has now become four (or five), and we need to recognize which language is appropriate for each. It can be easy for an analyst to mistake the level at which the work is taking place and to respond inappropriately in adult language when what is called for is the language and ambience appropriate to the presence of a child.

A table summarizing Hedgesís perspectives, the age range which they cover, their specific transferences and counter transferences, the emotional crises involved, and the chief people who have worked at each level is given on the next page to clarify and summarize the various interrelationships be tween them:

Table 6.1. The Use of Counter-transference

perspective	age	level	description	stage	transference	counter-transference	therapy style	emotional crisis	author
part self & part object	to 4m.	integrative	"psychotic" (organizing)	pre-verbal	connecting	chaotic *tenuous* *disconnected*		solidity boundaries trust bonding Erikson 1	Tustin, Little, Hedges, et al.
merger	4m. to 2yrs.	symbiotic	borderline	pre-verbal	fusing	mothering *dependent* *demanding*	"deficit" area	acceptance, dependence, separation 2	Ferenczi, Balint, Winnicott, Mahler, Stern, Bowlby, Bollas, et al.
selfobject	2-3yrs.	self-development	narcissistic		mirroring idealising *highly sensitive* *(→ "narcissistic wounds")*	being used *being admired* *drowsiness*		individuation 3	Kohut, Self-psychology, et al.
constant self & constant object	>3yrs.	relations with others	oedipal ("neurotic") classical	verbal	ambivalent relationship	conflict *exchange*	"conflict" (neurosis) area	independence, cooperation 4ff	Freud, Ego-psychy, Contemp Fr, et al.

(vertical text in description column: personality disorders)

+ mixture of all

Note: This table is based on Lawrence Hedges's *Interpreting the Counter-transference* (1992), 212–213

CONFUSION OF TONGUES

The muddling of levels is not imagined: it happens. It springs from and rein forces the confusion of tongues. While the preceding delineation of perspec tives concerns work within any model of psychoanalysis, the next two issues specifically involve failure to distinguish the difference between the levels or perspectives within classical psychoanalysis. They concern sharp contrasts in particular between the two psychoanalytic approaches dealt with in this book, the classical and, for want of any better word, the relational (or the human).

Perhaps the clearest example of the confusion of tongues which Ferenczi wrote about is to be found in what has become known as the erotic transfer ence. In the monograph on Freudís paper Observations on transference love (Person 1993), only one of the many contributions to the book (that by Takeo Doi on Amae) gives any hint of recognizing that the phenomenon might be something other than as labeled and described by Freud.

A further particularly stark example of differences between the two languages is the doctrine of the negative therapeutic reaction. This is a dogmatic feature of the classical withholding drive theory or instinct theory model of psychoanalysis, yet where it is a phenomenon self engendered by the model itself, although it is blamed on the patient. In the more relational approach honoring the child within the other person and using the language of tenderness, there is no need for this reaction to occur; and it duly doesnít.

Unfortunately people trained in the classical model tend to repeat it later in their own work, as if there is no possibility of achieving the same ends in a more benign or open manner. I am sure, for instance, that the confrontational and suspicious attitude that many therapists display in their work owes at least some of its origin to their having been treated in that way themselves in their own therapy, and they do not realize that there is any other way of being as a therapist. It is an inherited and self reinforcing feature of the particular school of training through which they have passed.

The "Erotic Transference"

The so called erotic transference undoubtedly confuses the languages of tenderness and passion. Working with transference is, as we have seen, one of the essentials of psychoanalytic work. One aspect of it is the transference of sexual feelings, which is what is sometimes termed the erotic transfer ence. The phrase owes its origin to Freud, and is an instance of applying the language of passion to all phenomena of analysis and therapy whether appropriate or not. It overlooks completely the realm of tenderness and inno cence, of deficit, of the child, of longing for what one never experienced: all is interpreted instead in terms of adult sexuality. The trouble is that a state of regression, which releases infant longing and yearning, can look superficially very like what Freud called the erotic transference (cf. Doiís paper [Person 1993] already mentioned).

This sort of transference can become extreme, especially if it is treated as being entirely sexual in nature and interpreted (fed back) as such, overlook ing any possible infant needs. One needs to question whether its content is in actuality sexual rather than being full of longing, yearning or admiring. When it occurs in the context of psychiatry, it has earned for itself the diagnostic label of a named syndrome: the de Clerambaut syndrome (as pictured in Ian McEwanís novel, *Enduring Love,* 1997). In more ordinary language it would be called stalking or persecution. I know, because I have been the object of it.

To understand the erotic transference more fully, an initial vital point about it concerns the meaning of eros and the erotic. The dictionary gives the meaning of the latter as pertaining to sexual love ; but it is a mistake to narrow the meaning of eros to this, or the meaning of the erotic transference to sexual, that is, genital, feelings for the therapist. The erotic (like the full meaning of sexual) has much wider reference: it is a total phenomenon of life, referring to our urge to connect with others reaching, touching, long ing, loving. The dictionary deals only with its genital aspects, but it is immea surably more than that. It is the life force for union, for integration; it is what drives human beings together. It therefore underlies all bonding, attachment and love. It is an underlying urge of our physical nature. For Freud, eros did originally have this wider meaning. It was a basic force in life, not just in adult sexuality: for him, it was what kept the death force at bay.

The dynamic of eros starts in childhood and continues throughout all human life; blocks on it cause great deprivation and pain and fuel the phenomenon of yearning. This yearning can then emerge later in the so called erotic transfer ence. In fact, it is almost bound to emerge, because of the intimate dyadic set ting of psychoanalytic therapy, however withholding the analyst may be. The crucial question is not whether the yearning appears but how it is treated when it does: whether it is blocked and rejected (as it may have been in childhood), to which further blocking and rejection there may well be a malignant reaction; or accepted, where there is the possibility of a benign (good) outcome. The malignant reaction may take all sorts of forms, well documented, though highly judgmentally, by those who have been at the receiving end of it; but its origin lies in the failure to see correctly what is happening.

Freud didnít see it, and treated the longing as if it were an unfortunate and aggressive intrusion into therapy. The psychiatric nomenclature awarded to it also misses its universality, urgency and pain. The fact is that the erotic trans ference can conceal immense childhood need and unfulfilled longings, and points to the essential place in our lives of the erotic in its wider connotation. Freudís failure to recognize its deeper springs is part of his failure to deal with the early mother and child aspects of life.

It is not surprising that this longing should enter into therapy, for therapy is intimately involved with connection and relationship: these are its primary concerns. Eros and the erotic are at its heart: one could say that eros is the body of therapy. It is sexuality in its broadest sense what we do with our bodies much wider than the restricted genital meaning that the dictionary surprisingly gives it. To reject it, or to rule it out of therapy rather than to understand it and integrate it into life, is to diminish the place of therapy and in consequence to make it largely irrelevant to our real concerns: yet that is what often happens to the erotic when it appears in the form of this urgent transference.

There is an important distinction needing to be made within the area of sexuality, that is, a distinction between adult genitality (the focus of Freud, though he also used the word sexuality to refer to physicality in general); and childhood physicality (the focus of Ferenczi). It is a distinction between the age of knowledge and the age of innocence; that is, between sexuality in its genital sense, and sensuality. Sexuality properly includes both, but Freud narrowed its meaning and spoke as if adult sexuality (i.e., genitality) was all that was at stake in transference love (as it does indeed sometimes appear to be and the person concerned may insist that it is). Ferenczi detected, cor rectly, that childhood longing was at the root of it: the longing for cuddling, warmth, skin and body contact, of which many people have been starved at the proper time, in childhood. It is, in short, a longing for love.

This longing can re surface later in life; but at that late time it can be mis understood as a desire for genital expression. If it is misunderstood by others, people who seek in adulthood only a loving human warmth feel outraged and dissatisfied if all they get is sex. Sometimes it can be misunderstood by the per son themselves, when they may think that in fact sex is all that they want, and they are bitterly disappointed when it does little to assuage their longing. The need can persist so acutely into adult life that it can undermine the possibility of any fulfilling adult relationship, and ruin lives. For its resolution it needs the possibility of acceptance, of understanding, of a therapy which perceives the child in the adult, and of regression within that therapy to work with it therapy that will allow the person to go back to the roots of the disruption in childhood without the distraction of trying to carry on a fully adult relationship at the same time. Tenderness, or human warmth, is a basic need of both men and women. If the blocking of it can be solved through therapy it can set the person free to live out a more equally balanced adult relationship.

Boss

Freudís famous paper Observations on transference love (1915) became fundamental to the psychoanalytic understanding of the phenomenon of the erotic transference. He had much valuable insight into its nature and its problems (see especially 20 25); yet even though he recognized some of its infantile roots he understood it in terms of adult sexuality, and brought to that understanding all the limitations and prejudices of his time. His paper betrays the therapistís fears of involvement and dependence; and it conveys a highly critical judgment of the unfortunate patient, though he did emphasize at the same time the need not to opt out but to stay with the transference as it was and to work at it, albeit on his own terms. Freud spoke, too, as if the erotic transference were a problem of women only, possibly because they formed the bulk of the patient population of hysterics with which he worked. He also treated it and spoke of it as if it were only a type of resistance, rather than a living sign of deep need and long standing pain (as resistance usually is when understood humanely).

If Freudís account in his paper is read closely, it seems to point to rather different conclusions, which were being explored concurrently by Ferenczi, and developed further by Balint. It is actually an excellent instance of the de velopment in Freudís patients of the need for regression. Freudís description of the beginning of an erotic transference in the course of a therapy (1915, 20) echoes almost exactly Balintís description many years later (1968, 131) of the phenomena which indicated a personís readiness for regression. Balint saw these phenomena as marking the entry into what he termed the arglos state, which he understood to be revealing an urgent need to go back into childhood to resolve lasting deficits from that period, and heralding a new beginning. Regression was then the work called for in order to deal with the void that had resulted from those early deficits.

Ferencziís papers (1931,1933) which were outlined in chapter 3 of this book, provide the foundation for this different understanding of the erotic transference. There is also an excellent book edited by Mann (1999), who accepts the erotic transference as an inevitable and essential component of therapy. He emphasizes that it needs working with and through, not reject ing or discarding. He clarifies how it can be both regressive (looking back to childhood / deprivation) and progressive (looking forward to adulthood / development). It is an instance of Fosshageís (1994) organization model of transference referred to on page 80 of chapter 5. If either the person in therapy, or the therapist, refuses to recognize its childhood origin and understands it only as a desperate longing for sexual union (which they are not going to get), the erotic transference can become a block on the therapy; if they are prepared to recognize its true origin, it can be a spur to progress.

If an erotic transference develops, how then can the therapist work with it? First, we need to take note of our own counter transference, to recognize the possibility that our adult sexuality is what is being aroused and we are actually attributing to the other person feelings which are our own. Next, that issue being clarified, we need to acknowledge the possible presence in the therapee of this sexual (connecting) form of transference, to bring it into the center of the therapy, and above all to accept it as real, and then, to work with the longing that lies behind it and empowers it. Denying the reality of this love or suggesting that it belongs only to childhood is a mistake: that can be an avoidance of any emotional closeness. The love is as real and present as the original yearning. It feels critically real to the person experiencing it; they feel dismissed and discarded if the therapist speaks of it as only trans ference or part of your infancy, or seeks some other way of avoiding its challenge and escaping its personal demands.

Such work can indeed be demanding, threatening, frightening, exciting, hopeful, bewildering, at times overwhelming, and very long term. However, if it is recognized for what it is, it is possible just to keep oneís head above water. The deprivation which gives rise to the need for tenderness can be so radical and early that it pervades every expression and wish; but it is not to be solved in a genital way, for that is not what it is, though it may well be made to appear so. The therapist has to communicate somehow that there are other ways of getting in touch than the genital and physical, and that there is a clamant earlier need for tenderness, for innocent sensuality, which underlies the needs of passion, for adult sexuality.

Our aim is to help people to connect with us and with one another, and to recognize each other as inter linked beings: neither dominating one another nor otherwise avoiding real connection. There can be enormous pressure both to dominate and to avoid in both therapist and therapee; but there can also be great rewards to be had in genuine sharing, giving and learning. It is dif ficult, but infinitely worth it: neither avoiding the erotic nor acting upon what it appears to be; that is, not dismissing the erotic transference as something perverted, nor feeling that genital sex is the answer to everything; but ac cepting the erotic transference as a sign of a deep, though temporarily maybe distorted, longing for human connection, bonding and love.

The "Negative Therapeutic Reaction"

The second example of the confusion of tongues between tenderness and passion lies in the concept of the negative therapeutic reaction. This is a particularly vivid example of something originating in classical psychoanaly sis which does violence to the child in an analysis, even though it is actually a misunderstanding of the phrase. Originally it meant a falling back in oneís progress in therapy; but by an alternative reading of the words making up the phrase it has come to mean conflict between therapist and therapee, held by some forms of classical psychoanalysis to be both inevitable and necessary. Evidence of being able to deal successfully with it is then required as the mark of a competent psychoanalytic therapist.

This understanding of it reflects, and encourages, a total confusion of tongues. The concept has been placed in quotation marks because it is badly understood and is muddled in its origin and its application, yet it has become an article of belief for some therapy trainings. In my own training I did not hear of the idea: many years later I learned from people in supervision with me that it had become a shibboleth of the local psychoanalytic therapy train ing. Trainees were required to experience it; indeed, it appeared, they were expected to bring it about, and finally to know how to deal with it. It is dif ficult to do that if it need not and does not happen.

The trouble is that the so called negative therapeutic reaction is an unfortunate artifact of the therapy situation when conducted according to the classical model. It is brought about by bad practice on the part of the therapist. When first used (Freud 1933a [1932]; Fenichel 1946, 298, 501) the phrase referred to a stage which sometimes occurred in an analysis when the analysand, threatened by the emergence of unconscious forces which they wished to keep under control, reacted against the analysis (not, neces sarily, against the analyst). One of its expressions was termed the flight into health, when the analysand decides they are all right after all and donít really need analysis. It is a negative reaction to the therapy rather than to the therapist; it represents peopleís ordinary resistance to change, however much it may outwardly be desired.

In distinction to this, the phrase nowadays has become displaced from the therapy on to the therapist. It is used in instances when negative transfer ence, which does properly refer to the therapist, would be a more accurate term. A strong negative transference is an understandable consequence of some analyses within classical psychoanalysis. In them the confrontational yet withholding stance of the analyst provokes, as might be expected, violent reactions in the analysand, or therapee. It is not stroppiness on the part of the patient but deliberate withholding on the part of the therapist which pro duces such an antagonistic stand off.

This had evidently become such a recurring pattern within the old model that it later came to be seen as an inevitable and indeed essential part of the therapy, which (together with the therapist) was held to be invalid unless it occurs. One of the aims of therapy in this style therefore appears as a result to be to produce, if not to provoke, such a hostile angry reaction in the thera pee, and to learn how to handle (or endure) it. One person whom I supervised appeared to be subjected to this model of provocation in their own training therapy. I used to hear bitter accounts of it. It seemed that their therapistís aim was to make them angry through goading questions, comments and criticisms. The therapist then retreated into the blank screen wall of silence and watched how the person coped. That was likely only to reproduce and reinforce a childhood trauma of frustration and of being blamed, and then not being allowed to defend oneself or to enter into any sort of dialogue with the persecutor. This time the trauma is inflicted by the therapist, and for the person to defend themselves is seen as further evidence of rebellion.

It would not be too far from actuality to see such a therapist, by their criti cal withholding of themselves, as deliberately seeking to produce a furiously angry reaction from the therapee in spite of their supposedly neutral stance. They seem to think that what they are required to do is to stay wooden, remote and unresponsive until the storm has passed and the therapee has learned the lesson that life is like that (as if they didnít know that already). It is not surprising if such a therapist gets the angry reaction that they expect, since the therapee is being cruelly frustrated in their search for some human help and support. They do not expect to get instead a reproduction of their earlier life, where adults around them may have been similarly withholding and judgmental: their frustration can know no bounds, yet the therapist denies all responsibility. It is a classic example of Ferencziís definition of trauma as the experience of an overwhelming force imposed by someone known and trusted by the sufferer, which is then denied by the perpetrator and others around them. It may teach furious resignation, withdrawal, and acceptance of helplessness as a way of coping with the world, but it is not very likely to lead to any sense of life or power or love. It can reproduce the very troubles from which the person is seeking release.

It is so unnecessary. No one should have to go through that. A more open and responsive attitude in the therapist means that such a negative thera peutic reaction need not, and does not, occur. It may happen in its original meaning, of the flight into health triggered by realization of the possibility of change: indeed it frequently does. We are all highly ambivalent about change, and it can be very much in the balance as to whether or not we de cide voluntarily to move into it. If someone does decide to proceed then they are entitled to an acceptance and an engagement which will support them in their struggle, rather than something which adds gratuitously to their pain and suffering.

A better criterion for a well trained therapist is to be someone who loves the people they work with, and certainly one who does nothing deliberately to provoke them to rage and impotence. We are there to empower people,

not to suppress or annoy them. Even with such a considerate therapist, inad
vertent slips and failures in sensitivity and understanding will provoke their
therapees often enough, especially in situations where narcissistic wounds are
re opened. The remedy is not to infuriate them further by added frustration
and coldness, but to acknowledge the happening, together with its failure
in empathy, and to seek to understand and heal it. It is one of the aspects
of psychoanalysis where the contrasts between adult and child, passion and
tenderness, confrontation and cooperation, are most marked not that such
aggravating withholding is suitable for an adult passionate encounter either.
In both types of work the therapist needs above all to be engaged and open.
That is the way in which liberating change can occur.

All in all, the general thrust of the insistence on experiencing the nega
tive therapeutic reaction as thus misunderstood is that anger is all right: love
is not. This was Suttieís (1935) main criticism of Freud and psychoanalytic
theory all those years ago. It is also worth noting that the same people who
promote such a fabricated situation as a core requirement of therapy are very
likely to be the same people who are most vociferous in decrying Franz Alex
anderís corrective emotional experience as a tool of therapy. It is, however,
just such an experience that they are trying to bring about. The difference is
that the apparently permitted corrective emotional experience is one of anger:
the rejected and criticized was one of love, seeking to undo the lack of it in
earlier life. The real fallacy in any imposed corrective emotional experi
ence is if it is contrived it must be genuine. We need to be real; and we
need to be careful in the selection and training of therapists: therapists who,
like good parents, will be alert to and wary of any hidden sadistic impulses.

Chapter Seven

Practical Issues

COMMUNICATION

We come now to some practical issues that result from the deepening and widening of psychoanalysis to include the earlier years and the child in the analysis. Work with the child necessarily requires a different approach from a psychoanalysis which works only with the adult. There is a child within that adult, and we have to get through to that child, remembering their fra gility and sensitivity, even if there is also adult strength and purpose. Not surprisingly, given the origins of psychoanalysis and the culture in which it grew, some of the issues raised by the different focus of the work result in considerable differences in practice. Some reflect contrasts between the vari ous models of psychoanalysis: some refer to more general issues which may arise within any model.

These practical matters relate to things which can best serve the aim and pur pose of the work. They are such things as promoting the growth of a relation ship, facilitating the recovery and expression of emotion within it, and reaching the person's deeply submerged early experiences. They could be said overall to be concerned with communication communication of the relationship itself, and communication within it. The first issue raised is that of respect, a quality already mentioned many times in passing. Respect for the other person can communicate both the fact of the relationship and the nature of it.

RESPECT

In the encounter of psychoanalysis or psychotherapy, there is one prime requirement for it to be a profound human interaction. Neville Symington

(1997, 190) puts it well: Respect for the other is the natural outcome of the emotional registration of the other as a person.   Respect for the other person is indeed, for me, the primary requirement of a therapist: it governs any feel ings that I might have about training, diagnostic labels and practice. It also rules out the antagonistic stance which many therapists seem to have towards their therapees: both the confrontational stance of Freudians, and the suspi cious attitude of Kleinians.

I was sent once a sample assessment written for the purposes of a training program. I hope it wasnít taken from an actual interaction, though I fear that it was. I was appalled by the language used to describe the   patient   and her perceived responses to therapy. It implied that she was out to defeat any move by the therapist to help her, and it assumed that this had been the previous pattern of her life, so that all sympathy should be with her partner. I cannot imagine anyone coming to therapy if their motive were indeed to undermine everything that therapy could do. Nor would they be likely to stay there, or benefit from it if they did stay, if they felt that that was the therapistís at titude to them. If they did appear to behave in the way alleged, it could only be because of earlier experience, not because of any personal antagonism to the therapist; although any response to the   patient   by the therapist of the nature recorded might well aggravate such antagonism and start off a vicious circle.

What is really needed is that the person be respected and their earlier experience be explored, understood, and reacted to in a new way; not aggra vated by the therapy. Possibly the ladyís reaction to the assessment, if it was recorded accurately, was because she sensed (if she wasnít actually told) that she was being seen with eyes of disapproval and oppositional judgment, and was being treated, and spoken to, accordingly. In this and in other respects, I feel that R. D. Laing was absolutely right in his criticisms of diagnostic practice (*Politics of Experience* 1967).

Failure to recognize the other as an equal, denial of their right to their own opinions, and any judgment of them that lacks sympathy and understanding are all instances of a lack of respect. Here I take pleasure in introducing my experience with a young man who was sent to me by his GP. He came having been diagnosed as schizophrenic by a psychiatrist. The label in this case re ferred to some instance of   disordered thoughts   (then, a standard diagnostic symptom). I found him to be a warm but damaged individual, a near genius in a family whose other members were anything but intellectual and who took out on him their differences from him. He was cooperative and interactive once he got to know me (and, for all I knew, before that), and possibly once he realized that I was not out to find fault. He had trenchant comments to make on medicine and on society: given his background these were perfectly understandable and ones that many might have shared. I was puzzled to know why he had been diagnosed as schizophrenic, so one day after we had got to know one another well I asked him. I asked if he could tell me anything about the disordered thoughts referred to in his psychiatric report. He said that it was when on one occasion he had asked his psychiatrist when she had last had sex. I said that that seemed a strange question. He said, Well, she had just asked me.

When working on this topic of respect for the other person in psycho therapy I was surprised as well as disturbed to find that there is little written about it by psychoanalytic writers. The one book which from its title might have been expected to deal with the subject, Roy Schaferís *The Analytic At titude* (1983), has nothing to say on this vital human aspect of the analytic encounter, although it is a touchstone in its definition of the analytic attitude throughout a wide range of its more technical aspects.

Some of the more blatant indications of a lack of respect are simple things like answering the telephone or the doorbell during sessions, or the analyst cleaning his nails or drinking coffee. Quite apart from being disrespectful of the other person, analysts and therapists would do well also to realize that the therapee can hear what they do, even if they canít see, and that any heard activity might arouse some feeling. Especially is this so for someone who at that moment is a child as well as an adult. Some of the feelings and memo ries might concern hearing but not seeing interactions between adults in their childhood. These could include, but certainly not be confined to, sounds of what is so delightfully called the primal scene in psychoanalysis (it makes one warm to the possibilities of primal therapy). The primal scene refers to parental intercourse: it is far more likely to have been fairly ordinary sounds of anger, dispute, or a disturbing silence.

The therapistís respect for the other person is shown, or not shown, in so many different ways. There was a school counselor who reported at a meeting on her work with one of the boys in her care, Iíve counseled and counseled him, but he still wonít do it . . . Bludgeoning is not a feature of respect. Or there is the dismissal through diagnostic labels, reflecting an unconscious dehumanizing attitude to people, speaking of them as less than whole per sons. It is difficult to maintain an arrogant position of power, or an attitude of disrespect, if the two people in the encounter recognize one another as equals. Making recordings of sessions without the other personís knowledge or consent is another example of overriding their humanity. Forcing interpre tations on them, as Freud himself records doing, is another. Thinking that we know better than the other person their meaning or their inner working is to lack respect, as is using judgmental, derogatory, dismissive or condemnatory language. It rides roughshod over them.

The one thing that matters is respect, and in order to respect someone we have to feel that they are basically the same as us. The undermining of such a feeling lies, for instance, behind military training which seeks to make the enemy seem alien beings, less than human. In the context of therapy, we need to feel that their experiences are basically one with ours (cf. Richard Bentallís *Madness Explained* 2004). This is one of the things that underlines the need for having our own therapy. Talking down to the other person as if they are an alien being is not likely to be a healing experience for them. We have to be aware that there is no basic difference between us: only circumstances. We hope indeed to help people to come to gain a respect for themselves which they have often lost, and to arrive at a feeling that they are ultimately the proud and autonomous agents of their own lives. Our respect for them affirms both of these things.

The need for respect would also exclude what is called back to backing. The usual custom of the analytic hour is to allow one hour for each person, divided into fifty minutes for the session, and the remaining ten minutes to phase over from one person to the next: in that ten minutes the therapist can attend to any personal needs or tasks. Back to backing means that only the fifty minutes for each person is allowed with no interval between, the subse quent patient being admitted immediately the previous one is released. One can get more people fitted in by this procedure but it is scarcely respectful, as it cannot possibly enable either full attention or full time to be given to either. It is also an extremely foolish and potentially draining way to work, likely to contribute to burn out (though that would assume a demanding commitment to each patient).

If there is no respect, we are going to damage both the people we work with and the work which we are seeking to do, and, of course, ourselves. Respect demands that full attention is given to the other person, with due regard for their personhood, throughout the full time that one is with them, without other activities intruding to break the mutual engagement. This works both ways: the analysand or therapee is expected also to treat the engagement as sacrosanct, not to be interrupted by any extraneous matter such as a mobile phone. The human interaction is what is crucial, and people may need to learn this basic fact.

This fundamental feeling about the urgent need for respect in psycho therapy was strengthened for me in later years when working in a therapeutic community. At a staff meeting one of the therapists referred to the members as being only a group of wonkies. Anyone with an attitude like that can scarcely hope to win the respect or cooperation of those with whom they work. In contrast, one of the non therapist members of the community said on one occasion, showing a much greater perception of reality, You can say what you like to us, as long as we know that you love us. Love, of which respect is an integral part, is the way to new life.

It became very obvious in that particular setting that those who had been trained as therapists without any recognized inner need of their own were very different in attitude and approach from those who had come to practice therapy as a result of their own need and who had experienced it themselves at the receiving end. It appears that training can sometimes be given for working as a therapist or counselor without any requirement that the trainee should understand it from the inside. One of the strongest features of the Guild of Psychotherapists, in contrast, which I discovered in my early search for training, was that they required of applicants that they should have had experience of pain in their own lives. I hope they still do.

People who are trained from above would appear to work, perhaps not surprisingly, on a vertical dimension: hierarchical, authoritarian, didactic. Others, who practice therapy in consequence of their own need, are working on a horizontal dimension: a companionship, going with the other on a journey. If therapists have not experienced pain in their own life, they can neither know what those in their care are talking about, nor the world that they inhabit. It is exactly like the difference alluded to earlier for those who have never known a damaged childhood. Never having been there it is like a foreign country, with strange inhabitants: it seems difficult for such practitioners fully to understand, empathize or identify with those who live within that world. Even if they respected and loved the person, there would unfortunately seem to be an innate difficulty in recognizing their experience or their inner world. I had the strange experience once of going with excruciating pain to a dentist whose receptionist said she had never known toothache: I felt I was on a different planet. To find someone who knows where you have been and what it can be like, and who honors you for having managed to cope so far, is itself a liberation.

Couch or Chair

One of the features of practice which is a bone of contention between different traditions and outlooks in psychoanalysis is the use of a couch. It might appear to be a trivial issue, but it has great bearing on the possibilities of mutuality, humanity and respect in the engagement.

Before I started therapy, one of the things I was sure of was that I didnít want to take it lying down. I wished to see my interlocutor, to see their face, their eyes, their expressions, their movements; to be aware how they were reacting to me as a whole, and where the words were coming from: what their attitude towards me was. I thus started off with a general feeling that the use of a couch was a peculiar sort of way to interact with anyone, but willing to try it if the person to whom I was committing myself felt it was necessary. Experience taught me that it can actually be a hindrance to the work: it inter feres with reality in damaging ways. I feel in consequence that the enforced use of a couch whether people want it or not is counter productive, and that there are strong reasons against it being seen as a sine qua non of psycho analysis and psychotherapy: it is by no means a trivial matter.

One reason for it being counter productive is that it puts people in a subor dinate position: one of them is lower than the other. My first training analyst commented that I behaved with him as if I was little psychotherapist; he, big psychoanalyst. This was intended to be a parody of what he thought I felt about the situation; but in fact it well reflected the actual position and what I sensed was his own attitude: I was lower than him. A prone position on a bed also implies illness and its frequent concomitant infantilization, although the situation of psychoanalysis is even more deeply depersonalizing as there is no physical necessity to be in bed. Further, in an illness, the doctor or nurse is usually at the side of the bed and visible to the patient, not beyond the head of the bed, invisible. Therapy is a paradoxical situation: we want to allow the person to be innocent and child like and to be able to re enter their early ex perience if they need and wish to, even if this means that they may sometimes behave in an infantile and childish manner. However, we do not want to force them from the start into such an infantile and petulant state.

A second reason why enforced use of the couch can be counter productive concerns the nature of human interaction. For one partner to be prostrate while the other is upright, particularly where this means that they cannot see each otherís faces, negates anything truly human. The contemporary findings of neuroscience (Schore 1994) suggest that being able to see another personís eyes is a vital aspect of human development. Deprivation of this visual and facial interaction in psychoanalysis by the use of a couch immediately de prives us of this aspect and sets psychoanalysis apart from the mainstream of human interaction and development. It effectively destroys any vestige of mutuality and any benefit that may come from gaze.

The origin of the use of a couch is declared to be that Freud did not like being stared at for hours on end. If so, that was his problem, from the conse quences of which hundreds of others have suffered since. It seems to be no good reason to ignore the wishes of anyone else. It was something to do with Freud as an individual, around which a mystique has been built up such as to perpetuate as essential for psychoanalysis what started out merely as an idiosyncratic artifact, as such things frequently do. The use of a couch lay ready to hand for him, because it developed from his earlier practice of hyp nosis. In actual fact what he used was not the flat couch, which is employed nowadays, but a chaise lounge, as can be seen in photographs of his study. The principal difference in that piece of furniture is that the person has the upper part of their body raised, more in the fashion of their posture in a chair. Where it differs from the normal use of a chair is that Freud sat behind the head of it, out of sight.

It was evidently not germane to him that invisibility favors impersonal ity. Together with the spatially lower position of the patient in relation to the analyst, it conformed to his model of a scientist studying an organism, rather than to one of an exchange of being. It was allied to a medical model of scientific treatment by an emotionally uninvolved operator, as indeed it was Freudís intention that psychoanalytic practice should be. It contrasts sharply with a model of open interaction between equals, where one person is prepared to become emotionally involved with the other in a fully human relationship, knowing that thereby lies risk but also the other personís hope of attaining their own personhood.

A more thought out reason sometimes adduced for using a couch, with the person lying prone, is that they are thereby enabled to reach deeper levels of feeling. This, in my experience both as a therapee and as a therapist, is not true; I have reached far deeper levels seated in a chair than I ever did lying down. The people with whom I have myself worked did not seem to have any difficulty in reaching their own deep feelings, whether of joy or of distress, in maturity or in regression. I think I have seen in print an argument that when lying down the head is lower, and emphasis is moved from the head to the gut; but it does not seem in practice to make any difference. What actually makes the difference depends on quite other factors, such as the atmosphere in which the two people meet. I personally found that isolation, such as I might feel when lying down with the analyst out of sight, actually inhibited the experiencing of feeling: I could only think about it. It was only when in company with another person and feeling that I was in rapport with them that emotions were able to come to the fore and be expressed. Someone to whom I mentioned this has told me that their experience was the opposite. Perhaps it depends both on the perceived empathy and receptivity of the other person, and perhaps on oneís earlier history.

Even if a couch should be used for the reason that it be thought to move the focus from head to gut, it does not require that the therapist be out of sight: it is being out of sight that makes the couch so antipathetic to its purpose and to a human encounter. If the person finds it helpful sometimes to lie down, the therapist can sit beside them as a caring equal, visible more like a nurse or a loving parent or friend than an uninvolved observer.

My strong antipathy to the use of a couch developed with my first train ing analyst, the classical Freudian with whom analysis degeneratcd into a crushing re living of early trauma. I had asked to use a chair rather than his couch when we first met. He never asked why. I think he saw it as a demon stration of stroppiness on my part, to be confronted and defeated. If he had asked, he might have discovered that my preference was due to a childhood trauma that had taken place when I was lying down; and the analysis might have taken a different course.

This emotional reaction, however, is not now my main reason for question ing the dogmatic use of a couch with the analyst hidden from sight. My main reason is that it obviates human interaction. This is reinforced significantly if the use of a couch is insisted on against the personís wishes, that is, to ne gate the therapeeís rights. The practice presumably reflects the attitude that the analyst knows best, and that his or her perception of reality is what is to prevail. Anyone who is suffering already from a perceived lack of freedom, or from a sense of exploitation or of being ignored, requires the opposite experience if they are to find release.

Chair and Couch

With my second training analyst, I stated my preference for a chair, and the request was accepted without question. He himself normally used a chair for his therapees, one like his own and opposite his, with nothing in between. We talked at times in the therapy about whether he made any use of the couch, since there was a divan beside him. His chief comment was that he used it mostly to sleep on between sessions if he was tired. Only sometimes was it used by therapees: if they asked about it, or he saw them looking towards it with what he interpreted as an attitude of longing, he would ask if they wanted to move there and lie on it.

I myself always followed this practice. Most people who came clearly had no thought of being anywhere other than in my matching chair, placed at an angle facing mine so that they did not have to look at me if they did not want to (and vice versa). There was no furniture between us. A few people, in contrast, especially psychotherapy trainees, came with a preconception that they would be required to lie down. I did have a divan in the room, beside my chair: it is what faced people when they came in. With those who expected to be made to lie on it I used to therefore discuss the matter, stating my own preference and the reasons for it. In every case I found that given the option they chose also to sit in a chair, at least for most of the time. I do not think that they were being conformist or bowing to my authority: if anyone did express a wish to move to the couch, they would do so, and I would alter my position accordingly so that they could still see me, and I them.

If people used the divan, they didnít often remain lying motionless on it for long: they sat up on it as well. More than one sat back against the cushions at the wall, using it as a seat but one which was nearer to me than their chair. Another used the cushions and the rug in autumn colours on it to make a nest of leaves, like a Babes in the Wood scenario. Sometimes, I would sit beside the person on the divan: on one or two occasions I held them if I felt that they needed to be held and if they shared that feeling, and we both felt it was OK to do so. Physical contact, for very good reasons, can sometimes not only be helpful but indeed necessary.

At one time I discarded my divan because no one was making any use of it, and moved it out of the room. The move lasted only a week: I got a strong feeling in its absence that there needs to be such a piece of furniture available, in case the therapee should ever want it. One person whom I was seeing at the time, having said that they didnít want to use it, changed their mind once it disappeared, and wanted it back. Without it, there was a void. It can, for instance, be useful for regressing to childhood (it is, after all, very like a childís bed); or for people to get more easily at their feelings if they feel that that position will help them do so; or simply to play; or to change their position in the room in relation to the therapist. To be entirely without such a facility deprives the person of a chance of doing something which they may desperately wish and moreover need to do as part of their therapy. The important thing is that it should be their choice; and that it is open to discussion. I moved the divan back. Like episcopacy in the church, it is of the *bene esse* of analysis, not the *esse*.

A recent article in the *IJPA* (Celenza, 2005, **86**, 6, 1645) would indicate that a greater openness towards the use of the couch is developing in modern psychoanalysis: this is a very welcome change.

BYPASSING DEFENSES

The next major practical area relating to the orientation of psychoanalysis towards a more child friendly model is the facilitating of emotional exploration and the reaching of the pain and tangles of the buried years. This moves from communication of the relationship to communication within it. The first aspect of the latter which we shall consider is ways by which we can reach someoneís core, the second is the place of words in that. A third aspect is the use of physical touch.

In order to enable us to make our way through life we develop various ways of coping with its hazards: we use whatever proves to be both possible and effective at the time. These used to be called defenses or defense

mechanisms, and their varied forms were elucidated many years ago by
Anna Freud (1937). Defense mechanisms served to enable people to deal
with the effects of trauma, to avoid pain whether remembered in mind or in
body, and to cope with interactions with others. From the different point of
view of a modern, respectful psychoanalysis, the means by which they do
it would be better called coping mechanisms. People could benefit from
an understanding of how much they have had to cope with and the several
ways in which they managed to do so. They could do with credit for coping.
Unfortunately their methods can get fossilized and carried over into situa
tions which are markedly different from the original. In these new situations
they are inappropriate and can frequently be provocative and self destructive.
Until such a response is rendered unnecessary, any attack or perceived at
tack naturally arouses anxiety and serves only to strengthen the defenses (or
coping mechanisms). In the old model such strengthening was termed re
sistance and was spoken of disapprovingly, as if the patient was thought
to be resisting the efforts of the well intentioned analyst to help; whereas the
analyst might actually be reinforcing the need for the defensive actions.

Defenses are indeed needed to cope with unexpected happenings and
threats to balance and composure posed by life, by other people's behavior,
and by the world of passion, however unhelpful those defenses may prove to
be in the long term. In psychoanalysis they are obviously also necessary if the
analyst is felt to be part of that world. If he or she is aggressive and confronta
tional, the person will react in the same way as to any other assault. Defenses
are particularly called into play with a confrontational model, though it is
difficult for any approach to avoid touching on sensitive topics inadvertently.
People will defend themselves vigorously, if only by resentful silence, and
will naturally and instinctively cover up any sensitive spots. Such defenses
are less necessary if the analysis is conducted on a more cooperative level, in
a world of sensitivity and concern (i.e., of tenderness), where people need not
feel so threatened. There is then not so much need for defenses to be evoked
(though it is impossible to avoid it completely), and one can get fairly directly
to the underlying anxieties and hidden feelings.

In this new model, resistance, if one has to use that term, is seen more to
show where pain and danger are located, equivalent to our reaction when a
sore spot is touched; it is a helpful indicator to the therapist of where trouble
lurks, and of the need to proceed with caution. It might better be termed
sensitivity, and it needs equally sensitive response and exploration. It needs
a cultivated gentleness of touch until such touch becomes instinctive: what
Ferenczi called the exercise of tact. This contrasts sharply in practice with
treating people aggressively, confrontationally and judgmentally as if they
are the wayward adults they may appear to be or indeed that they may have

become: this is more likely to be the result of reaction to confrontational treatment rather than expressing their true character. Ferenczi indeed believed that the resistance . . . belonged to the analyst, who, if not actively disliking patients . . . was often afraid of them . . . and drew back from the intensity of the therapeutic encounter (Kirshner 1994, 239).

A word is called for about a well known and much used model for working with defenses. I refer to David Malanís triangle of conflict, or triangle of defense (1979, 92), involving defense, anxiety and the feeling or emotion which arouses the anxiety and which the defense is trying to protect against. Malan suggests that it is necessary first to tackle the defense: but this is likely only to increase the anxiety and to strengthen what we are trying to get past. What is vital to tackle first is the anxiety: to acknowledge it gently and to identify its content; thence to understand why the particular feeling or emotion that stirs it needs to be defended against in the first place; and why the emotion is painful. Often the anxiety is founded on a misunderstanding or misperception. Once that is cleared, the defense may lose much of its power and permit working with the emotion which it protects. Even just to have it recognized that anxiety is present, and to have it brought into the open, can result in a considerable lowering of tension. It makes the defenses, or unsuitable mechanisms of coping, less necessary.

Along with treating peopleís coping mechanisms with respect and understanding such that they can be worked with and made matters of choice rather than of blind and panic filled compulsion, it is clearly important that we also develop and use avenues of inquiry and exploration where possible which do not call these mechanisms into action in the first place. To this we now turn.

Metaphor

The first of these avenues is the use of metaphor. With metaphor peopleís coping mechanisms do not need to be called into play, because they are not roused or challenged. If there is no threat, there is no need to protect oneself. Metaphor gets through, or rather under, peopleís defenses, by carrying no threat. It works with anxiety in a way which provides a benign alternative to tackling directly either anxiety or the defenses which anxiety calls into play. The subtitle of Murray Coxís book on metaphor expresses this beautifully with his choice of *The Aeolian Mode* to suggest its mode of working (Cox and Theilgaard 1987; see also Hobson 1985). Like an Aeolian harp, or wind chime, metaphor stirs answering chords as it passes into and through us. It stirs chords, because it uses a relevant image but from another context, especially a physical image touching the core of our being, which is able to move us in a non threatening way.

The power of metaphor springs from the earliest days of life, when interac
tions are bodily, and physical imagery expresses emotional meanings. Only
gradually do we come to use the symbols of language: the symbolic then
gradually takes over from the somatic, though the latter continues to persist
unattended. The development of language is cognitive coding being overlaid
on sensory, as a result of which we come to describe emotions in physical
language and use such metaphors to convey what we are feeling; but the sen
sory experience is nevertheless still there. Metaphor is therefore something
which is physical at root, then symbolic, and in consequence has multiple
meanings. Examples abound, such as words sticking in the throat, insults
canít be swallowed, someone is a pain in the neck, I was paralyzed
with fear, I have a weight on my shoulders, she is head over heels in
love (cf. Trad 1993, 318). Feeding metaphors are particularly plentiful: be
ing fed up, having something gnawing at my vitals, or many others that
people use without thinking.

Using this sort of language and being alive to its reverberations gets past
defenses: it makes them unnecessary and therefore does not evoke them.
At a group therapy session, a lady whose everyday life involved making
cakes, especially sophisticated wedding cakes, mentioned more than once
the tiers of a cake on which she was currently working. The repetition
seemed to have some significance. When this word was fed back to her in a
questioning tone, it immediately brought up in her the other word with the
same sound, tears, and she started to weep. Those tears, and their connec
tion with her own marriage, were what she had been talking about without
realizing it. The instance of getting into hot water mentioned earlier in
the book is another example of conjoined meaning expressing two things
simultaneously at different levels. If we are alert to the use of words and
phrases with multiple meanings, it can be helpful just to repeat them back.
On the repetition they may strike the person who used them with the full
impact of their manifold meaning. Metaphor can touch the heart of the mat
ter directly, but gently.

Questions and Suggestions

A further effective way of avoiding stalemate, and of letting people go at
their own pace of self revelation without feeling that they are being attacked
or confronted, is by phrasing inquiries as open ended questions. These are
questions which do not immediately demand nor indeed do they permit a
monosyllabic answer of yes or no. They do not put an abrupt stop to the
process. Instead, they open out discussion and lead to an expansion of pos
sibilities: not were you frightened? but how did that feel to you?

Open ended questions require to be accompanied by tentative statements and suggestions; not laying down the law or speaking as if the therapistís per ception is the only reality, but seeking to elicit the other personís being. The exact reaction of the other person to such provisional and evocative remarks needs in addition to be observed sensitively, and recorded in some part of the therapistís being: it may be a significant pointer to things that might other wise remain concealed. The therapist is required to offer hypotheses that can be accepted or rejected without the other person feeling that they are defying an authority. Examples of such evocative comments could be that sounds like what you were saying the other day, or, I wonder if that reminded you of anyone : the briefer, the better. It is definitely not good therapy to make a pronouncement stating a conviction of oneís own as if that is the only true interpretation of affairs, or implying that differing from it can be seen only as perverse opposition. Perhaps, maybe, it sounds as if are frequent starters to therapeutic sentences: they may be repetitive for the therapist who makes them hour by hour; but hopefully the therapee doesnít hear them fre quently enough for them to stale.

The last starter, as if, draws attention to the frequent use of simile as well as metaphor as a highly useful way of suggesting an explanation, a parallel or an alternative way of seeing reality. It is different from metaphor; and in its extreme form, when the as if actually becomes the perceived reality, it is taken as a sign of psychosis: when being Napoleon is taken as the reality rather than reflecting on what it might be like to be Napoleon. To suggest a different way of seeing or interpreting things can open a door to new life and new possibilities, which is what psychotherapy is about.

Humor and Paradox

We seek also to promote emotional openness and interchange. Anything that will do this is grist for the psychotherapeutic mill. A further invaluable tool in this regard is the use of humor and paradox, which both touch emotion. They are things that can be shared and enjoyed by both parties and which, like metaphor, make defenses redundant. I read once a ponderously solemn article in a counseling journal about the propriety of humor in psychotherapy, as if the interaction must be preserved from anything so trivial, and as if we can only be healed in an atmosphere of gravity, solemnity and sacrifice, not of fun and enjoyment. Freud defined maturity as the ability to love and to work. He did not mention play: he may have regarded playing, like childhood, to be immature, not to be indulged in by adults.

Laughter, on the other hand, is a releaser of emotion, and a great strength ener of friendship. To be able to laugh together, to become children again and play together, is a great asset in life and love: it strengthens our common foundation, cements our bond, and represents a true maturity. People who cannot play miss out on life, often to their great distress. Laughter and emo tion are linked, often unfortunately at other people's expense: it is one way of connecting with our deepest feelings about ourselves. One theory of laughter suggests that we laugh when a strong, unexpected emotion is released which we do not immediately recognize, and which we do not have the time to process and identify. Instead we laugh: in laughter we are unusually open to one another. Therapy may have its problems, its tragedy and its solemnity: so does life. But that is not all that there is to it, either. Hopefully there can also be comedy, lightness and joy.

Closely associated with the exercise of humor is the making of blindingly obvious, bizarre, enigmatic, plain silly, or paradoxical remarks (and gentle teasing, if suitably timed). They have the power to bring people up short and break through an established mood. They shake logic, and move firmly into a right hemisphere emotional world. This is not the same as the paradoxical imperative of behavioral therapy, where the therapist enjoins the therapee to carry out actions which are the opposite of what is actually intended: this strikes me as distinctly unethical. The sort of paradox to which I refer as being invaluable in analytic therapy is best illustrated by an example of an appropriately bizarre comment.

An angry therapee described their partner as an arsehole: he doesn't give a shit. Not a very efficient arsehole, I muttered. It brought the person to a halt. What did you say? they asked suspiciously. I repeated my remark. What do you mean? they demanded. Well, the purpose of an arsehole is to give a shit. The incongruity resulted in laughter and a reversion to a slightly more realistic approach to the subject of the person's partner. Ben Churchill told me once that anything useful said in psychotherapy was always either obvious, obscene or absurd. I don't know if the observation was his own or came from someone else, but it is very true: such remarks penetrate defenses and stir the substrate of our being and emotion.

WORDS

We have been speaking in the last section about promoting effective com munication between the two people involved in the therapy relationship that will help it to achieve its aims. A very important additional aspect of this is the use of words.

The use of metaphor, of open ended inquiry, of tentative hypotheses and of humor and paradox highlights the importance of the precise language that we use. Ferencziís papers stress the need for us to speak child language even in the analysis of adults. One of my supervisors made the point touched on earlier (in chapter 3). That was, always to use language that was as childlike as possible, and as earthy as possible. It helps people to get out of their heads, to get into their bodies, to have their feet on the ground, and to remain close to the level of childhood, where most troubles have their origin.

Being earthy in speech has this effect because it serves one of the same functions as metaphor: it connects with the physical substrate of early living and childhood and it links that with the more symbolic and cognitive use of words. Language and feeling find connection; understanding and experience are brought together. The use of physical language is vivid and fresh: it can surprise, and, as in metaphor, without the need for thought, send us back to levels which otherwise might take a long time to reach.

This attitude towards language is in marked contrast with that of classical psychoanalysis (if only to judge by its literature). The classical model proj ects the view that conflict is the problem, and that an often highly academic interpretation is the answer: rationality rules. The analyst is a detached figure uncovering the patientís inner conflicts, and, using only words, communi cates understanding and explanation. It echoes the medical model, but is one in which the patientís words represent the disease and the analystís words are the diagnosis and the cure. The latter constitute the understanding and expla nation of the disease. The analyst in the classical model is thus the possessor of truth and the perceiver of reality; through interpretation he or she imparts this superior knowledge to the analysand.

Verbal Interpretation

In spite of that, it is nevertheless emphasized in classical theory that mere intellectual converse is not adequate for change in therapy: for interpretation to be mutative it has to conform to certain requirements. It has to be related to what is happening between analyst and analysand (i.e., to the transference), it has to be suitably timed, and, most important of all, it has to have emotional impact (Strachey 1934). Strachey says that the patient must experience something actual (127). This, from within the mainstream of classical psy choanalysis, is astonishingly parallel to Ferencziís insistence on re experienc ing rather than merely remembering, which so upset Freud. Again, it makes one wonder about the latterís objection to what Ferenczi said. If verbal in terpretation conformed to the above characteristics then it was held to be the absolutely essential element in psychoanalysis. Unfortunately in some hands it could and did become mere intellectual understanding, which was in addi tion sometimes forced upon the patient whether they agreed with it or not.

It is assumed within classical psychoanalysis that it is this verbal inter
pretation which brings about change. But is it indeed interpretation, or is it
something else, such as understanding, explanation, insight, containing, or
just being there? In the light of the essentials of psychoanalysis which we
picked out earlier, what place does interpretation play in psychotherapy, and
what is the relevance of the sole use of language?

Interpretation was originally considered to be essential, and within classi
cal psychoanalysis it still is. Its two invariant components in that model have
been understanding, and explanation, both expressed verbally. Laplanche and
Pontalis, in *The Language of Psychoanalysis* (1967), say Interpretation is
at the heart of Freudian doctrine and technique. Psychoanalysis itself might
be defined in terms of it, as the latent meaning of given material (cited in
Lomas 1987, 16). While initially interpretation meant explanation in terms
of drive theory, even within that theory its meaning changed. First it meant
making the unconscious, conscious; then with Freudís later structural model
it became where id is, there shall ego be, its purpose being to strengthen
the ego, our responsible adult part, in its control of the id, the source of our
primitive instinctual life. But whatever the model in classical psychoanalysis,
verbal interpretation remained the recognized agent of change.

As other models of psychoanalysis, namely deficit models, regressive mod
els and relational models came to the fore, the precise meaning of interpretation
changed further. It now has a much wider application and has come to be seen
more as leading to an overall integration (Lomas 1987). It still plays an es
sential role, but the emphasis has shifted. Increasingly it is seen as not the only
essential; as also that verbal interpretation and conflict interpretation are only
part of it; they are not all the occasions of interpretation that there are. This has
been especially so with the development of regression (Balint, Winnicott), and
with the concepts of containing and holding (Bion, Rycroft). The verbal is only
a part of this (Stolorow et al. 1994). The focus has shifted to the interaction of
the couple, to what is happening between them as well as inside one of them.
The arena of interpretation has thus come now to refer to all of that: to words,
feelings and movements covering not only occasions of conflict, but also occa
sions of deficit, of developing relationship, and of sheer confusion.

Kohut (1977) says, in criticism of a wooden classical approach to inter
pretation: an inhuman computer like machine which gathers data and emits
interpretations does not supply the necessary psychological milieu for healing
(Siegel 1996, 137). What is needed is a quite different approach to the person;
one of sensitivity and respect, regarding them as responsive human beings,
seeking to understand their world, how it might have gone wrong, and how they
are feeling about it. The therapist then offers an understanding, an interpreta
tion or an explanation in congenial and empathetic terms, trying to find the

meaning of their experience together, and seeing if it makes sense to the other person often revealed by a jolt in the gut rather than an assent in the brain.

Interpretation in consequence involves all the many varied happenings of therapy: free association, dreams, parapraxes; transference, counter transfer ence, and the ambience of the entire situation; language and metaphor; feel ings, body language, and symptoms. Within this whole range, interpretation extends far beyond words, and yet, within both models, whether drive or re lational, it is still seen as having two parts understanding, and explanation. It stands as the executive agent in the overall aim of the four essential tools of psychoanalysis; that is, the search for meaning.

Other Ways of Making Sense

As recorded earlier in this chapter Balint pointed out some years ago that classical psychoanalysis is based on the principle of interpretation leading to insight, rather than on relationship leading to maturation. Interpretation of that earlier nature was for people with an intact sense of self, who were able to use verbal communications such as ideas and symbols; it belonged to the level of neurotic conflict, and can mean little to someone working in a pre verbal state. With the latter one has to work more through the relationship itself with its transference and counter transference, using non verbal com munication, and bringing feelings into the open.

Balint further says, in relation to his own developing work (1968, 14), we found that there are at least two levels of analytic work; consequently it is very likely that there are two levels of therapeutic processes . . . one aspect of this difference is the different usefulness of adult language at the two levels. Balintís finding is echoing Ferencziís (1933) work in identifying and teasing apart the languages of tenderness and passion, and underlies the contention of this book that there is need not only for a recognition but also an imple mentation of the difference between the two levels. In the previous chapter we dealt with some of the phenomena involved in working at a level where adult language can be contra indicated. We saw that since the time of Balintís words these levels which refer more to the child in the adult and to the power fully active buried remnants of childhood, had widened into three major sub divisions (organizing/psychotic, borderline and narcissistic).

Balintís and Ferencziís work links with that of Winnicott, Bion and oth ers on holding or containing as being an essential accompaniment of interpretation at this level which involves engaging with the child. We need therefore as always to be careful to recognize which of the languages is the more appropriate for the particular therapy in which we are engaged. It can be very easy for an analyst to mistake the level at which analytic work is taking place, to respond inappropriately with the adult language of passion to someone who is at the more primitive, innocent level, and to omit what the child might desperately need.

I listed factors at the beginning of the previous subsection (verbal in terpretation) as possible components of the curative process involved in interpretation. They were understanding, explanation, insight, holding, con taining, and being there. They are all present and all closely connected with one another to make a whole, particularly when we are working with the child (which is most of the time). Above all, it is most important that the therapist should just be there. I was told early on by a supervisor that this was more vital than anything one might ever say, however perceptive or clever. The fact that the therapist is there, whatever happens, come rain or shine, is the most important factor in holding and healing.

TOUCH — *excellent section*

The last form of communication to be considered is the physical; that is, touch. Touch is essential to embodied people. Without it, we become schiz oid, divorced from earth and reality. Yet deliberate touch, and indeed any physical contact (other than, in some countries, a handshake), is generally understood to be forbidden in classical psychoanalysis, and in psychoanalytic psychotherapy: it is ruled out ab initio.

This is perhaps partly out of a fear of psychoanalysis losing its scientific standing: partly, because of the original growth of psychoanalysis out of medicine; partly, a consequence of having its roots in the classical, verbal, ab staining tradition; partly, because of fears of sexual activity (as are put ironi cally in Freudís letter to Ferenczi rebuking him for his permissiveness, on the lines of cannabis leads to heroin); partly, from a fear of the unknown; and partly also, perhaps, the embargo on touch might reflect an analystís own fears of closeness. There would appear to be all sorts of possible origins and dynamics for the ban. Touch certainly can lead to complications, and if one wants to play safe, any physical contact is best avoided. Whether or not that is necessarily best for the other person is a different matter. If, on the other hand, one is willing to take the risk, and to allow holding, it is almost cer tainly a phase, like dependence, that passes, as it does in childhood. It is not likely to be required forever   and it can always be renegotiated.

The question arises acutely in psychoanalytic psychotherapy because of its development beyond the verbal and classical approach, together with the opening up of the area of early childhood and infancy, where touch is an im portant avenue of both experience and nurturing. Several of those who have pioneered work in this area have used touch: Ferenczi and Balint among them, also Winnicott and Little. They have touched, and held, regressed patients.

Balint changed his mind about touching and clinging from an initial refusal to do so, when he realized that the desire for it was not so much a yearning for primary love as a reaction to trauma, an expression of, and a defense against, the fear of being dropped or abandoned (Stewart 1996, 43). As a result of his realization Balint came to permit touch not in order that the therapist might be a better mother, but to enable the developing of an atmosphere of trust that might overcome the fear of abandonment. He felt that that made a considerable difference; though separation of the two aspects seems somewhat artificial, and the desire could be for both. Primary love (the quality of a good mother) is itself a remedy for abandonment: Balintís distinction makes it sound as if there is something inherently wrong with being loving. Possibly love is understood even in such discussions as being something to do with passion rather than with tenderness, with the adult rather than with the child.

Casement (1985) devotes a chapter to his inner struggle with whether to al low finger holding or not: it has become a classic account of the dilemma that a therapist might face. He eventually decided not to accede to his patientís request. Regardless of any opinion about that particular decision, I would say, with respect, that having read and re read his account carefully I do not feel that he was working with someone who was in deep regression. His account seems to show that the therapy was at the verbal, and therefore at the adult, passionate level: though there might still have been other reasons against granting the request.

Harold Stewart advises against any form of touching, one of his grounds being that it may conceal more going on than it reveals. The difficulty con nected with the subject is shown by the manner in which it is so easy to slip into discussing it from the viewpoint of passion. I feel that Stewart himself may risk confusing the two languages, of passion and of tenderness, of adult and of child. He says in another place concerning hand or finger holding, that he has only been asked by females, because, to quote, he has no experi ence of work with homosexual males (1992, 121). That is an adult, genital, passionate reference: in regression at the level of the basic fault, people are not at the adult hetero or homo sexual level. They are at a child level; sen sual, but not genital. At this level it is not only homosexual males who might have a need or craving for warmth and bodily contact. All males might and all females. It is something belonging to the child, to all, to the language of innocence and tenderness, of comfort, contact and warmth, to sensuality and bonding. Yet at the same time we have to take note of the fact that it can very readily become generalized when one or both of the parties is adult; including in the therapy situation.

The question of touch and physical contact is raised even more acutely by the work of Lawrence Hedges on his listening perspectives. As one goes fur ther back through the eras of development, words give way to other means of getting into touch with the person. As far as physical touch is concerned this would involve acting in such a way as might be comforting to the child in the adult but might possibly be misinterpreted by the adult. A child might not misunderstand; but this child is also an adult, for whom its meaning might be something quite different, as Stewart also would appear to be saying. It needs most of all to be discussed thoroughly by the people involved. Lawrence Hedges suggests (1994.2) the use of a signed contract of informed consent: this point is returned to in chapter 9.

Touching in psychotherapy obviously connects also with the general ques tion of boundaries. Gabbard and Lester (1995) deal excellently with this topic in their book *Boundaries and Boundary Violations in Psychoanalysis*. They deal extensively with Ferencziís work, and, though written from a generally conservative viewpoint, their book does set out the relevant issues, both in Ferencziís work and generally, in a way that I have not seen elsewhere. Its ac count of what they call the love sick, and I might prefer to call the love starved, therapist brings a great deal of clarity and understanding to a very important subject. But chiefly, it points out the critical difference between boundary vio lations and boundary crossings: the latter might on occasion be beneficial to the therapee (1995, 123). In this regard, in relation to the questions concerning tenderness raised in this present book, it is worth noting the further distinction which has already been made implicitly; that is, between breaching an adult sexual boundary, and permitting sensual human touch at a child level.

More recently, writers of papers presented at the John Bowlby Memorial Conference 2003 (reprinted in White 2004) have been bold enough to attempt to bring discussion of this hidden topic into the light of day. This has been fol lowed with the publication by Karnac of *Touch Papers: Dialogues on Touch in the Psychoanalytic Space* (Galton 2006) which builds further on the issues raised. In the latter book there is an excellent paper by Camilla Bosanquet cit ing an instance in which she used touch as part of the healing process. There is a further excellent paper by Nick Totton on Body Psychotherapy, though it is both significant and regrettable that he had to go outside the bounds of analytic psychotherapy to develop his approach.

Overall, one can say with confidence that it is important to touch; but it is also important to remember that there are other ways of touching people than the physical. On one occasion when I spoke to a training course about Ferencziís work and the challenges with which it faces us, all that one of the senior therapists could ask at the end was do you touch your patients? I should have answered I hope so.

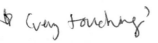

Chapter Eight

Some Clinical Aspects

A HUMAN RELATIONSHIP

All that I have mentioned of my experience persuaded me that what is tak
ing place in the strange situation of psychotherapy is an ordinary human
relationship, and that the phenomena occurring are those which occur in any
ordinary human relationship. The fact that the psychotherapy interaction
takes place in a particular setting for a particular purpose under particular
circumstances may make it special; but it does not mean that the processes
involved are any different from those in everyday life, merely that the pur
pose and setting enables us to identify, study, promote and make use of those
processes. This is saying no more than Peter Lomas (1993) has said about
therapy, and Richard Bentall (2004) has said about madness. The clinical
consequences of such a very ordinary human approach to psychoanalysis,
with a child at the heart of it, are many.

Thus the first meetings between the two people are laying the foundation
for the sort of relationship that may develop, determining whether we will
wish to meet again, and whether we feel that the possible outcome will be
something that we want. Essentially it requires some degree of rapport: if
that is not present, it is not likely to augur well for either process or outcome.
This is in keeping with the observation by Atwood and Stolorow (1993) that
someoneís analyzability is not assessable on the therapeeís psychological
structures alone, but on the interaction: it is a property of the therapee thera
pist system. Above all, the first meetings are to test the creative possibilities
of continued encounter, whether it will be sufficiently fulfilling for each of
the people involved. This may be in respect of the healing of disorders or the
satisfaction of aspirations and longings on the part of the therapee, and career
satisfaction on the part of the therapist. However, most of all, the fulfillment lies

just in the being together. With some partnerships this will be more so than with others; but in this again it is similar to relationships outside therapy.

Where the special experience that therapy offers can be of particular value is in situations in which the ends hoped for are difficult to achieve in other relationships of life. Therapy is valuable where the need of the one person is deeper than can be satisfied ordinarily: where it is difficult for them to form a relationship at all; where the person may be too damaged; where more restraint is called for than can be expected from an ordinary partner; where understanding of the past and study of the present are needed beyond the point that is usually possible because of the everyday demands of life; and es pecially where the unresolved residues of childhood demand that one partner needs to be allowed to become a child again and to be engaged at that level. Sometimes, if one is lucky, it may be possible to find that these conditions can be met in an ordinary friendship with a unique friend, or in a partnership with an understanding partner. One needs the partner to be someone who is able not only to recognize and contain the needs of the other, but also to be able to regress to the childhood state themselves, and to restrain their own needs from interfering too much with this.

Sometimes, however, the needs and demands of the one partner are too deep to be understood by someone who has not had any similar experience, or are too clamant for the other to cope with, and they put a strain on the relationship which it cannot maintain. Those are the sort of situations where psychotherapy can help: where these early tangles and urgent longings can be worked with outside the everyday relationship, both to take the strain off that, and to give some hope of resolving the dangerous subversive dynamics that are so damaging to it. That is the difference between psychotherapy and relationship counseling such as Relate. The focus of the latter is on the relationship, to deal with problems arising from the sharing of a common life by two individuals. The focus of psychotherapy is on the earlier life of one or both of the individuals, and on the potentially disruptive life experience which they may have imported into their relationship. All psychotherapy can help with some problems, but intensive psychotherapy in particular can assist the damaged child in one or both partners to grow so that they can enjoy a more fulfilling equality within an adult relationship.

FORMATION OF BONDS

The first requirement in forming a relationship is to form a bond between the people concerned. The formation of bonds in psychotherapy is also the same as in any other relationship, in spite of the constraints of time, setting, schedule of appointments, rules, conventions, and payment of one participant by the other. These provide the framework within which the work of forming bonds can be carried out. Their actual creation, though largely spontaneous, may be a more self conscious process than normal because of the setting. Much depends on there being an initial rapport between the two parties, and on the development of a firm mutual commitment strong enough to survive upsets, disappointments, misunderstandings and the surfacing of long buried emotions and of challenges to trust. Yet it still occurs in the same instinctive way as between child and mother; the underlying process that carries the interaction on its way does its unseen work.

As sessions progress there comes the click of a bond being formed, of a developing attachment, and of a relationship, however tenuous, becoming established. Suddenly the attachment is there, and with it the possibility of change. This moment can be quite frightening: to realize sharply that it has happened, and that one is now committed to a lengthy and costly engagement. For me, it was as if I had a spare valency, to use an analogy from chemistry, waiting to find someone with whom it could bond. The experience of losing at an early age someone to whom I was deeply attached seems to have pre pared me for it it left an antenna searching for its home. I would conclude from other people's responses that something similar happened for them; in my role as their therapist I was supplying a lost connection for which they, in turn, had been searching all their lives.

This again is something which occurs in ordinary encounters in daily life. What happens in therapy is an extension of a process which takes place every day, but one which through focused attention, understanding and training it is possible to hone into a valuable instrument of healing. This may not be a highly scientific explanation of what happens, but in some at least of the first encounters in psychotherapy it is what appears to me to occur: and the journey of psychotherapy begins.

Some people find it extremely difficult to form a bond, reflecting early obstacles and confusions: some may be aggressively antagonistic; some may be almost completely shut off. There nevertheless seems to be some core in people somewhere where the yearning for connection remains and a deep bond can in fact eventually be made which carries the couple through the upsets, the conflicts and the inner vicissitudes which arise along the way: these are inevitable daily happenings of psychotherapy as of life. The latent longing for that profound bond brings them to therapy and the grow ing sense that they may have found it keeps them there and enables them to be open to the process that is taking place between themselves and the therapist. This is in spite of all the old entrenched dynamics which conspire against it. The therapist has to develop skill and sensitivity in nurturing the bond, in recognizing its possibilities, and in overcoming obstacles to its formation and development.

Above all perhaps, the therapist has always to be prepared for the unex pected, and to have no preconceptions. Preconceptions cloud perception. As Kohut (1985) put it: nothing interferes more dramatically with acquir ing a deep understanding of a patient than premature closure. If you think you know, then you cut yourself off from taking in more and more details with that pleasurable expectant puzzlement, until you finally see a totally unexpected configuration (266 267). I had that quotation fixed inside the cupboard above my desk for all my working life, and used to pass it on to trainees at lectures and seminars which I conducted.

Someone who had come through years of therapy full of unfulfilled long ing gave me a passage expressing this need to have no preconceptions which I have kept ever since inside the same cupboard, beside the quotation from Kohut: He walked right into the dark caverns of my doubt and confusion and fear. He did not stand at the entrance of the cavern and shout at me to come out. He did not pose foolish questions about how I got there in the first place. I guess that I was most surprised that he did not even blame me, either for being there or for not being able to muster enough strength to find my way out. He just walked in and shared the darkness with me. I did not have to explain it to him. He knew that I could not. Most of all, he knew how dark it really was. He had been there before.

It goes almost without saying that I believe Bowlbyís Attachment Theory to be of supreme importance for psychotherapy. Psychotherapy repeats the processes of attachment, and for its success especially in work with the child in the analysis, it depends on the formation of bonds. To omit Bowlbyís work is an impoverishment, depriving psychotherapy of something essential to its work and understanding. The work of Bowlby and his successors, like that of Erikson, is based on observation, as well as, in the case of the former, on experi ment. It thereby has a firm scientific basis; something on account of which he was extruded from the psychoanalytic establishment, to the latterís great loss. It seems so self evident that his work is both scientific and true to experience that it is hard to understand why his exclusion (like Ferencziís) is not immedi ately acknowledged and his work restored to the mainstream of psychoanalytic thought and development where it belongs: but to do that, the mainstream would have to widen its flow and to some extent alter its course.

The Underlying Process

Mention of processes raises the question of what it is that takes place in psychotherapy to enable change. One perception is that of a happening below the level of consciousness which carries the encounter along despite what may appear to be happening on the surface. Trust the process, the Ameri cans say. The substrate of what is occurring can seem an almost mystical thing, though again it is very much an ordinary phenomenon of everyday life once one is aware of it.

Stolorow and Atwoodís book *Contexts of Being* (1992), which was com mented on previously, brings out this reality, as do the teachings of various philosophers and practitioners throughout the ages. Supervision, de briefing, and staff discussion after a therapy group all have as their purpose (not neces sarily explicitly acknowledged) an attempt to discern this process: to see how the events happening on the surface point to or reveal what might have been happening below it. This is connected with wider questions about the phenom ena of mind which are ceaselessly occurring outside our focal awareness.

Much happens there. That is an understatement: most happens there; we have only a limited span of attention. Learned habits are one example of such things. Another is feelings not consciously remembered. More than that, there are the undercurrents of our interactions with other people which lie behind the phenomena of perception and transference. Behind these there are the expectations, and the relational matrix of experience with others, which have been laid down since birth (Stolorow and Atwoodís pre reflective un conscious, 29, 33). Most of all, and most important of all, is the emotional interplay between people. Some of this is conscious: we are aware that we are moved, angered, saddened, enlivened by someone. Some if it is unconscious: counter transference in psychodynamics in particular bears witness to this very natural happening. Some people may be more aware of the interplay of unconscious currents, or more open to the possibility of it, than others. Most of us have to learn to cultivate the gift.

We do undoubtedly, for instance, already pick up other peopleís feelings without them having to be expressed in words. One of the deepest, most meaningful and most rewarding of my relationships in therapy was one in which my emotions were stirred at a profound level just from being in the room with the other person. I felt always on the edge of an emotional ocean as if a door were opened on to a boundless expanse of feeling. I found the sharing (or concealing) of this to be a challenge. My training was to conceal, to keep myself and my own feelings, concerns and past out of the interaction. The intention of this embargo is no doubt good, so that the therapistís mate rial doesnít interfere with the other personís feelings and concerns; but this policy did not match this particular partnership: there is no allowance in the embargo for individual differences. It was, on the contrary, failing to share my emotions that interfered. I found instead that when I was open, and said something about how I was feeling and why, in relation both to the present and the past, it had a reciprocal effect on the other person. It freed them in their turn to be more open to me in response, and to be more in touch with their own feelings, and with our joint feelings (like Ferencziís experience with Elizabeth Severn see chapter 2). The experience was remarkable at variance with all the classical theory.

A further aspect of things of which we may not be aware, and of the underly ing process that subsumes both therapy and life, concerns issues of synchronic ity, coincidence and other matters sometimes placed in the realm of parapsy chology. They occur astonishingly often in strange and challenging temporal juxtapositions: dreams, letters, simultaneous occurrences, shared meaning. Both Freud and Ferenczi had a great interest in this, especially in its relevance to the unconscious, and writers such as Stolorow and Atwood give it a good experiential basis. These issues then spread out to take in concerns of spiritual ity, and of underlying purpose and meaning in the unseen current of life.

FIRST SESSIONS

To get down to the actual practical details of psychotherapyís encounters, the initial meeting is exciting, and anxious for both parties. Remember Bionís remark about there being two frightened people in the room. For myself, I always anticipated the possibility that this first encounter might develop into a long term commitment, though it most commonly took two initial sessions to be sure that psychoanalytic psychotherapy was the right course of action. I used in opening the first session to ask the person to tell me whatever they wished concerning what had brought them to me: and I tried not to interrupt. By doing that I sought to gain a general feel of them and of their commitment to the task ahead. At some time in that first session I would ask if they had any questions that they would like answered if it were possible to do so. That, I hope, gave them a feeling that they were being listened to, and that their opinions, hopes and fears were being taken into account.

Taking a detailed history and assessment is counter productive at this ini tial stage, and unnecessary at any later date. It feels distancing, appearing to treat the person concerned as if they were a thing to be slotted into a precon ceived pattern, their own concerns being of lesser importance than those of their interlocutor: one will discover soon enough as therapy goes on any facts that are relevant to the personís life and problems. A preliminary diagnosis is not actually called for in psychotherapy: a supervisor attributed to William Gillespie the dictum that psychotherapy is the one field in which diagnosis, prognosis and treatment go together. They each change as the therapy pro gresses and different levels are reached. After some time it may become dif ficult to recall what the person came about in the first place. The presenting problem, and the problem presented, frequently conceal something far more important that only emerges as the work progresses.

In the initial sessions I used to say little about the process of psychother apy, except, if asked, that it needed to be experienced to be understood. Since people are naturally anxious about committing themselves to a process which they do not yet understand, I used to add that it should be possible for the per son to tell after a few sessions, say after a month, if anything is happening and if they feel it is worth it. That usually gave them sufficient reassurance to go on for long enough to see if it felt right. We then entered into an open ended commitment to continue until one or other of us (usually if not invariably the other person) felt that we had done enough. People appeared generally happy with that, except for natural questions in the course of a long therapy as to when it was likely to end.

People were free to stop at any time. I did tell them that if they were to decide to do so, it would be preferable to discuss the matter first so that we might end it mutually, rather than just have them disappear. Disappearing without a word of explanation feels like a regrettably inconclusive display of either fear or anger, which could do with being looked at. Otherwise, taking such a course is often rather pejoratively called acting out, that is, acting on some feeling which is felt to be too strong to be put into words. It is therefore a very natural reaction, like the way people may try to avoid saying good bye at any parting because they fear they cannot contain their distress; but such strong feeling, if it is not to continue to interfere with life, needs to be brought into the more manageable realm of words. Telephoning to cancel at least gives an opportunity to discuss what is behind the decision and possibly, by helping to put the feeling into words, to alter it   that is, if the therapist can think quickly enough on the telephone, which I find very difficult to do.

If someone were to arrive with a letter of reference I would put it aside to read at the end of the session. I explained that if I read it first it ran the risk of foreclosing on what the person themselves might tell me or want me to know   like putting on a pair of blinkers; or premature closure. Frequently the story they told turned out to be very different from what the reference said, so that not reading it was a good precaution against prejudging the issue.

The personís story may not always be very clear. As I have written earlier in the book, the vaguer the story is, the more it suggests that the damage occurred very early in the personís development. There are no words at that time with which to name or describe experiences or, particularly, feelings; but they are nevertheless experienced. They are likely, therefore, to go instead into our bod ies, so that if a person tells of repeated childhood illnesses and ailments, that too proves to be an almost infallible sign of some deep, early disturbance.

At the end of the first session, which always tended to take slightly longer than the usual fifty minutes, I tried to leave time to explain the geography of the house and to clarify any expectations of the therapy hour. My front door was left unlocked, so that people could walk straight in and wait, without ringing or knocking. The chief aim of this was that they might feel welcome, and feel they were entering a home rather than an office. An added advantage of the door being unlocked was that the sound of a doorbell did not disturb the session with the previous person. Most people were in fact invariably punctual, arriving within a minute or so of their appointed time, which was some minutes after the previous person had left. Some people expressed concern that I might be leaving the house open to burglary; but I could always hear from my room if the front door were opened, and I did keep the door locked once it was dark.

Since psychotherapy works primarily with emotions, which are not the field of physical medicine, it usually was not necessary to insist on medical cover, unless there were other indications making it important to do so. Many people who made the decision to seek therapy themselves did not feel it re quired endorsing by a doctor, especially if it was a doctor whom they hardly ever saw and who might know nothing of the particular difficulties with which they came. I was, on the other hand, careful to ensure medical cover from a GP or psychiatrist for anyone whom they sent, and for anyone else if I felt that there might be a possibility of needing it. I usually telephoned rather than wrote, as notes tended to get into a personís file and remain on record. If I felt a possibility of breakdown strongly and the person concerned refused consent for me to approach their GP, I would not take them on   for their own protection as well as mine. I was also helped by the unofficial support of a local psychiatrist, who was willing to advise me in cases of doubt, and to be the nominee for the medical cover that training courses demanded.

Understanding the Other

Although I didnít make use of any initial formal investigation or history tak ing by way of diagnosis, I found that my own experience was always a useful tool, both at the initial encounter, and frequently, too, in the later course of the therapy. On hearing of some apparently bizarre phenomenon I would reflect on whether I had ever experienced anything like it in my own life, whether in person or in therapy. Often I had, or I could recognize it as not being far off something that I had known: this is in accord with Richard Bentallís (2004) emphasis on psychiatric disturbances representing one end of a spectrum of everyoneís ordinary experience.

If that failed, I reflected on whether I had heard anything similar from anyone else in therapy: again, often I had. Both these identifications put the phenomenon within the realms of the bearable, understandable and solvable. If these first two reflections failed, I might next reflect on how I thought my therapist would have reacted, or on what a supervisor might have said. Only after that did I think about what I might have read in books (whose authors usually seem only to describe their successful experiences), or what I might have been told in seminars during training. That order of putting things rep resents fairly accurately the relative value and usefulness in my eyes of the various authorities and of the official emphases of training.

Such a reflective approach to diagnosis and to the course of therapy means that waiting plays a large part in the work of understanding. Books which give case histories frequently reveal analysts and therapists leaping in too soon with interpretations, which are also far too long and involved. Peopleís attention span is limited, and in their often inwardly absorbed state they are not able to follow involved reasoning or a detailed intellectual argument: this is in addition to the fact discussed in the previous chapter that verbal interpretation is not the proce dure of choice for people who have been badly damaged. If verbal interpreta tion is given, it is, further, commonly based on the therapistís theory rather than on the therapeeís story, which is in consequence not fully attended to (Broom 1997). The premature speed of giving an interpretation would seem to arise from a mixture of arrogance and impatience on the part of the analyst, many of whom seem to find either silence or not knowing difficult to deal with.

Several writers, on the other hand, have made valuable remarks about the need to listen concentratedly, to wait, to restrain oneself, and to put up with long periods of obscurity. Kohut (1985), for instance, made the remark about premature closure reproduced earlier. Comments of especial power include: one by Nina Coltart (1986, 187) . . . the stress which Dr. Bion laid on the need to develop the ability to tolerate not knowing, the capacity to sit it out with a person, often for long periods, without any real precision as to where we are, relying on our regular tools and our faith in the process to carry us through the obfuscating darkness of resistance, complex defenses, and the sheer *unconsciousness* of the unconscious. Another is by Christopher Bollas (1987, 203), The most ordinary counter transference state is a not know ing yet experiencing one. I know that I am in the process of experiencing something, but I do not as yet know what it is, and I may have to sustain this not knowing for a long time.

Understanding emotional as well as intellectual is closely linked with Sternís (1985) concept of attunement, referring to a motherís instinctive re sponsiveness to her infant. To be understood in this way; to feel that someone knows what you are experiencing or expressing and what makes you tick; and to have someone who can respond in exactly the right way before you have framed your wish or even become conscious of your need, is a supreme gift. It is this understanding which therapists need to nurture. A failure in attunement can lead to all manner of harmful outcomes, both in infancy and in therapy.

WORKING WITH EMOTIONS

In any meaningful relationship, we are working with emotions. The aim of psychotherapy is to draw these emotions out. Emotional states are sensitive, so that we need to take particular care, especially when we are engaging with the child in the other person. Emotions at that period of life are especially fragile, sensitive and easily damaged. It cannot be stated too strongly that the release, healing and harnessing of purposeful emotion is what psychotherapy is, or should be, about. One has nevertheless to be aware that anything can happen in this quest: we may experience love, joy, anger, sadness, yearning; depression, elation, silence; mania, paranoia, admiration, hatred; devotion or fury.

These are all part of the province of psychotherapy, just as our physical well being is the province of physical medicine, although there is consider able cross over between the two: psyche and soma at core are one. Emotions are the prime area of psychotherapeutic work, even if appreciation of this was obscured by the original emphasis on the unconscious. This did not make it sufficiently clear that unconscious conflicts were caused by the repressed and unrecognized emotions of everyday life. Neither was it helped by psycho analysis traditionally referring to emotions as affect (cf. Stein 1991).

Emotion, affect and feeling are used more or less interchangeably to refer to much the same phenomena, but with insufficient definition to make their finer differences clear. These differences are important. Affect was originally part of the tripartite division of human function in philosophy, which later passed into the subject divisions of psychology, namely, cognitive, affective and conative: cognition referred to thinking, affect to the emotional or feeling aspects of life, and conation to the will and doing. Psychology nowadays calls these divisions cognition, emotion and motivation and does not use the word affect. Definitions of the three words (emotion, affect and feeling) have become somewhat conflicting as a result. I think the best is that affect is seen as the unconscious aspects of emotion, that is, its automatic physiological stirrings; feeling refers to the conscious physical signs of emotion; and emo tion itself means its more ordered purposive content (Basch 1992). Emotion is what moves us, and its harnessing is the goal to which we aspire.

In normal development a child is helped to identify feelings and to label them as particular emotions. On the basis of that and over a long term, they learn to decide what action is both needed and appropriate for their expres sion. When development is not ideal, the moral bar is pushed back from the choice of what to do about one's feelings or emotions to the possession of feelings per se. The child comes in consequence to absorb the conviction that emotions are wrong in themselves, and has no chance either to discover what they are, what they mean, or how they may best be expressed. As a further result of this, feelings and emotions can become totally suppressed and de nied (by others) or repressed (by ourselves); or both: but they do not go away. They remain under the surface to affect our bodies and our lives, often in the unhappy ways that bring people to therapy. As a further, and inevitable, part of this since our emotions are integral to us as embodied beings, the person comes to feel that it is they themselves who are wrong.

A therapist's first task may therefore be so basic as to get people to become aware of what emotions are, how much a part of us they are, how important to us they are, and what is their intended place in life. This will initially in volve identifying the physical stirrings or feelings that indicate the presence of affect or emotion. The therapee may have been ignoring or indeed denying these stirrings all their lives. The task for both partners in the therapy is then to permit the feelings to emerge and to accept them, after which the task may be to help the therapee to recognize clearly the emotions which the feelings represent, to label them correctly and to learn how to express them appropri ately. It can be a long, radical and testing process of education.

Working with emotions in this way can perhaps be clarified by considering briefly two other areas of activity which might be thought to overlap with the field of psychotherapy. What makes the difference between them is that emo tions are the specific arena of psychotherapy, and not of the others.

Psychotherapy and Physical Medicine

The first of these possibly overlapping areas is that of physical medicine. Physical medicine may deal with our bodies and with physical complaints such as are often presented in psychotherapy, but it does so usually at the expense of emotion. So far as is possible emotion is excluded both from diag nosis and from practice. It is seen as interfering with the medical process, and is only given a place in so far as it can be eliminated by psychotropic drugs. People who are classed as untreatable are in consequence frequently so only because the root of their problem is not physical, and is therefore outside the remit of physical medicine.

This is especially so for the group of ailments known as psychosomatic. In these, because verbal expression was unavailable at the time of their develop ment, mishandled emotions find their voice in the body and its ills. In going for physical medicine the sufferers are going to the wrong place even though they may be presenting with disorders that appear to be physical. Their problem is actually emotional, but medical doctors are not usually trained to deal with emotions other than to give medication to suppress them. Emotions donít like this sort of treatment: they are doing their best to bring their needs (and ours) to our attention, and they therefore continue to do so. Emotions are the proper work of psychotherapy. If people were fully aware of that dif ference they might be helped to take their problem to the right place, where emotions are welcomed and, in spite of it often being through considerable turmoil, harnessed as a source of power.

Psychotherapy and Sex Work

In its emphasis on emotions psychotherapy contrasts equally sharply with another way of dealing with lifeís problems which does not involve feelings; that is, by way of sexual activity. This, I imagine, could be one reason why so much energy is put into avoiding sexual contact, intimacy and genital passion in psychotherapy: it would be a diversion from and an avoidance of the real challenge. It is a pity, though, that in consequence any infant need for warmth, sensuality, touch and tenderness is also excluded. It is very literally a case of throwing out the baby with the bath water. It is also a pity that some of the energy put into the exclusion of sex is not mirrored by attempts to exclude cold ness and lack of humanity. This too departs from a truly therapeutic attitude, which works ideally with a full range of emotion, warm and human.

Early in my training I sensed in the work of psychotherapy a certain parallel between psychotherapy and prostitution. Frequently the therapist feels used: sometimes there are overt sexual demands made; money changes hands. I raised this question in one of our training seminars, only to be greeted with cries of indignation at my suggesting such a thing. When I mentioned the seeming parallel between the two professions to my therapist, I was pleased that he took the topic and the comparison seriously. He agreed, and pointed out in addition that the sessions are for much the same length of time, the fee is commensurate, and the purchaser is often referred to by the same word, client. The difference, notwithstanding, is as radical as that between psychotherapy and physical medicine. Psychotherapy works with emotions: they are its raison dí tre, its modus operandi, its cause, its tool, and its goal. Prostitution essentially works without emotion: that is the one thing that must be excluded if sex workers are to survive.

On one occasion I was very puzzled by someone who came for therapy. She was a beautiful woman, poised and apparently healthy, but very con fused and, on account of the confusion, in considerable distress. She threw me off balance by insisting on paying me at the beginning of each session, in spite of my demurrals. I never normally expected to be paid until the end. A supervisor to whom I mentioned this realized immediately why. It took me longer: it was only as we progressed through the therapy that I realized that the lady was a call girl, for whom it was customary for payment to be made at the beginning of each encounter. She had fallen in love with a client, and had no idea what had hit her. She thought she had gone mad. Psychotherapy essentially includes, sex work has to exclude, emotions.

I was glad to see recently that this paradoxical analogy with prostitution has been dealt with openly by Hoffmann (1998) [cited in Buechlerís *Clinical Values* 2004].

INTRUSIONS

I mentioned that I tried not to interrupt the personís story. I tried also not to allow extraneous noises and disturbances to intrude on the personís therapy. I turned off the telephone and the telephone bell   answering machines can take care of that. The rest of the house was also always closed off from my study, though this might not be possible for everyone. The one exception which I used to make was to answer the front door if the bell rang and there was no one else to answer it. Often I would ignore it in the hope that whoever it was would go away; but if they persisted I would excuse myself to go and see what it was. It was unlikely to be the next person for therapy, as they almost always arrived on time in the gap between people; but it might be a delivery which demanded attention and which I felt should receive it. On my return from answering the door we could deal in the therapy with any feelings aroused by the interruption, such as that I might be held to consider a parcel delivery to be more important than the person engaged with me.

Most people were relatively unaffected by this practice and didnít appear to mind: at least, they never said so. One person minded very much; though nothing was said until after the damage was done and had become irreparable. The sudden break in the session when I went to answer the door had evidently been too much for that person to bear. A short time later they broke off therapy, citing as the reason my evident disregard for them in going out of the room. They broke off, I realize now, without letting me know   which seems a reasonable tit for tat. That happening was fairly later on in my practice, but it made me re think whether it was really necessary to answer the door: callers, including deliveries, can always either leave the package or a note, or they can call back later. Nothing is so urgent as to warrant an interruption which might be misinterpreted (or interpreted correctly?   the therapist might want a break) by someone whose history has been such as to make them ultra sensitive to being abandoned.

One of my supervisors had long before given me a piece of excellent advice, linked with the general advisability of bringing any experienced or sensed feelings into the open: it was, that if I knew in advance of the likeli hood of some unavoidable interruption, I should mention the possibility at the beginning of a session. This lets the other person know that their feel ings are being taken into account, as well as the fact that they are allowed to have feelings about such an apparently everyday and trivial occurrence. My sense is that people always accepted this, and it did not have any dire effect.

In this particular instance I did not know in advance, and was therefore not in a position to give any warning. The person who broke off may in fact have done so partly in order to get back at a man: most events in therapy (and outside it) are multiply determined; and it had happened with that person before, in their life outside therapy. If so, I should at any rate have been more sensitive: I feel that I deserved what I got. If they felt that way, they presumably had good reason to do so, which had needed to be uncovered. The chief trouble was that I did not realize that that was where the person was in their inner development; they seemed so competent and adult even in therapy that I failed to see the wounded child. I knew nothing of the reaction which my answering the door had aroused until they failed to reappear. I should have remembered how angry (and silent) I had been myself with a psychiatrist in Bangalore who, when I was consulting him, allowed the telephone to interrupt us repeatedly: his full attention never seemed to be on me.

The effect of intrusions and of other things that trigger off explosive emo tions can be examples of narcissistic wounds (see the following section), although they do not always cause as much overt upheaval as the latter do. Something has gone wrong in infancy, usually with the primary carer, such that sufferers have not received something that is essential for development, as Kohut made clear. This need, bugging them all their lives, can then surface with immense strength in therapy. We are in consequence dealing in therapy with the lost child (Ferenczi): therapy becomes a recrudescence of infancy.

What is called for most of all in responding to such reactions is that the person be held firmly throughout any crisis. What is inexpressibly damaging is if they are responded to as if they have launched a personal attack on the therapist. Their reaction needs to be understood rather than attacked in return. This holding is the human response which any caring parent knows: to assure their child that they are loved and contained, and that they need not be afraid. It is one of the challenges of tenderness when we are working with an adult who in this moment is also a child: we want to respond in a way that is hu man, effective, and appropriate to their present state.

NARCISSISTIC WOUNDS

The sort of intrusion which brings on such a reaction as that just described is one example of what Kohut (chapter 1) called a narcissistic wound. The work of regression in particular requires us to accept that the person with us is a child in respect of the satisfaction of narcissistic needs, amongst other things. If in therapy their narcissistic needs are once more not met we have to be aware that there is likely to be an occurrence, or recurrence, of a narcis sistic wound. This refers to people's reactions to gross episodes of failure on the part of their carer. The reaction is what is often popularly, and accurately, seen as an outburst of infant rage.

If essential narcissistic needs have not been met at the appropriate time in childhood, people look for their satisfaction in family and friends in later life; but they are still primitive needs which are not well understood by those who have not themselves suffered from that type of deprivation. They are, notwithstanding, universal and real; and psychotherapy should be a human relationship in which such continuing needs, if unmet earlier, can be faced and supplied. In spite of that, being only human, therapists are not perfect and, even if working at a child level, do not always either remember their own childhood, or cannot in advance be totally prepared for the particular deprivations that their therapees might have suffered, which the therapist may in consequence inadvertently repeat.

There is therefore always a possibility that the therapist will not be suf ficiently attuned to the other person to anticipate or provide what they might be seeking (often the person doesn't know that themselves, or they might be better able to obtain it more readily). When the possibility becomes an actual happening this is what constitutes the narcissistic wound, and it can bring about a tumultuous reaction. The person frequently lapses into either a with drawn silence or a violent rage, and may fail to interact or respond in what we might think is any reasonable manner; or, in the extreme case, they may just fail to appear for the next session. Probing or inquiry on the part of the therapist often sets off further turmoil: it merely underlines that we haven't understood. It is as if a bond has been violently ruptured, and the hope of any good outcome or even of any future for the therapy is in the balance.

The therapist usually has no idea what has gone wrong only that some thing has. They don't realize what it was they did or said (or didn't do or say) to cause the rupture. It is exactly like the situation where a child has been let down, misunderstood or misinterpreted by his or her carer as if the bottom had dropped out of their world. One reaction would be (and I fear often is) for the therapist, or a parent, to react indignantly and defensively, and to attack the person or child for behaving in this way. Such a response only aggravates the situation. A different and more creative approach is for the therapist to indicate their awareness that some cataclysmic failure in attunement has occurred (such realization being in itself a sign of the attunement needed), and slowly, and frequently painfully, to explore what happened, and to understand how the person had perceived the situation that caused the breakdown. This may make it possible to find out what the occasion had triggered off or echoed from their past. The road is then clear to explore that in turn and to build on the happening in a new and constructive way.

The Best of Intentions

From the last illustration it should be obvious that the road of psychotherapy is not all smooth and a pattern of perpetual tolerance. I give one more vi gnette. Someone came to me whom I knew was experienced as prickly, and had had none too happy experiences of counseling. I was confident that I would be the one person who would be able to help (the savior of the world syndrome from which some therapists suffer). I would last out the storms and the bullying, the caustic wit and the aggressiveness. I would see and love the tortured child beneath the fa ade: there had been a very difficult childhood in the background. I would show an exemplary acceptance and a creative tolerance.

Unfortunately it felt that the therapeeís chief aim in every session was to try and make me angry. One day they succeeded. Instead of some vacuous reflective comment such as you seem to want me to respond to you in some particular way, or, better, a more firmly based statement such as I am feel ing angry, I felt goaded beyond endurance, and let fly. The person looked at me in sorrow and pity and said, Donít you know that as a therapist you are not supposed to show anger? They added that I was no use to them, and left. I was not of use.

I imagine that that person was hoping that one day someone would love them enough to accept all that they threw, and still love. Unhappily their ways of testing that love and patience and of holding people off for fear of getting hurt if they let them get close were too successful, and brought only constant repetition of what at some level was feared most deeply. I hope that someone since has been able to do what seemed well nigh impossible and overcome the personís rigid defensive shell. I feel that what they might really have needed was to be held tightly if anyone could ever get close enough to do so, and be allowed to struggle and protest to their heartís content, until they should fall quiet and know that their holder was still there, and all right. That is the way in which a parent might respond to a childís rage and fury.

Part Three

CONCLUSION

Chapter Nine

Further Challenges

THERAPEUTIC POSSIBILITIES

While it is extremely demanding and testing to be with people sensitized to rejection, pain and narcissistic failures, there is a further group of people who pose an additional challenge. I do not think that this challenge has been faced adequately in the psychoanalytic and psychotherapeutic world. It concerns the needs of and therapeutic possibilities for the particular group of people with early damage mentioned earlier in the book whose early deprivation was of such a nature as to rob them of the experience and comfort of human touch and body contact. Their resultant yearning for that sort of sensual tenderness unconsciously seeks its fulfillment in the joy of warm and loving physical contact. In my practice I noticed that these needs were present to a high and crippling degree in a small but significant proportion of people who came for therapy.

In addition to Ferenczii's highlighting of trauma as the determinative fac tor in mental or emotional illness, and of regression and relationship as the means of dealing with it, his identification of the stage of tenderness at the start of life is equally important (FC 1955, 163). This, with its immature, as yet guiltless, connotation, is as we have seen in chapter 3 the corollary of innocence. Ferenczi was identifying something which is essential for a full human life, and which every child should receive; that is, the experience of an accepting tenderness, of cuddling, holding and sharing bodily warmth, non genital in its intention. It is something that we always need, whose de privation leaves a potentially destructive vacuum.

Ferenczi was not to know it, but his stress on the formative role of tender ness in early life has been greatly strengthened by work since his day on

the vital part that touch plays in early experience, both for humans and for
other animals (Barnard and Brazelton 1990). It resonates too with the work
of modern neuroscience with regard to emotional development, where right
hemisphere interactions between mother and child, brought about by close
ness and gaze, are so important (Gerhardt 2004; Schore 1994 et seq.).

Ferencziís writing made sense in itself and in the light of this later work,
both in respect of my own life and the lives of those in therapy with me.
It made me wonder if therapists always find in therapees a background
experience and disturbance similar to their own; the occurrence of simi
larities seems frequently to be remarkably greater than might be expected
by chance. It would appear, for instance, that people who look for oedipal
conflict find it, and those who donít, donít. In Ferencziís case, however, it
is clear that he was not initially looking for instances of trauma. Their uni
versality forced the issue on to his attention as a result of his clinical work,
even though he might have been sensitized to the possibility by his own
earlier experience. Further, while a therapistís own life might well alert him
or her to similar issues in others, it cannot very well determine the content
of the actual experiences reported.

Be that as it may, for the many people with whom I worked some early
trauma inevitably appeared to be the original cause of trouble. Later imagin
ings and fantasy may have embroidered it, and later experience with the mal
adaptive responses developed to cope with its results may have exacerbated
it but it required no fantasy additional to or aggravating of the trauma to
suggest that anything other than the trauma itself was the primary cause of
disturbance. In this I believe that Freud was quite wrong, and Ferenczi right:
not in everything, but in many things, and certainly on this point of trauma.
In this comment I am reflecting what Ferenczi himself said in his introduction
to his paper Child analysis in the analysis of adults. He said, Nor can I say
that Freud himself agrees with all that I publish. He did not mince matters
when I asked his opinion. But he hastened to add that the future might show
me to have been right in many respects (1931, 127).

Ferencziís emphasis on trauma, his interest in the earliest years, his focus
on early interactions with the mother, his gentler, more maternal approach,
his cooperative accepting way of working rather than that of confrontational
aloofness, his stress on the ambience of innocence and tenderness in all
these he was an essential corrective to Freud. This maternal element is
an integral and inseparable part of life, and the deprivation of it can cause
urgent, long lasting and interfering needs. It was therefore bound to sur
face again at some time in psychoanalysis in spite of the suppression of
his work, just as it does in individuals who are affected by such maternal
deprivation.

New Methods

Although I wanted to help people who were so deprived, I remained for years, as described earlier, in a state of considerable ignorance as to how it might be done. I went along with my trainings for psychoanalytic psychotherapy feel ing that everyone else must be possessed of much clearer vision than myself and that they all knew exactly what they were doing: at least they appeared to do it with a greater sense of purpose and a deeper conviction of success than me. I seemed in contrast to be stumbling along in parallel with the trainings, in them but not quite of them, more and more puzzled as to what was going on or how to formulate it, and tending to agree at some level with those in volved in my formation who told me that as far as they could see nothing seemed to be happening in my work.

Nothing, at least, of the nature of what they were talking about: and yet, the people I worked with still came, hour after therapeutic hour, day after day, week after week, month after month, year after year. At a different level I knew very well that something deeply significant was happening, both to them and to me. Small changes occurred that both they and I could see at the time. Larger changes took longer, but could be seen on looking back. Some people came only for a short time and went away with immediate problems solved. Others came and stayed for years, to experience a gradual transforma tion of their life.

The reasons for finding the old way unsatisfactory were two fold. One was that the people who came for therapy were different from those of Freudís day: they had less focused problems. From the evidence of Freudís and othersí writings, patients in the early days were nearly always labeled as hysteric. They were people, usually but not always women, who suf fered from emotional problems converted into bodily symptoms and neurotic conflicts. The task of analysis was to bring the things responsible for those conflicts which were buried in their unconscious into consciousness, where they might be resolved. In my day, the people who were coming for therapy had vaguer problems, though equally unconscious. I came to recognize that they fell under the general headings of borderline disorders, narcissistic disturbances, or long standing personality problems, as these have been delineated earlier. Their origin was very early in a personís development, and their consequences were as a result more diffuse and difficult to identify. The request for help itself served as sufficient indication of the need for it, and gave whatever hope there might be of a positive outcome.

Any diagnosis of hysteria, or any reference to someone as hysteric, needs to be treated nowadays with great suspicion, whatever it meant in the past (hypochondriac appears to be the male equivalent). Apart from hys terical conversion, which means conversion into physical symptoms rather than neurotic ones (though why that should still be called hysterical is a mystery), it seems to be used simply to mean that there is something radi cally wrong with the person, but that the person making use of hysteria as a diagnostic term doesnít know what it is that is wrong. It becomes a dismis sive title, and is frequently used pejoratively, implying that the person is greedy, and an attention seeker. They are actually attention needers: needy, not greedy. They seek recognition, acceptance, tenderness and warmth, of which there was a radical absence in their infant lives, and they are searching for some redress of the resultant ill effects. These are instead frequently rein forced by the attitudes they meet and the treatment they receive: they do not find the tenderness that is needed so urgently. They are in addition unable to verbalize their need directly, because it happened in their infancy the word infant means without a tongue, before language. The experience stays as an emotional yearning disconnected from intelligible explanation.

The people with whom I worked most intensively belonged to this group. They usually had only an imprecise though disturbing sense of unrest; they had physical complaints of unknown origin; and were again and again at the end of the line in their search for helpers, or had been passed on to me by doctors who themselves would have liked to help but were despairing as to how to do so. I soon learned that all these features were most commonly signs of profound damage in the personís life which had happened early in their emotional de velopment. The more blurred the complaint and the harder it was to formulate, the deeper and earlier the trauma was likely to have been, and the longer and more intensive the therapy that was likely to be necessary. Those who came from doctors had been rightly perceived to be not medically ill at all, but rather emotionally needy or damaged, often desperately so in spite of appearing to lead otherwise normal and responsible lives. The damage went far, far back.

A different type of therapy was called for to work with people who had this wider range of problems with their earlier origins. This was the second reason for finding the old ways unsatisfactory: such people required a new approach. Development of appropriate new ways of working had occurred in parallel with the discovery of the different types of person, and over the years, it had resulted in all the various adaptations, modifications, discoveries and shifts in methods, theories and applications which we have looked at in this book, even if the par ticular pioneers did not realize or like to claim how radical they were being.

THE RESURGENCE OF CHILDHOOD

A dominant finding in the newly discovered methods was that to cope ef fectively with such early traumas and deficits through any therapy which was carried out in adult life meant having to re visit childhood. This is no easy thing to do; and to do it in therapy comes up against many obstacles. There is for instance in psychoanalytic therapies a sensed prejudice against the expres sion of love; there is the taboo already cited, both analytic and cultural, on tenderness; there is the prohibition of touch. There used also to be a certain prejudice against childhood and immaturity: deliberately to permit it to re surface was not thought to be a good idea. It was considered an indulgence by Freud. Part of this was undoubtedly a fear of dependence, boosted by a fear of gentleness, and underpinned by a fear of emotionality, that is, of the more stereotypically feminine characteristics. There is in addition the large practical stumbling block of the cost of a long therapy. This will, I suppose, be always with us; and we have to solve that one as best we can.

I did nevertheless find that alongside the considerable amount of more straightforward work of psychoanalytic psychotherapy in my practice there was a constant call from a sizeable group of people whose primary need appeared to be this earliest of all the need for holding, for shared bodily warmth, for contact with a human skin within a warm emotional relationship. I wrote about my first recognition of this need towards the end of the Intro duction. As discussed later in chapter 1, this group might be seen as synony mous with, or a subgroup of, people at what Hedges termed the organizing level. For them Hedges sees physical touch as essential; though the need for touch which I am now describing is rather more fundamental and less cogni tive than organizing. To the end of supplying it Hedges suggests the enter ing into of a signed consent between the therapist and the person concerned, permitting such contact as is necessary, non intrusive and non threatening (1994.2). The signed consent appears to be particularly relevant to America where there is a tendency to bring lawsuits against therapists: its relevance to the different conditions of Britain was questioned by Mollon in his review of Hedgesís book. The recent incidence of legal actions in both countries against people who have pastoral responsibility towards those in their care would seem to indicate not only how great the yearning for tenderness is, but also how powerful and driven it can become if it cannot be channeled into some safe, healing, acceptable expression. Passion takes over instead.

I have therefore come up against, both in writing this book and in life, a problem which, thanks to Ferenczi, is beginning to be recognized but is not yet being fully engaged with; that is, the need to be allowed to be sufficiently a child in an adult world for any deprivation of body contact in earlier years to be overcome. The lack of affectionate handling in infancy means a conse quential deficit in attachment and bonding, since touch is basic to those pro cesses. The problem is how we can enable unfulfilled but continuing child hood needs to be met in physical reality, and not just recognized in verbal symbol: the symbol does not connect sufficiently deeply with the actuality. This is especially a problem when the lacuna which meant that the childís needs were not met in the first place has as one of its effects that in later life they cannot be met in ordinary adult fashion through an adult partnership and affection. The agonizingly demanding needs are too radical and, once released, too fierce to be contained happily within such an ordinary relation ship, and they are in consequence extremely difficult for the partner as well as the sufferer to understand or cope with.

Even if the need is recognized and initially accepted, it may place insuper able strains on the partnership or friendship and on both parties within it. These can then lead to tensions and misunderstandings too great to tolerate; and the partnership peters out, or breaks up more explosively. What is needed to avoid this is for someone outside the couple to hold and satisfy the infant longing, taking the pressure off the personís partner; the intention being that when the deficit of the deprived party is sufficiently understood, accepted, satisfied and healed, the two original partners can come to enjoy a fully adult relationship with each other. The obvious safe place for this longing to be satisfied is via a therapeutic relationship which recognizes the child within the adult. However, is it possible to provide the needed warmth and physical contact in such a setting?

Misunderstandings

The concept of the language of tenderness makes good sense of both every day and therapeutic experience; yet it can so often be misunderstood and mis interpreted by the language of passion: we have already touched on some ex amples of this in therapy. It is also frequently misunderstood in relation to the ordinary human phenomenon of friendship, which is itself an exemplar of the therapeutic relationship. An instance is the confusion between genitality and affection whereby same sex friendships are almost immediately seen nowa days in terms of sexual activity and genital exchange, and not just in terms of being close friendships sharing emotional warmth. One should not have to distinguish friendships in this way, but people readily jump to passionate rather than tender conclusions. Perhaps this is one of the reasons why people can be suspicious of any mention of love or closeness in psychotherapy.

A further set of misunderstandings relates to the search for closeness itself. If tenderness is not given and received in infancy and childhood, it gives rise to a constant yearning. It makes sufferers look constantly for comfort, warmth, bodily closeness and touch; but the search has to be furtive and concealed because of peopleís fears. By processes of reaction formation and avoidance of further pain people may therefore fight fiercely against their desperate need ever being uncovered: more than one therapee has identified themselves with a cactus or a hedgehog. Those deprived are therefore left with either yearning or avoiding, or both together. The word yearning, like the words longing and missing, has a significant emotional undertone; I use it as expressing deep emotional pain with its roots in infancy, caused by the absence or loss of something which is sensed as vital to well being.

There are two constituents of this yearning; a taking and a giving. The latter is frequently ignored or overlooked even more than the former; people are gratuitously assumed to be selfish, wanting only to take and not to give. Anna Freud put the contrary beautifully when she said many years ago a baby wants to love its mother with all its bodily powers (Milner 1969): every fiber of the babyís being strives towards this end. It is the original dynamic of care. The blocking of this bodily urge to love is another part of what lies behind the frustrated longing and enduring yearning for physical touch. It is a two way exchange: not just a longing to receive, but also, and perhaps more deeply, a longing to give.

If the need for tenderness and touch should have been fulfilled in child hood, that experience hopefully will feed into and meld with more adult sexual longings, so that in adult intercourse both aims can be simultaneously fulfilled, sensuality and sexuality together. If, on the other hand, people have been deprived in their search, the missing touch and sensuality can become all that they truly want at the deepest level of life later. Unfortunately, due to the tendency to see such longing in terms of passion, their subsequent search for closeness and warmth is likely to be seen as solely a quest for sex, and responded to accordingly. This can then lead to a feeling of violation and out rage. One partner may be seeking only fulfillment of the longing for holding, warmth and closeness, but if the other moves unquestioningly to intercourse it leaves the former with a sense of dissatisfaction, of misunderstanding, of being used, and of deeply confusing anger. It can represent a misattunement and deprivation as profound as the original.

I may speak as if the misunderstanding is intentional: it is not. It is a natural response to the overtures for closeness; but because these particular overtures are coming from such a primitive level, they need to be accompanied by a verbal (adult) explanation if misunderstanding is to be avoided. One trouble is that the person seeking closeness may not have any adult explanation to offer for why it is so agonizingly urgent and exclusive: the matching dif ficulty is that any adult who has themselves experienced sufficient warmth and holding in infancy and has been able thereby to integrate their child and adult sensuality is likely to find the explanation difficult to understand (Fe renczi 1931/1955, 132). It is like inhabiting two different worlds: it seems well nigh impossible for someone who has not experienced deprivation of the tender component of infant life to appreciate or enter into the world of those who have.

For those who have grown up with the longing satisfied, tenderness and passion both subsequently pass through benign phases of development where the one becomes a part of the other so that they become inextricably inter twined, in thought as well as action, and can be expressed in full emotional sexual exchange. Those who lacked this tenderness in childhood can be stranded at that earlier phase without ever being able to reach full maturity and integration or to know this entwining. Being adult, they can experience and share in physical sex, but there is something missing.

After years of trying to explain the difference between the infant longing for tenderness and the adult expression of passion, I came to realize that it might well be impossible to separate the two except for those for whom they were already separated. Anything said in the way of describing, or seeking the fulfillment of, the sensual infant yearning was interpreted as being an account of, or an attempt to find, adult sexual gratification. It didnít matter whether this was in relation to opposite sex or same sex relationships. It might be a more natural interpretation when the sex of the partners is op posite, though even then it seems presumptuous; but any reference at all to affection or tenderness between two people of the same gender is also almost always interpreted with a homo genital twist. What hope is there for those who yearn for the touch that they have never had if it is always going to be misinterpreted? Some of them look to therapy.

TOUCH AS NARCISSISTIC NEED

The need for touch and skin contact has not, so far as I know, been explored as a specific narcissistic need like those others identified by Kohut (see chap ter 1), however, it shares nevertheless in the same accompanying phenomena. That is, it can give rise to narcissistic wounds if frustrated or transgressed, and to narcissistic rage if crossed or denied. Furthermore, the other person in the search for its provision is treated as a selfobject, valued only for their part in supplying the need. This is confirmed both in thought and in experience. The other person has no significance in their own right, only in relation to the searcher: in any other respect their reality is unimportant. They are a selfobject fulfilling the need for touch and contact in exactly the same way as others fulfill the needs for mirroring and idealization. There can of course be several selfobjects for any one person, each supplying a different narcissistic need: it does not have to be one person who supplies them all. It might be that there is something here, too, about Kohutís alter ego, the figure like oneself who ap pears in life and in dreams as providing a fulfillment of the search. In infancy the frustrated need would understandably become turned in on oneself.

The difference between the need for touch and contact and the other nar cissistic needs is that this one is yet more primitive. It is perhaps the most basic and radical of all, prior even to Hedgesís organizing level, and basic to the feeling or atmosphere of acceptance. Touch is an essential part of the communication of that acceptance (cf. Tustin 1986). It feels as if it is prior too to Stolorow and Atwoodís (1992) pre reflective unconscious, formed of the organizing principles that shape a person s experiences (33). These are likely to be the material of Hedgesís organizing perspective. The experience of touch and body contact would be deeper than this, providing the basis for it. It would supply the foundation for the integration of life; a bedrock of so lidity, confidence, stability and trust. The question is whether this particular narcissistic need can be met and supplied by any form of psychotherapy.

Meeting the Need

Part of this question has already been looked at in the section on touch in psy chotherapy, though there it was dealt with more as a form of communication. Here it re surfaces not just as a form of communication but as an essential experience in establishing a solid foundation for life. The need for touch as something essential for development and therefore ranking as a narcissistic need in Kohutís terms lay outside Freudís awareness, though it was sensed by Ferenczi. Many subsequent workers pointed to it, especially those mentioned extensively in this book as working with the earlier years of a childís devel opment, but so far as I know they did not explicitly formulate this specific foundational need nor did they identify the particular group of people whose experience might call it forth.

They also did not discuss regression work, or work with the child in the adult, as providing a means of meeting the need for touch per se. Touch was introduced only in relation to fulfilling other needs the assurance of love, or the avoidance of the fear of abandonment. These are important consequences and motivators of touch, but touch itself is more basic and less sophisticated. Bowlby was the closest to it. Holmes (1993) makes the valuable point that

Attachment Theory throws an interesting light on the dilemma posed by the problem of touch in therapy. Bowlby emphasizes the importance of real at tachment of patient to therapist. Because attachment needs are seen as distinct from sexual or oral drives, there is therefore no intrinsic danger of gratifica tion or seduction. Attachment provides a quiet background atmosphere of security within which more dangerous *(sic)* feelings can be safely explored (167). The therefore in the third sentence sounds a bit starry eyed, as if such needs do not automatically interact with one another when they coexist within one person, and especially when that person is an adult: it requires dili gence, renunciation and hard work to keep them apart. This is possibly one of the difficulties with Ferencziís teasing out of the two languages, of tenderness and passion. Even Bowlby, though, does not seem to have identified touch as an essential foundation of attachment. There is, for instance, no mention of either touch, contact or body in the indices of Bowlbyís three volumes on Attachment, Separation and Loss (1969, 1973, 1980).

The satisfaction of this profound longing, which has such power to impov erish and unsettle peopleís lives (oneís own and othersí) is thus a great prob lem. The ongoing yearning needs first to be recognized, and then, if possible, to be satisfied. Therapy can do the first, but can it do the second? It might be suggested that a person so afflicted should find this fulfillment or satisfaction in a friend or partner; but there is the problem previously aired that a partner who is themselves without this lack in their background does not understand the problem and cannot enter into the experience of the deprived one. They will always, and very naturally, want to follow any contact through to genital completion.

That in turn raises the important question as to whether tenderness in adulthood (the attachment needs) must always be infused with adult genital sexuality (the sexual drives). The clearest instance of where it is not so in fused is in parenthood. A therapist is therefore required in this sort of situa tion to act as a parent in addition to his or her other roles. Their maternal or parental counter transference indeed suggests this to them and guides them in its implementation. There are of course other instances in ordinary life where tenderness and passion, sensuality and genitality, caring and desiring, innocence and sophistication, are kept apart: one is in the practice of physical medicine and another is in the related practice of nursing, in both of which a non sexual touch is employed for purposes of healing. This comes very close to the specific use of touch as the healing agent.

Basic requirements in satisfying the sensual infant longing without it cross ing over into adult sexuality would seem to be one or both of two. The first is that the therapist be sufficiently secure in his or her own sexuality to be able to offer holding and closeness without expecting genital activity or feel ing that they have to respond to any request for it. It goes without saying (so for some reason I say it) that they would not demand that themselves. They would offer the warmth of close contact with the restraint of tenderness, and accept (but not act on) whatever the effect of that may be on themselves. The second requirement is that the therapist understands what is needed, maybe from having suffered a similar lack in their own background: they are thereby enabled to provide it without misunderstanding and to guard against letting it overspill into a more mature adult genitality. On account of this, and of the various caveats entered both previously and subsequently, the number of people who can enter freely into this sort of tactile exchange may be very small; but it would still be worth it even if only for those few. It should be added that a rare sufferer might be fortunate enough to find one or both of these conditions met in a partner.

These arguments and possibilities belong to any pairing of therapist and therapee, whatever their gender. It is possibly easier for the therapist with members of the same sex: if the requirements described are fulfilled, this is less likely to turn into a genital event. A mixed gender dyad, if both are heterosexual in orientation, is likely to rouse more powerful forces at the level of passion and to bring more difficulties. Fairness would suggest that a same sex dyad, if both parties are homosexual in orientation, would have the same problems.

Consideration of this sort of therapeutic action within psychotherapy raises once again the question of what defines psychoanalysis, and why touch has to be so strictly forbidden within it. Even if a more tactile approach is used within work carried out using the essentials of psychoanalysis as defined in chapter 5, it is likely notwithstanding to be looked at askance by rigorists. That does not mean that it must inevitably be ruled out ab initio: they might be wrong.

Caveats

Several qualifications have to be made about seeking to satisfy any need for the experience of beneficial touch. One is that there can be a surprising ambivalence of feeling among those who have lacked it in their early experi ence. The very lack of it can bring about a situation apparently directly op posed to the clamant need for it. The personís longings can be disguised so successfully as to make them appear to be withholding or withdrawing from people, or even actively pushing them away, like the cactuses and hedgehogs referred to earlier. They can be so tortured by their need to keep their yearn ing hidden that it makes them aggressive and destructive at the same time as parasitic and irritating. They long for warmth and acceptance, but are fearful and panicky that they wonít get it and instead will be rejected and excluded. Or, perhaps, they fear that once aroused their longing will know no end, so that they have to suppress it; similar to Suttieís hypothesis (1935) as to what may lie behind the taboo on tenderness. The longing can be so chaotic and paradoxical that it can even result in attack and refusal if the supply of it is offered. I can say this without feeling that I am being judgmental or dismis sive, because I know it to be true of myself.

Two other qualifications need to be made: not only can those who have lacked the experience of touch be ambivalent, but the meaning of touch can also be highly equivocal. Thus first, while some people may have been deprived of loving touch in childhood, others may have had too much and been traumatized by it, for instance by some form of abuse, whether spring ing originally from love, from anger or from the other personís need. In the former case, of deprivation, touch may be urgently needed as a part of psychotherapy; in the latter, equally urgent abstention might be called for. I worked with one person for whom a hug would have meant feeling trapped forever: they feared that it would repeat their experience with their mother. For others it might have brought up even worse feelings. The essential thing is that possibilities and their meanings need to be talked about before they are ever acted on; and that contra indications are rigorously observed.

The second additional qualification is that some people may have experi enced both too little and too much touch at the same time. They may have been twin and simultaneous features of their childhood; that is, the deprivation of loving touch and cuddling, together with at the same time the infliction of the savage touch of physical abuse. For them, touch is highly charged and ex tremely ambivalent; desperately longed for and simultaneously deeply feared. A loving non sexual touch, very gradually introduced, with careful discussion of its meaning and with sensitive and exhaustive handling of its emotions, might be the only answer. It is important for healing that the feelings that might be aroused by touch are brought fully into the open and dealt with.

For those who have suffered deprivation, touch may be needed to show that it is a way of conveying love; for those who have suffered abuse, abstention may be needed, to show instead that there are other ways of conveying love; for those who have suffered both deprivation and abuse, loving care and sensi tivity around all that surrounds the subject is most needed to convey the reality of love. One cannot be too careful. A therapist, though of a different tradition, wrote an article some years ago about just such a procedure. I understand that the articleís reception had the result that the person now regrets writing it. I will therefore not give the reference, but merely say how courageous and valu able it was, and express regret that our environment appears to be such that prejudice and misunderstanding in these matters can almost be assured.

Setting Out

My questionings as to how the need for human contact might be met in a therapeutic situation could not remain unanswered forever. The issue is particularly acute within one to one therapy, where the dyadic situation can awaken echoes of the mother child relationship, and where it is certain to raise questions of closeness and dependence. I suggested that it might be possible to meet the need if the affected person were to work with someone sufficiently secure in their own sexuality. For myself, I could not offer my self as someone secure in my own sexuality (I do not think that I have ever reached that stage); but I could offer myself as someone who shared the need and did not necessarily want a more adult or passionate sexual encounter. I was therefore open to the possibility as an adult of working and staying at the child level of interaction.

That then became one aspect of my practice of psychotherapy; large in conception, small in point of numbers. I had a wish and a willingness to try to ease people's yearning and despair by extending to them on occasion the pos sibility of physical closeness and holding. Sometimes it worked; sometimes it didn't. Sometimes it was ruled out because adult genitality might intrude. Sometimes people didn't want it: even if they didn't have a history of abuse, being held had quite other meanings for them than warmth and tenderness.

It worked better with men. With them I felt less potentially sexually in volved, and less threatened. It held risks, but I felt that that was worth it: risk is a part of anything on the edge of experience and of anything hoping to alter the status quo. I also feel that, even if such ventures did not always turn out as hoped they were not unique in that, and they always in some way enabled the person to find the strength to make significant and needed changes to their lives. There are of course one or two instances where I do not know the outcome. I can only trust the process.

BRAVING DEPENDENCE

It might be thought that a therapeutic situation such as I describe, where therapist and therapee are able to work closely because they share the same infant needs, might go on forever as a cozy twosome, without any possibility of change or growth. My experience of that was the same as with all of life: it doesn't stand still. When a person's primitive needs are met sufficiently they will instinctively and automatically want to move on to more adult encoun ter. Sometimes this might be by leaving therapy and finding the more adult relationship outside. Sometimes it might need more work in therapy, much more work, of growing slowly through subsequent stages of development, too, until a reasonably independent maturity is reached. A fear is that the nec essary experience of pain and loss when such an attachment is relinquished might be avoided by never letting go: this did not prove to be the case. Per sonal, financial and therapeutic pressures combined to ensure that growth and separation took place, even though it may have been sad for both participants at the time. Handled with awareness, such separation constituted a rich and valuable experience of a loss which could be mourned, and as a result of the mourning new and mature attachments could be formed in the world outside. This is the normal human template of good relationships.

In the long run closeness may thus lead to freedom, but if closeness had never been experienced earlier there can in the short term be a period of intense dependence, possibly mutual. Therapists are too often advised not to take on people for therapy who are likely to be or become dependent; and, that if dependence develops it is essentially a bad thing which should be avoided if possible. Independence (the stiff upper lip) is held to be the desir able norm. It might, I suppose, be thought to be so for someone for whom ear lier deficits have either not arisen or have been made good: but it seems to me that the embargo on dependence is fuelled largely by fear. A therapist fears that someone may become dependent on him or her forever, which will both be currently demanding and also contain the possibility that it might never be resolved (cf. Freudís Analysis terminable and interminable 1937).

This is also the fear of a parent regarding a dependent child, or of most ordinary adults facing any limitation of their freedom. It is a deep fear of never being free, of perpetual clinging, and of not being able to cope with the demands that that might entail. When parents shy away from allowing dependence in their children, the child is as a result forced into an early, and false, independence, which inevitably masks the universal underlying longing to have someone to depend on and to be attached to. It leads, in its denial of this, to the Ferenczian concept of the wise baby (chapter 3). There is a hu man need to be allowed to depend on someone outside oneself until one has found oneís own feet and strength and can proceed to a strong independence throughout the rest of life: it is a natural part of development.

Many people are in therapy because of this need having been unfulfilled. They have at some time in the past suffered refusal of their longing for con nection and have not been permitted to be dependent. To refuse it again in therapy is to add insult to injury; in the same way as Ferenczi pointed out that an analystís abstinence from other sorts of engagement might be repeating a childís experience of unresponsive parents. Some years ago I came across some psychological work which showed that the more a child is allowed to enjoy dependence in early life (i.e., at the right time), the more truly inde pendent that child will become as an adult. The deprivation of the chance of early dependence, on the other hand, results in an insecure attachment and an insecure adult; one who develops and lives out a false independence which they do not feel. It conceals an agonizing void. Unfortunately, not anticipat ing writing a book, I failed to preserve the reference. I did not realize at the time how important that work was. It is borne out by the predictions and find ings of Attachment Theory, and is an alternative way of saying what Kohut says in his concepts of selfobject and narcissistic needs.

As far as a therapist is concerned they thus have nothing in the long run to fear. That still might not overcome a prejudice which I feel is reinforced by psychoanalysis, that fierce independence is the desirable norm, together with an aggressive judgment that those who do not possess this independence are lifeís failures, to be condemned and dismissed. This characteristic of psycho analysis could be the result of inheriting Freudís hostile attitude to people who found it hard to cope, or it could be just the result of absorbing popular prejudice. It may be a very long haul to be caught up closely in the demanding life of a therapee, and it may mean frequently being tried and tortured by it. It does nevertheless come to an end for most people even if it takes several years to do so (as it does in infancy). The therapeutic pair can then move on into a more balanced and enjoyable relationship. There is always the potential for a process of growth.

If the therapist is not prepared to enter this dark and uncertain partnership they are limiting the possibilities of what can be achieved by psychotherapy: they are protecting themselves, but at the cost of continuing or aggravating the deprivation of the therapee which outwardly they are undertaking to relieve (this reminds me of some of Ferencziís words in his *Clinical Di ary* (1995), about the analyst pretending to listen while secretly harboring contrary thoughts). They are also depriving themselves of an experience of growth, their own as well as the therapeeís; and are foregoing the joy of de veloping a fully adult mutuality of relationship with that particular person. As Winnicott says (1958, 261) It is commonly thought that there is some danger in the regression of a patient during psychoanalysis. The danger does not lie in the regression but in the analystís unreadiness to meet the regression and the dependence which belongs to it.

With all this as background I accordingly moved to greater closeness with some people whose needs appeared to be of this nature: a need to have someone to cling to, though not necessarily to touch. My counter transference towards them was of a strong maternal or parental feeling, which I had early learned to recognize as an indicator of infant deprivation. It invariably turned out to be so. All of the people whose journey I accompanied in this way moved into a regression (recognized or unrecognized by them) into child hood, and the therapy could be seen to progress in that regression through the various stages of child development. Not all the people with whom I worked through regression suffered from an early deprivation of holding and bodily contact: there are other aspects to deprivation as well an inability to make sense of the world, an inability to express feelings, and a difficulty in trusting and hence in forming and maintaining relationships. These people required a different, more separated approach; but their therapy was also long. They all needed to be allowed a lengthy period of dependence in order to win the time to grow through their difficulties.

Risks

There were some, especially women, for whom a greater closeness might have become a sexual encounter. This was not because they were women, but because they were women and the therapist was a man. It was therefore better for the therapy if I and they exercised a painful but necessary restraint. M. Scott Peck (1978) said that he would be prepared to have sexual inter course with a patient if he felt that it would help the personís therapy, but that he had never found any circumstances in which he felt that it would. I would agree. A sexual relationship is a chimera, promising liberation and fulfill ment, but providing disappointment and void. It can be wanting a dummy at the wrong end, as a supervisor said to me once: a desire for something much earlier. It can be an avoidance of something infinitely closer and much more valuable; as so often it can be too in ordinary life, steering clear of deep com mitment. Tenderness is the need, not passion: a lasting emotional relation ship, not a passing thrill.

When I started my work, one of the first people to come to me was a woman who had been unloved as a child and knew nothing of trust or security. Her subsequent insistent search for love only succeeded in provoking the original reaction that she had gotten in her childhood, of people avoiding her. One of her first actions early in the therapy was to come into my room, remove all her clothes, and seat herself on my divan. She said that she had always wanted to do that with her father, but had never been allowed to. I didnít quite know what response I was supposed to make: an answering nakedness was not the right one. She might have thought that that was what she wanted, but would in reality also have been terrified. The perception of threat would need to be dealt with first. She might have wanted to invite tenderness (she had indicated the childhood origin of her action), but was frightened as an adult by the pos sibility of receiving passion. At that time I donít think that I had learned to formulate the difference. What she needed was a long, steady, holding which she could come to trust and build on.

I was only able to work with one person at a time who was in an absolute state of dependence: the task was so demanding as to be impossible with more than one. Twins must be a real challenge to parents. When that one person moved on, they were almost immediately succeeded by someone else who needed equally intensive tending. I had experienced the same in my ministry. It was like a sort of inbuilt homeostatic control of my capacity to care. At any particular time, the one person took over a large portion of my life, such that I was always aware of their needs, even through the night. I would be told the next day that they had wakened at such and such a time; and I would think how strange (and annoying: I wished they wouldnít) because so had I. I am not a multitasker at the best of times; and certainly not when my full attention and emotional engagement are being demanded by any one individual.

Intensive work with one person nonetheless did manage to proceed in parallel with other less demanding work with many others, though it was not necessarily any shorter in duration. I could manage to sustain perhaps up to fifteen people at any one time, working for up to nine hours a day, six and a half days a week. Some people could only come on a Saturday. Saturday was also indicated when people needed three therapy sessions per week if the sessions were to be optimally spaced. Some of those therapies extended up to ten to fifteen years, which seemed to surprise some colleagues but which was necessary in view of the depth of the work to be done. When I came to end my active work I realized with a start of surprise that the five people whom I was then still seeing had been with me for a total of seventy seven years between them. It was a humbling realization.

Early on also someone came who longed for touch but for whom touch evidently meant the release of insatiable and insistent wishes for something ever closer: sex was the panacea for all ills rather than the provoker of some of them. Physical contact was definitely not the answer. It seemed impossible to fulfill that personís longing and yearning, however much I felt it to be my task. I still do not know what the answer can possibly be in such a situation. Denial and refusal was always experienced as rejection, and merely provoked intensification of the distress and the demands. Possibly the firmest observation of boundaries and limits might have succeeded, if both the people involved had been able to stand the strain; but such a policy would almost certainly instead have put paid to any chance at all of relieving the personís situation: it would have made them withdraw from the therapy. It was a disturbing dilemma, and seemed to be an insuperable problem   perhaps it must remain regrettably so for some.

Rewards

I was fortunate that my sensitiveness to another personís frustrated need for mothering could pick this need up also with men who had been deprived. It was more possible to respond to men with a closer physical care without it crossing over into adult genitality. Contrary to many peopleís assumptions, about as many men as women came to me for therapy: human problems are ipso facto universal. One man, whose life was disordered, doubting and directionless, required virtual reconstruction from the start. He was almost unbelievably obsessive, and asked unanswerable questions of a nature that one might expect from a persistent child who wanted to know the secrets of the universe. To find the answer, such children need, as he did, physical ac tion rather than intellectual reasoning. He had attempted suicide at least once, and was in despair.

Obsessions and compulsions always mask some intolerable hidden emo tion or emotions: that is their purpose. With this person the obsessions seemed to have been a fairly successful attempt up to that date to conceal a profound uncertainty as to his own existence or worth, a doubt about the trustworthiness of anyone else, and a general naivety about the world around him. He had no solidity. This was indubitably caused in the first instance by a mother who was always pushing him away and giving him extremely mixed messages. It soon proved that the only way I was able to put a stop to the endless bouts of dithering, niggling and nagging was to hold him tightly, as one might a painfully anxious child. He was then able to stop the maithering (as dithering was known locally), and calm down. This went on for a year or so, and was succeeded by a further two years, when for every session we sat together on the divan holding one anotherís hands: the physical touch was able to convey mutual trust. The instinctive human response to children in distress would seem to be an excellent model for how to respond to adults in a similar state.

It was very noticeable when we were holding one anotherís hands that we communicated in a totally different way from the usual adult exchange. We were not separate people, addressing one another from outside; we were con joined, inside a sort of invisible membrane, communicating largely through touch, holding, and feeling, as children might do. Emotion was conveyed at several levels; while sentences were short and words were simple. It was, in fact, impossible to talk sense, that is, to talk about something outside us, or to offer a reasoned commentary on or explanation of what was happening or what was said. The result was that the hand holding gradually became a felt hindrance to more adult and cognitive communication, such that we grew out of it, gradually abandoning that means of communicating and adopting instead a sitting apart, talking in more adult language, and offering explana tions and interpretations. In that mode we found that we talked to each other more from out of our separate existences, rather than communicating from within a mutually shared experience.

When we started, the person was on medication to deal with his anxiety: this had the effect on some occasions of making him like a zombie, going through the motions of life without being able to enter into real engagement with anything or anyone. Emotions were absent. It was pointless trying to conduct psychotherapy of any sort with him in this state: there was no com munication. He himself did not want to live like that, and on turning his atten tion to what was happening it became clear that it depended on the dosage of his medication. With his supportive doctorís consent and cooperation he was therefore encouraged to regulate the dose himself, so that it was sufficient to calm his anxiety but not so much as to make it impossible for him to have any emotional engagement with me in the therapy.

For several years the therapy took place within a context also of telephone calls every day, first thing in the morning, last thing at night, and sometimes at times in between, including over holiday periods to wherever I happened to be. They appeared essential to keep the person on an even keel, to enable him to cope with a low level of medication, and to supply the base from which he could grow. On one occasion, before I went on holiday I was touched to receive from him the gift of a St. Christopher medallion: he had written to keep you safe . . , which I felt was very touching and caring, but on reading further found . . . for me. This also was touching but in a different way: it revealed the childlike state in which he was living, at least in his relationship with me: I was a selfobject. His need centered on his safety rather than mine.

Childlike is a good word: one that allows us to do justice to the child within every adult, who is always there but who surfaces especially at moments of stress. Childish is not a good word: it is pejorative, and suggests that one should snap out of it (if only people could, they would have done so long before). It has the same flavor as the critical use of the word dependence. There seems to be a prejudice against infant need and behavior, in spite of (or perhaps because of) it being there in all of us.

In the first year of this therapy, too, it became clear that the twice weekly meetings which had been scheduled were not enough. For over a year we moved to sessions every day of the week, including weekends: this was in addition to the telephone calls. It was a total commitment, on both our parts. For myself, I had at the beginning undertaken to do whatever might be neces sary to get him well. I therefore did it within the same weekly fee structure as for the two sessions he was already paying as much as he could afford. Taking the time to attend therapy so frequently, together with the drain on his finances, was a great demand on him as much as his needs were a demand on me; and his responsive total commitment was a salutary lesson. I had thought initially that he was unlikely to stay in therapy for long, he being a somewhat skeptical professional man. It is indeed amazing how so many people are liv ing the lives of useful and apparently well balanced citizens when underneath they are barely able to cope: this is a feature of being borderline. One justi fication of a financially costly procedure such as psychotherapy is that through engagement with one person (the therapist) many others (the therapees) are

able concurrently to keep working themselves and to live useful and reward
ing lives with others in society.

This particular person was a most lovable and loving man: perhaps I could
equally well say   child. His naivety and trust showed an idealization of
people which can only have come about in reaction to not having been able
to trust at all in his earliest years. It flew in the face of reality, but it was
perhaps the only way he could cope with that. He reminded me of Parsifal:
he had no guile. I still remember his charming figures of speech, and treasure
his thoughtful gifts. I loved him, although to say so opens up the possibility
of imposing the language of passion on our experience of tenderness. The
reality was rather different. It felt more like my entering into a state of pri
mary maternal preoccupation, which Winnicott has characterized as that into
which every mother needs to allow herself to move, and which he sees as so
essential for a babyís growth. Life becomes different: it revolves completely
and for as long as necessary around the needs of the infant. It is one part of
the complex phenomenon of tenderness.

My friendís childlike trust and behavior kept the interaction at this level.
He knew passion, but that was separate from the therapy. His increasing well
being and inner strength was demonstrated by his going through a revived
period of suicidal impulses. It is said that people do not contemplate suicide
when they are at their lowest point: it requires a certain detached resolve to
consider it and execute it. They turn to thoughts of suicide when they are
on their way out of the trough and have some energy to carry it through. I
am assured by historians that this is paralleled in the development of social
revolutions: they occur as conditions are getting better, not when they are at
their worst. They reflect an inability to see any other way out of the present
situation, any other possibility or opening, or any other means of using the
nascent energy.

So it is with people in the grip of internal oppression: suicide is when
there appears to be no other way. One person who had just started therapy
with me committed suicide. He had, I believe, caught a glimmer of hope
that life could be different, but the difficulties opposing any change made
suicide seem the only way. There had not been time for a bond to develop
that would have held him in life. Helping people to see other possibilities
for their lives and other ways of coping with situations is one of the great
tasks of psychotherapy. So much goes wrong because we tend to continue
using the same techniques that we have always used   long after they have
outgrown their usefulness and indeed their relevance to the situation at
hand. Sometimes we need to turn and look in another direction, to see a
possibility we had overlooked; a door we hadnít noticed; a different way of
doing things. We then have a choice.

My man child eventually came through the missing phases of his growth as well as anyone else does, and achieved a reasonably settled and confident life, with new and mutually satisfying relationships. His need for close and basic mothering had been met. Through dependence he had found independence. It would appear that it is indeed possible through psychotherapy to do something about the fundamental lack of love and warmth which a surprisingly large number of people have experienced in their infancy, even if it should be only in limited instances. It is by working in the world and language of childhood and of tenderness.

THE NEED MET

I experienced another instance in which the need for physical closeness could be met. It convinced me that provided certain conditions can be fulfilled it is possible at least sometimes to satisfy this need. I found that I was able, without misunderstanding, to share and satisfy longings and yearnings for warmth and closeness. This was with someone whose very physicality seemed to cover up a lack of loving touch in early life: his mother had been preoccupied with other things.

He was a man in early middle age, involved with physical training, stocky, round faced, and totally cut off from his feelings. He had the deepest worry lines in his brow that I have ever seen, like the ramparts and ditches of the fortress which he had to defend in an early dream. The dream came at the start of his therapy, when he possibly sensed that I might storm the bastion and get through. It struck me that Simon and Garfunkel's I Am a Rock might have been written specially for him: his fortress was so that no one might get through to him, his feelings were buried so that he might feel no pain. He suffered from bouts of blackness, especially if he wakened in the night; he was highly sensitive to any narcissistic injury, such as any feeling that he was being ignored, excluded or overlooked (an inevitable hazard of many sports). He had been married, but was now in a relationship with someone else, which seemed to be a continuance of a care which he had received from them during an illness.

One feature of our early meetings was that at the beginning and end of each session he insisted on shaking my hand. This was not my custom, and it felt uncomfortable. I was confused as to whether the discomfort was because I felt it to be a formal social gesture without meaning, an expression of a buried need for human contact, or an uninvited crossing of my boundaries. I was not particularly concerned with whether or not it broke some psychoanalytic rule. Where rules were concerned I was careful to observe those which I felt were soundly based and had good reason behind them; and to ignore such as I felt were not and had not. The custom of not shaking hands had seemed to me to be a good one: it helped to avoid the therapeutic session being misunderstood as some conventional encounter, or it being treated as some sort of everyday social event. Touch has its very important place, but only when it arises out of the relationship and is not imposed on it from outside.

I mentioned my unease with the hand shaking. The man gave it considered thought, as he always did to anything I said, but responded that he liked to shake hands: it meant a lot to him, though he didnít seem to know quite why. He said he would continue to proffer his hand: whether I took it or not was up to me (he was a highly independent spirit, and in spite of his diffidence and troubles knew exactly what he wanted and what he intended or was prepared to do or not do: he was a most commendable example to us all). I still felt uneasy. I felt it was only a partial, unsatisfying, gesture. Perhaps it was awakening buried longings for contact within me, which I shied off: it might release too much.

I sensed him as being a very down to earth person in spite of living con sciously in his head. His main mode of being was thinking rather than feeling, although his chief form of spontaneous self expression was through the phys ical, and he unconsciously yearned for physical expression in return. Yet the physical too was a defense against feeling, and against anything emotional. It made him very vulnerable to the rejection which he feared, and made me think that the remains of both his longing and his fear might be unconsciously expressed in the handshake, which was at the same time contacting and hold ing at a distance. I suggested that it might be better and more meaningful if instead of that rather formal gesture we exchanged a hug. This he agreed to whole heartedly, or rather whole bodiedly.

We continued for some time thus, with me feeling increasingly that I might be able to communicate with him better physically than verbally. Physical touch might be more able to convey some feeling of concern for him   a real ity which he appeared to find it difficult to grasp. Our verbal exchanges did not get very far, and he was somewhat impatient of them. I felt that a combi nation of psychoanalysis with a more physical approach might get through to the bits that needed engagement. Bioenergetics, and massage, came to mind; not as ends in themselves but as means to stir the unconscious, ancillary to words and shared presence; a bit like the physical connotations of metaphor. Some parts of Lowenís (1976) book on bioenergetics struck me as relevant, and I gave copies of extracts from the book to him: he felt the same.

I suggested therefore that we might try massage as well as talking, physical communication as well as verbal; in the hope that it could meet some of his deeper needs and enable him to feel safe and secure enough to let his blackness emerge into full consciousness. This was not an idea unique to me: several ear lier workers have made similar suggestions (Whiteley and Gordon 1979). The purpose of the massage would not be just to convey the sensation of physical touch but would be a means of communicating strong emotions of affection and connection which lay beneath it and which words alone could not do. It might be possible to allow himself then to experience the dread again, but this time feeling himself supported in his adult strength, from which place he might find he could deal with it sufficiently effectively to overcome it. The blackness seemed to come from his infancy, from some gap in maternal care. He certainly spoke as if it were so, and I in my counter transference felt strongly that he had suffered some radical deprivation of human contact and holding at that time.

An unforeseen result of moving into massage in tandem with talk was that I found it was also meeting a deep need of my own, allowing me to love someone for themselves without it being rejected, or its origin and motive being questioned. Because of this I ceased to charge him any fee. That felt fair, though no doubt as always purists and critics will find some darker motive in my decision. The benefit of the therapy was mutual, and if he was prepared to give the time for it, then so was I. It also avoided transgressing psychoanalytic rules if it was unconditionally mutual rather than carried out for a fee: he accepted this.

We continued to meet on this basis twice a week for several years, until enough work had been done for the blackness no longer to trouble him. He became able to make major changes in his life, and to move with greater confidence into other more adult relationships including finding a new partner. Our own relationship had done its work of satisfying to a sufficient degree his yearning for physical warmth and closeness, such that he no longer needed me to provide it. I am not sure that I was quite so ready to move on myself, but that was a necessary consequence of the way in which we had come to meet and the inevitable cost of committing myself to his cure.

This experience pointed to the possibility that the longing for human touch and warmth can be met, though the presence of strong genuine feeling made it all the more challenging to maintain the difference between sensuality and sexuality. It made it clear that it is actually possible to work at the child level of innocence and tenderness, passion taking a back seat. My therapee at least made sure it stayed there, and had the urge and good sense to move off to a more realistic partner when the appropriate time came.

INTEGRATION

The two people mentioned, the man with whom I moved into massage and the one who was so dependent, reflect the two extremes of reaction to deprivation of physical contact. The two extremes are identified by practitioners of body therapy as being situations in which that therapy is considered to be the most appropriate form of work (see Nick Tottonís chapter in Galtonís *Touch Papers*, 2006, 160). Like metaphor, it offers a bridge between somatic and psychic modes of experience, though in this case the bridge is physical rather than verbal. The one extreme of reaction represents people who have taken refuge from their emotions in their body and their physical existence, who are exclusively in their bodies, and who need to be met there before they can explore other modes of feeling and experience. They are fiercely inde pendent, denying any needs. That was the situation of the man with whom I used massage: he had gone entirely into his body, using that to defend against emotion.

The other extreme represents people who are disconnected from their bod ies and have taken refuge in their heads, in verbal and intellectual modes of existence: this was the man who had such a tenuous connection with any thing solid and who proved to be so dependent. He had dealt with emotional deprivation by going into his head, masking his pain through his obsessions. The first person needed to be helped by means of his bodily feelings and the interpretation of them to recover his emotional ones; the second needed to be helped to connect again with his bodily experience, especially his feelings, and to integrate that with what went on in his head. Both needed to become emotionally alive once more; this required renewing the bond between body and mind (which is emotion). In both cases, touch and physical contact formed the bridge.

A FINAL QUESTION

What remains is the question as to whether work such as this, which requires touch and physical holding, can be recognized within, or absorbed into, the gamut of psychoanalysis now that its boundaries have been pushed back to the earliest years of life. It meets the essential characteristics of psycho analysis as described in chapter 5: it does not correspond to psychoanalysis as defined by the British Psychoanalytic Society, or in the terms of the classical approach to psychoanalysis, for which touch is forbidden. Brett Kahr, in his chapter on Donald Winnicott in *Touch Papers*, (Galton 2006) points out the absolute prohibition on touch within orthodox psychoanalytic circles which highlights the acute question which such an embargo raises. If touch is for bidden ipso facto, then any psychotherapy using it is automatically excluded from psychoanalysis. If, on the other hand, the absolute exclusion of touch is not regarded as a necessary condition, then psychoanalysis is defined by other characteristics, which is important to clarify.

The work which I have been describing can certainly meet a definition of psychoanalysis if it is defined by its essential characteristics in practice rather than by adherence to a particular theory or training. It ventures, though, into the uncharted areas where Ferencziís explorations met such condemna tion and misunderstanding. Let us hope that things may have moved since Ferencziís day. Such work essentially requires tenderness, not passion: it is an impoverishment of psychoanalysis if it is to exclude any attempt to meet these very early needs. The result is that tactile approaches, like body therapy or bioenergetics, have to be carried on as separate professions, which only reinforces the split between somatic and symbolic, body and mind, soma and psyche, which is what psychoanalysis is in theory attempting to heal. It would seem to need a more inclusive name, a name which would embrace a conjoining of verbal and physical work, a conjoining which in turn might set free our most deeply buried potential.

Perhaps, though, a more fundamental question is whether this deficit in human warmth and closeness can ever be supplied by therapy, whatever name it might go by, or whether some people are always going to be left out. The book of some years back to which I have already made reference expressed the need in its title *Touch: The Foundation of Experience* (Barnard and Brazelton 1990). That book was at the time the most expensive that I had ever bought I had ordered it without noticing its price. It was well worth it. Touch is an absolutely fundamental human need, ensuring that our human experience is firmly grounded and lovingly integrated. Touch shares with emotion the function of binding mind and body, especially in the earliest days before emotions are fully realized. It is feeling (a word with the most basic of double meanings) that defines them both. Although touch has this vital function it remains something about which professionals continue to be very sensitive, in spite of such basic research demonstrating its necessity. It is indeed a most significant word, with an expansive range of meaning. Touch could be said to be the touchiest of questions.

The answer to the earlier question, as to whether such a deficit in human contact can be supplied within the remit of psychoanalysis or psychotherapy, requires separating tenderness from passion. Maybe there are not sufficient people who are assured in their sexuality or who have shared in this deficit and are comfortable with acting at the level of tenderness to supply the need. The real answer, of course, would lie in better and more informed parent ing; though reality would also suggest that some people are still going to be deprived.

Towards the ending of my own practice there was someone in therapy with me, a woman, who had suffered a lack of loving handling in childhood. This is not the same as mere physical care, which many people starved of love may in fact have received. Stern (1985, 207) points out that an almost complete lack of attunement is possible even while physical and physiologi cal needs are being met. Distressingly, it was not possible to help her by any direct method of holding or touch. She was extremely attractive, and tender ness would certainly have turned into passion. The result might have been feelings of outrage and exploitation rather than of love and fulfillment. They were instead, as an outcome of this further deprivation, more often of frustra tion and anger, together with distress and resignation that her infant longings might never be fulfilled.

It seems to be a counsel of despair if we are always going to say that the work of psychotherapy is to get people to realize that some yearnings are never going to be fulfilled. They have been made aware of that throughout their lives and rebel against such a cruel fate: its results have already led them into therapy. A medical man said recently that initially he thought he could cure people, but now he realized that his task was to help them to put up with things as they are. Perhaps this is reality, but to accept that judgment without trying to alleviate it feels heartless and feeble. It feels that it is setting an un duly restricted limit on healing, equivalent to Freudís remark about the aim of psychoanalysis being to replace neurotic misery with ordinary human unhap piness. There can surely be more to it than that. I do not feel that it is being impossibly idealistic: perhaps that is what Freud meant when he attacked Ferenczi for his *furor sanandi.* There is no knowing where such passion to heal might end up: fears abound. But it might end well: it might end in tenderness. Psychotherapy is about possibilities. One of those possibilities is that we can recover the language of tenderness and innocence. Whether it be expressed physically, verbally or emotionally, that language needs to be recovered for its own sake, for the sake of sufferers from lack of it, and for the sake of a more human psychotherapy.

References

Aron, L. (1996). *A meeting of minds: mutuality in psychoanalysis*. Hillsdale, NJ: Analytic Press.

Aron, L., and A. Harris, eds. (1993). *The legacy of Sandor Ferenczi*. Hillsdale, NJ: Analytic Press.

Atwood, G. E., and Stolorow, R. D. (1993). *Faces in a cloud* (2nd ed.). Northvale, NJ: Jason Aronson.

Bacal, H. A. (1987). British object relations theorists and self psychology: some criti cal reflections. *International Journal of Psychoanalysis* 68: 81 98.

Bacciagaluppi, M. (1993). Ferencziís influence on Fromm. In *The legacy of Sander Ferenczi*, ed. Lewis Aron and Adrienne Harris, 185 198. Hillsdale, NJ: Analytic Press.

Balint, M. (1968). *The basic fault: therapeutic aspects of regression*. London: Ta vistock.

———. (1969). Trauma and object relationship. *International Journal of Psycho analysis* 50: 429.

Barnard, R. N., and T. B. Brazelton, eds. (1990). *Touch: the foundation of experience*. Madison, CT: International Universities Press.

Basch, M. F. (1992). *Practising psychotherapy*. New York: Basic Books.

Bass, A. (2004). Book review. *International Journal of Psychoanalysis* 85: 249.

Benedek, L. (1993). What can we learn from Ferenczi today? In *The legacy of Sandor Ferenczi*, ed. Lewis Aron and Adrienne Harris, 267 277. Hillsdale, NJ: Analytic Press.

Benjamin, J. (1992). Recognition and destruction: an outline of intersubjectivity. In *Relational perspectives in psychoanalysis*, ed. Neil J. Skolnick and Susan C. War shaw, 43 60. Hillsdale, NJ: Analytic Press.

Bentall, R. (2004). *Madness explained*. London: Penguin.

Bion, W. R. (1990). *Brazilian lectures*. London: Karnac.

Bokanowski, T. (1996). Freud and Ferenczi: trauma and transference depression. *International Journal of Psychoanalysis* 77: 519 536.

. (1997). Book review of Falzeder et al. 1996. *International Journal of Psy choanalysis* 78: 395 398.

Bollas, C. (1987). *The shadow of the object*. London: Free Association Books.

Bosanquet, C. (2006) Symbolic understanding of tactile communication in psycho therapy. In *Touch papers: dialogues on touch in the psychoanalytic space*, ed. Graeme Galton, 29 48. London: Karnac.

Boschan, P. (1996). Psychic reality and the Freud Ferenczi controversy. Panel report by J. Roiphe. *International Journal of Psychoanalysis* 77: 135 139.

Bowlby, J. (1969,1973,1980). *Attachment, separation and loss: vols. 1 3*. Harmond sworth: Penguin.

. (1988). Foreword to *The origins of love and hate*, by Ian D. Suttie (1935). London: Free Association Books, 1999, xv xvi.

Boyle, J. (1977). *A sense of freedom*. London: Pan.

Brabant, E., E. Falzeder, and P. Giampieri Deutsch, eds. (1992). *The correspondence of Sigmund Freud and Sandor Ferenczi: vol. 1, 1908 1914*. Trans. Peter D. Hoffer. Cambridge, MA: Belknap Press of Harvard University Press.

Broom, B. (1997). *Somatic illness and the patient s other story*. London: Free As sociation Books.

Buber, M. (1937/2004). *I and Thou* (orig. publ. T & T Clark, 1937). London: Con tinuum.

Buechler, S. (2004). *Clinical values: emotions that guide psychoanalytic treatment*. Hillsdale, NJ: Analytic Press.

Casement, P. (1985). *On learning from the patient*. London: Tavistock.

Celenza, A. (2005). Vis vis the couch: where is psychoanalysis? *International Jour nal of Psychoanalysis* 86: 1645 1660.

Chediak, C. (1979). Counter reactions and countertransference. *International Journal of Psychoanalysis* 60: 117 129.

Coltart, N. (1986). Slouching towards Bethlehem. In *The British School of Psycho analysis: the Independent Tradition*, ed. Gregorio Kohon, 185 199. London: Free Association Books.

Cox, M., and A. Theilgaard (1987). *Mutative metaphors in psychotherapy: the Aeo lian mode*. London: Tavistock.

Cozolino, L. J. (2004). *The making of a therapist*. New York: W. W. Norton.

Dicks, H. V. (1967). *Marital tensions*. London: Routledge and Kegan Paul.

Doi, T. (1993). Amae and transference love. In *On Freud s Observations on transfer ence love*, ed. Ethel Spector Person, 165 171. New Haven: Yale University Press.

Dupont, J., ed. (1995). *The clinical diary of Sandor Ferenczi*. Cambridge, MA: Har vard University Press.

Erikson, E. (1950). *Childhood and society*. London: Penguin.

Falzeder, E., E. Brabant, and P. Giampieri Deutsch, eds. (1996). *The correspondence of Sigmund Freud and Sandor Ferenczi: vol. 2, 1914 1919*. Trans. Peter D. Hoffer. Cambridge, MA: Belknap Press of Harvard University Press.

. (2000). *The correspondence of Sigmund Freud and Sandor Ferenczi: vol. 3, 1920 1933*. Trans. Peter D. Hoffer. Cambridge, MA: Belknap Press of Harvard University Press.

Fenichel, O. (1946). *The psychoanalytic theory of neurosis*. London: Routledge and Kegan Paul.

Ferenczi, S. (1926, 1994). *Further contributions to the theory and technique of psy choanalysis*, ed. John Rickman (orig. publ. Hogarth, 1926). London: Karnac.

——. (1955, 1980). *Final contributions to the problems and methods of psycho analysis,* ed. Michael Balint (orig. publ. Hogarth, 1955). New York: Brunner/Mazel.

——. (1926). The dream of the clever baby. *(Paper 58 in Further contribu tions).*

——. (1927). The problem of the termination of the analysis. *(Paper 7 in Final contributions).*

——. (1929.1). The unwelcome child and his death instinct. *(Paper 9 in Final contributions).*

——. (1929.2). The principle of relaxation and neo catharsis. *(Paper 10 in Final contributions).*

——. (1931). Child analysis in the analysis of adults. *(Paper 11 in Final contribu tions).*

——. (1933). Confusion of tongues between adults and the child. *(Paper 13 in Final contributions).*

——. (1932, 1995). *The clinical diary of Sandor Ferenczi*, ed. Judith Dupont. Cam bridge, MA: Harvard University Press.

——. (1993, 1996, 2000). *The correspondence of Sigmund Freud and Sandor Fe renczi: vols. 1, 2, 3.* (see also under Brabant et al. [vol.1], Falzeder et al. [vols. 2 and 3]). Cambridge, MA: Belknap Press of Harvard University Press.

Fortune, C., ed. (2002). *The Sandor Ferenczi Georg Groddeck correspondence 1921 1933.* London: Open Gate Press.

Fosshage, J. L. (1994). Toward reconceptualising transference: theoretical and clini cal considerations. *International Journal of Psychoanalysis* 75: Part 1.

Fraser, S. (1989). *My father s house.* London: Virago.

Freud, A. (1937). *The ego and the mechanisms of defence.* London: Hogarth Press.

Freud, S. (1896). The aetiology of hysteria. *Studies in hysteria,* with J. Breuer. *Stan dard Edition* 2. London: Hogarth.

——. (1900/1976). The interpretation of dreams. *Standard Edition* 4/5. London: Hogarth, 1953; Pelican Freud Library Vol. 4.

——. (1901). *The psychopathology of everyday life,* vol. 5. London: Pelican Freud Library.

——. (1915). Observations on transference love. *Standard Edition* 12: 159 171.

——. (1923/1962). The Ego and the Id. *Standard Edition* 19: 3 66.

——. (1931). Female sexuality. *Standard Edition* 21: 221 246; *PFL* 7: 367 392.

——. (1933a). On femininity. *Standard Edition* 22: 112 135; *PFL* 2, 145 169.

——. (1933). Sandor Ferenczi: obituary. *Standard Edition* 22: 227 229.

——. (1937/1964). Analysis terminable and interminable. *Standard Edition* 23: 211 253.

——. (1993, 1996, 2000), *The correspondence of Sigmund Freud and Sandor Fe renczi: vols. 1, 2, 3.* (See also under Brabant et al. [vol.1], Falzeder et al. [vols. 2 and 3]). Cambridge, MA: Belknap Press of Harvard University Press.

Gabbard, G. O., and E. P. Lester. (1995). *Boundaries and boundary violations in psychoanalysis*. New York: Basic Books.

Galton, G., ed. (2006). *Touch papers: dialogues on touch in the psychoanalytic space*. London: Karnac.

Gay, P. (1988). *Freud: a life for our time*. London: Macmillan.

Gerhardt, S. (2004). *Why love matters*. Hove, UK: Brunner Routledge.

Ghent, E. (1993). Foreword to *Relational perspectives in psychoanalysis*, ed. Neil Skolnick and Susan Warshaw. Hillsdale, NJ: Analytic Press, xiii xxii.

Gomez, L. (1997). *An introduction to object relations*. London: Free Association Books.

Green, A. (1990). *Le complexe de castration*. Paris: Presses Universit de France.

Greenberg, J. R., and S. Mitchell. (1983). *Object relations in psychoanalytic theory*. Cambridge, MA: Harvard University Press.

Greenson, R. R. (1967). *The technique and practice of psychoanalysis: vol. 1*. Lon don: Hogarth.

Hazell, J., ed. (1994). *Personal relations therapy: the collected papers of H. J. S. Guntrip*. Northvale, NJ: Jason Aronson.

Heard, D. (1988). Introduction to *The origins of love and hate*, by Ian D. Suttie (1935). London: Free Association Books, xix xlv.

Hedges, L. E. (1983). *Listening perspectives in psychotherapy*. New York: Jason Aronson.

. (1992). *Interpreting the countertransference*. Northvale, NJ: Jason Aronson.

. (1994.1). *Working the organizing experience*. Northvale, NJ: Jason Aronson.

. (1994.2). *In search of the lost mother of infancy*. Northvale, NJ: Jason Aronson.

Heimann, P. (1950). On counter transference. *International Journal of Psychoanaly sis* 31: 81 84.

Hobson, R. F. (1985). *Forms of feeling: the heart of psychotherapy*. London: Tavis tock.

Hoffer, A. (1991). The Freud Ferenczi controversy a living legacy. *International Journal of Psychoanalysis* 18: 4, 465 472.

. (1996) Psychic reality and the Freud Ferenczi controversy. Panel report by J. Roiphe. *International Journal of Psychoanalysis* 77: 135 139.

Hoffmann, I. Z. (1998). *Ritual and spontaneity in the psychoanalytic process: a dia lectical constructivist view*. Hillsdale, NJ: Analytic Press.

Holmes, J. (1993). *John Bowlby and attachment theory*. London: Routledge.

Home, H. J. (1966). The concept of mind. *International Journal of Psychoanalysis* 47, 42 49.

Jacobs, D. et al. (1995). *The supervisory encounter*. New Haven, CT: Yale University Press.

Kahr, B. Winnicottís experiments with physical contact: creative innovation or chaotic impingement? In *Touch papers: dialogues on touch in the psychoanalytic space*, ed. Graeme Galton, 1 14. London: Karnac.

Kirshner, L. A. (1994). Trauma, the good object, and the symbolic: a theoretical inte gration. *International Journal of Psychoanalysis* 75: 235 242.

Klein, G. S. (1976). *Psychoanalytic theory: an exploration of essentials*. New York: International Universities Press

Klein, J. (1987). *Our need for others and its roots in infancy*. London: Routledge.

Koestler, A. (1964). *The act of creation*. London: Hutchinson.

Kohon, G., ed. (1986). *The British School of Psychoanalysis: the independent tradi tion*. London: Free Association Books.

Kohut, H. (1971). *The analysis of the self*. New York: International Universities Press.

———. (1977). *The restoration of the self*. New York: International Universities Press.

———. (1979). The two analyses of Mr. Z. *International Journal of Psychoanalysis* 60: 3 27.

———. (1985). *Self psychology and the humanities*. New York: W. W. Norton.

Laing, R. D. (1967). *The politics of experience and the bird of paradise*. London: Tavistock.

Lake, F. (1981). *Tight corners in pastoral counselling*. London: Darton Longman and Todd.

———. (1986). *Clinical theology* (abridged version, orig. publ.1966). London: Darton Longman and Todd.

Laplanche, J., and J. B. Pontalis. (1967, 1988). *The language of psychoanalysis*. London: Karnac.

Levin, F. M. (2003). *Mapping the mind* (first publ. Analytic Press, 1991). London: Karnac.

Levine, H. B. (1994). The analystís participation in the analytic process. *International Journal of Psychoanalysis* 75: 665 676.

Lichtenberg, J. D., F. M. Lachmann, and J. L. Fosshage. (1992). *Self and motivational systems*. Hillsdale, NJ: Analytic Press.

Lomas, P. (1987). *The limits of interpretation*. Harmondsworth: Penguin.

———. (1993). *The psychotherapy of everyday life* (2nd ed. of *The case for a personal psychotherapy*. OUP, 1981). New Brunswick, NJ: Transaction.

Lowen, A. (1976). *Bioenergetics*. London: Penguin.

Maddox, B. (2006). *Freud s wizard: the enigma of Ernest Jones*. London: Murray.

Malan, D. H. (1979). *Individual psychotherapy and the science of psychodynamics*. London: Butterworth.

Mann, D., ed. (1999). *Erotic transference and counter transference: clinical practice in psychotherapy*. Hove, UK: Brunner Routledge.

Maroda, K. J. (1991). *The power of counter transference*. Chichester, UK: John Wiley & Sons.

Mart n Cabr , L. (1997). Controversy terminable and interminable. *International Journal of Psychoanalysis* 78: 1, 105 114.

McEwan, I. (1997). *Enduring love*. London: Jonathan Cape.

McGuire, W., ed. (1974). *The Freud Jung letters*. Princeton, NJ: University Press.

Miller, A. (1985). *Thou shalt not be aware*. London: Pluto Press.

———. (1987). *The drama of being a child*. London: Virago.

Milner, M. (1969). *The hands of the living God*. London: Hogarth.

Mitchell, S. A. (1997). *Influence and autonomy in psychoanalysis*. Hillsdale, NJ: Analytic Press.

Mollon, P. (1996). *Multiple selves, multiple voices*. Chichester, UK: John Wiley & Sons.

References

Ogden, T. H. (1989). On the concept of an autistic contiguous position. *International Journal of Psychoanalysis* 70: 127 140.

——. (1994) The analytic third: working with intersubjective clinical facts. *International Journal of Psychoanalysis* 75: 3 19.

Orange, D. (1995). *Emotional understanding: studies in psychoanalytic epistemology*. New York: Guilford.

Person, E. S., ed. (1993). *On Freud s Observations on transference love*. New Haven, CT: Yale University Press.

Rayner, E. (1991). *The Independent mind in British psychoanalysis*. London: Free Association Books.

Reisner, S. (1992). Eros reclaimed: recovering Freudís relational theory. In *Relational perspectives in psychoanalysis*, ed. Neil Skolnick and Susan Warshaw, 281 312. Hillsdale, NJ: Analytic Press.

Rogers, C. R. (1967). *On becoming a person*. London: Constable.

Roiphe, J. (1996). Panel report on Psychic reality and the Freud Ferenczi controversy, chaired by Andre Haynal. *International Journal of Psychoanalysis* 77: 135 139.

Rychlak, J. F. (1973). *Introduction to personality and psychotherapy: a theory construction approach*. Boston, MA: Houghton Mifflin.

Rycroft, C. F. (1979). *The innocence of dreams*. London: Hogarth.

Ryle, G. (1949). *The concept of mind* (reprinted by Penguin). London: Hutchinson.

Sandler, J., ed. (1991). *On Freud s Analysis terminable and interminable*. New Haven, CT: Yale University Press.

Schafer, R. (1976). *A new language for psychoanalysis*. New Haven, CT: Yale University Press.

——, ed. (1997). *The contemporary Kleinians of London*. New York: International Universities Press.

——. (1983). *The analytic attitude*. London: Hogarth Press.

Schore, A. (1994). *Affect regulation and the origin of the self*. Hillsdale, NJ: Lawrence Erlbaum Associates.

——. (2003). *Affect dysregulation and disorders of the self*. New York: W. W. Norton.

——. (2003). *Affect regulation and the repair of the self*. New York: W. W. Norton.

Scott Peck, M. (1978). *The road less travelled*. New York: Touchstone.

Shapiro, S. A. (1993). Clara Thompson: Ferencziís messenger with half a message. In *The legacy of Sandor Ferenczi*, ed. Lewis Aron and Adrienne Harris, 159 173. Hillsdale, NJ: Analytic Press.

Siegel, A. (1996). *Heinz Kohut and the Psychology of the Self*. London: Routledge.

Skolnick, N. J., and S. C. Warshaw. (1992). *Relational perspectives in psychoanalysis*. Hillsdale, NJ: Analytic Press.

Solms, M., and O. Turnbull. (2002). *The brain and the inner world*. London: Karnac.

Spinelli, E. (1989). *An introduction to phenomenological psychology*. London: Sage.

Stanton, M. (1990). *Sandor Ferenczi: reconsidering active intervention*. London: Free Association Books.

Stein, R. (1991). *Psychoanalytic theories of affect*. New York: Praeger.

Stern, D. N. (1985). *The interpersonal world of the infant*. New York: Basic Books.

Stewart, H. (1992). *Psychic experience and problems of technique*. London: Rout ledge.

———. (1993). Clinical aspects of malignant regression. In *The legacy of Sandor Ferenczi*, ed. Lewis Aron and Adrienne Harris, 249 264. Hillsdale, NJ: Analytic Press.

———. (1996). *Michael Balint: object relations pure and applied*. London: Routledge.

Stolorow, R. D., and G. E. Atwood. (1992). *Contexts of being*. Hillsdale, NJ: Analytic Press.

Stolorow, R. D., G. E. Atwood, and B. Brandchaft, eds. (1994). *The intersubjective perspective*. Northvale, NJ: Jason Aronson.

Stolorow, R. D., and F. M. Lachmann. (1980). *Psychoanalysis of developmental ar rests*. New York: IUP.

Strachey, J. (1934/1969). The nature of the therapeutic action of psychoanalysis. *International Journal of Psychoanalysis* 15: 127; 50, 275.

Suttie, I. D. (1935, 1988). *The origins of love and hate*. (orig. publ.1935). London: Free Association Books.

Symington, N. (1997). *The making of a therapist*. London: Karnac.

———. (2007). *Becoming a person through psychoanalysis*. London: Karnac.

Totton, N. (2006). A body psychotherapistís approach to touch. In *Touch papers: dialogues on touch in the psychoanalytic space*, ed. Graeme Galton, 145 161. London: Karnac.

Trad, P. V. (1993). Previewing and the therapeutic use of metaphor. *British Journal of Medical Psychology* 66: 305 322.

Tustin, F. (1986). *Autistic barriers in neurotic patients*. London: Karnac.

Van Heute, P. (2005). Infantile sexuality, primary object love and the anthropologi cal significance of the Oedipus complex: re reading Freudís Female sexuality. *International Journal of Psychoanalysis* 86: 1661 1678.

Victoria Butterfly Gardens, Brentwood Bay, British Columbia. http://butterflygardens.com/learn. Accessed on 3 April 2006.

Vogel, L. Z., and S. Savva. (1993). Atlas personality. *British Journal of Medical Psychology* 66: 323 330.

White, K., ed. (2004). *Touch: attachment and the body*. London: Karnac.

Whiteley, J. S., and J. Gordon. (1979). *Group approaches to psychiatry*. London: Routledge and Kegan Paul.

Whyte, L. L. (1978). *The unconscious before Freud*. London: Julian Friedmann.

Winnicott, D. W. (1958). *Through paediatrics to psychoanalysis*. London: Tavis tock.

———. (1965). *The maturational processes and the facilitating environment*. London: Hogarth.

Index

abandonment, fear of, 11, 44, 127, 155
abstinence/withholding, 10, 27, 49, 58, 91 94, 106 7, 160
abuse, 26, 29, 42, 59, 87, 158
acceptance, 41, 65, 90, *100,* 103, 107, 155
acting out, 135
activity, 88
Adler, A., 22
Aeolian mode, 119
affect, 3, 86, 138. *See also* emotion/ feeling
affection, 152, 154, 169
Alexander, F., 108
alter ego. *See* Kohut, H.
 Amae, 101
ambivalence, *100,* 157
analytic attitudes, 24, 31, 36, 42, 48, 101, 110 11, 116, 161; relationship, xvii, 11, 17, 25, 46, 48, 51, 63, 68, 90 93, 95, 99, 115, 125, 152, 161; third of Ogden, 94
anger, working with, xx, 90, 108, 144
anxiety, 118 19, 164
Aron, L., 96
arrested development, xxii
 Atlas personality, 44
atmosphere of childhood, 79, 82; of therapy, xxii, 29, 38, 80, 90, 99, 127

attachment, xxi, 11, 15, 80, 102, 131, 155
attachment theory, 10, 132, 155, 161
attitudes. *See* analytic attitudes
attunement/misattunement, 68, 137, 144, 153, 172
Atwood, G. E., and Stolorow R. D., 129
authority/authoritarianism, 25, 53, 57, 121
avoiding/avoidance, 79, 105, 140, 162
awareness/consciousness, 13, 49, 74 75, 79, 84, 86, 133, 149, 168

Balint, M., 5 6, 15, 18, 31, 70, *100,* 125; arglos state, 18, 37, 41, 67, 104; basic fault, 5; *The Basic Fault,* 4, 19; colleague of Ferenczi, 6; new beginning, 37, 67, 104; preserver of Ferencziís works, 6, 52; primary love, 5, 8, 63, 67, 127; and regression, 5 6, 18, 64 67
Barnard, K. E., and Brazelton, T. B., eds., 87
behavior, meaning of. *See* meaning of behavior
behavioral therapy, 80, 122
being used, 98, *100,* 153
Bentall, R., 87, 112, 129
bioenergetics, 168, 171

About the Author

Robert W. Rentoul became a minister of the Church of Scotland after obtaining a degree from the University of Oxford. As a minister he was a member of the Iona Community and worked in India for more than a decade. After returning to Britain he earned a degree in psychology from the University of Bristol, became an associate fellow of the British Psychological Society, and practiced psychotherapy for more than thirty years in an industrial city in the English Midlands, where psychotherapy was a new concept. He is now retired and lives with his wife in Wells, Somerset.